K.T. MITCHELL

Business Ethics
and the 21st Century
Organization

Business Ethics and the 21st Century Organization

Edited by

Peter Whates

To Gem, Tris and Oli – for always starting with unconditional love then going way past the extra mile.

First published in the UK in 2006 by
BSI
389 Chiswick High Road
London W4 4AL

Typeset in Sabon by
Florence Production Ltd, Stoodleigh, Devon
Printed in Great Britain by
Hobbs the Printers Ltd, Totton, Hampshire

British Library Cataloguing in Publication Data
A catalogue record for this book is available from the British Library

ISBN 0 580 45465 7

Contents

Notes on the Contributors

Sir Geoffrey Chandler was Founder-Chair of the Amnesty International UK Business Group from 1991 to 2001. He began his career as a journalist on the BBC and *Financial Times*, subsequently spending 22 years with the Royal Dutch/Shell Group in a number of posts in the UK and overseas. He was a director of Shell Petroleum, Shell Petroleum NV and Shell International and was the initiator of Shell's first *Statement of General Business Principles* in 1976. He was Director General of the UK National Economic Development Office 1978–83, Director of Industry Year 1986 and chaired the National Council for Voluntary Organisations, 1989–96. He has honorary degrees from a number of universities and is the author of books on Greece and Trinidad and of numerous articles on corporate responsibility and human rights.

Professor Philip A. Dover assumed the position of Dean of the Buckingham Business School and Professor of Marketing at the University of Buckingham in March 2004, after serving for five years as Faculty Director at the School of Executive Education, Babson College, USA. He has also held marketing management positions with British Petroleum and Nestlé. He continues to conduct custom executive education programmes on strategic management and marketing topics for leading multinational companies while offering open enrolment programmes on such topics as strategic alliances and services management. He pursues an active consultancy practice in the areas of strategic business planning and corporate entrepreneurship, mainly within technology-based enterprises, where many of his academic interests also lie.

Philippa Foster Back is Director of the Institute of Business Ethics. Philippa has over 25 years of business experience. She began her career at Citibank NA before joining Bowater in its Corporate Treasury

Department in 1979, leaving in 1988 as Group Treasurer. She was Group Finance Director at D G Gardner Group, a training organization, prior to joining Thorn EMI in 1993 as Group Treasurer. She was appointed IBE's Director in August 2001. She has a number of external appointments, including at the Ministry of Defence, the Institute of Directors and the Association of Corporate Treasurers, where she was President from 1999 to 2000.

Dr Kevin Franklin is an associate at Warwick Business School (WBS). He has a PhD in Industrial and Business Studies from WBS and a strong practical background working on the economic, social and environmental domains of sustainability. Kevin has more than eight years' experience in facilitation and advising companies on business ethics and corporate citizenship issues and strategy in both developed and developing country contexts. He is a professionally qualified and experienced auditor to both the ISO 14001:2004 and SA 8000:2001 standards, has published widely and co-authored numerous reports for high-level international agencies and forums.

Kathryn Gordon is a senior economist in the Investment Division of the Organisation for Economic Cooperation and Development (OECD). She is responsible for the OECD's work on the *OECD Guidelines for Multinational Enterprises*, a multilaterally endorsed code of conduct with a government-backed follow mechanism. She is also responsible for the research on corporate responsibility that supports implementation of the guidelines. Prior to taking her position at the OECD, Kathryn was a professor at a French business school (ÉSSEC) and she participates in numerous French research networks, including that of the Research and Management Centre at the University of Paris Dauphine.

Patricia Greaves is a Mexican social anthropologist, Professor and Researcher at the Research Institute for Sustainable Development and Social Equity of the Iberoamericana University in Mexico City and a member of the Puentes Network. Currently she is in charge of a project on social responsibility and corporate culture in Mexico, which implies extended fieldwork throughout the country. Since 1999 she has specialized in research on corporate social responsibility and the third sector. She has written *Business and businessmen: some actual trends in Mexican corporate philanthropy* (2000), and co-authored *Some Characteristics of the Non Profit Sector in Mexico* (2001) and *Private Funds for the Public Good: Mexican Funding Institutions* (2002).

Patricia Hind is currently Director of the full-time MBA programme at Ashridge Business School, as well as running open and tailored executive development programmes for a wide range of clients. She joined Ashridge as a member of the faculty in November 1996. After obtaining her degree in psychology, and a Masters degree in industrial psychology, she completed a doctorate on managing volunteers within the charitable sector. She has lectured at Leeds and City universities on organizational psychology and also worked for some eight years in the House of Commons, researching many current issues. She has published widely and regularly presented at conferences on topics related to organizational change, personal leadership and employee motivation.

Albrecht Mueller graduated from the University of Hamburg with the degree of Diplom Kaufmann (Business Administration and Economics). After working as an assistant to a board member in a fertilizer and then an aeronautics company he continued as project controller in the latter company. He was granted a scholarship for the European training programme in Japan sponsored by the European Commission. After working in the management team of a larger European defence programme, he joined a Belgium imaging technology company to work in Japan, Brazil and Argentina as local and later regional CFAO and assumed also the local MD position for Chile.

Dr Justin O'Brien runs the corporate governance programme at the School of Law, Queen's University, Belfast. He is the author of *Wall Street on Trial* (2003) and the editor of *Governing the Corporation: Corporate Governance and Regulation in Global Markets* (2005). His current research, funded by a major grant from the Economic and Social Research Council, examines the international implications of Sarbanes-Oxley. A former investigative journalist and television editor, he has written extensively on ethics, corporate governance and political and economic corruption. Dr O'Brien received his doctorate in political science from Queen's University, Belfast.

James Oury is Senior Partner of Oury Clark Solicitors, a Solicitor Advocate Higher Court (Criminal) Proceedings, Vice Chair of the International Bar Association Human Rights Committee, Special Advisor to the Defence Function of the International Criminal Court and a practising Solicitor and Chartered Accountant. He is also, along with Sune Thorsen, a Director of Corporate Social Responsibility Limited.

Andreas Prindl holds a BA from Princeton and a PhD from the University of Kentucky. He spent 20 years with Morgan Guaranty in New York, London, Frankfurt and Tokyo, where he was General Manager. He set up Nomura International Bank in London and was its Chairman until 1997. Dr Prindl has been Chairman of the UK Banking Industry Training and Development Council, President of the Chartered Institute of Bankers and the Association of Corporate Treasurers. He was appointed CBE in 1999. He is a member of Lloyd's Council, Junior Warden of the Musicians Company and agrees with Nietzsche that, without music, life would be a mistake.

Phil Rudolph is a partner in the Corporate Social Responsibility Practice Group of Foley Hoag LLP, where he provides a range of CSR advice, counsel and support to global brands and other clients. Prior to joining Foley Hoag, Phil was a Vice President at McDonald's Corporation, where he served in several capacities, including those of US and International General Counsel, and Head of Vendor Compliance. Phil also served on McDonald's Social Responsibility Steering Committee, which provided strategic CSR advice to senior management. Phil writes and speaks extensively on CSR and ethics issues. He graduated *magna cum laude* from the University of California at Irvine in 1980, and received his JD from the University of Chicago Law School in 1983.

John Sayer was a farmer in Wales before moving to Asia in 1976. He worked on rural development projects in India before settling in Hong Kong where he lived for 25 years. He joined the Asia Monitor Resource Centre (AMRC) to research the impact of foreign economic involvement on Asian economies and workers. As Executive Director of AMRC he worked with trade unions and NGOs in Asia on research and information systems, computer communications and occupational health and safety. In 1991 he joined Oxfam Hong Kong as Programme Director and later became Executive Director, working on relief and development in Asia and Africa. In 2001 he moved to Oxford to take up the post of Executive Director of Oxfam International for an interim period. His subsequent role involved consultancy for Oxfam on relations between NGOs and the private sector and he completed a Masters degree on the same subject. He is currently Director of Africa Now, a development agency working on market-based solutions for small-scale producers in Africa through business services and the promotion of ethical trade among international companies doing business in Africa.

Professor Alyson Warhurst is a leading authority with 25 years' experience exploring the roles and responsibilities of business in society – a field sometimes referred to as 'business ethics' or 'corporate citizenship'. Her special focus is research and teaching about business strategy and management systems relating to human rights, labour standards, humanitarian relief, health and education. She is currently Chair of Strategy and International Development at the world-leading Warwick Business School. Professor Warhurst is also an academic fellow of the World Economic Forum and the inaugural winner of the European Faculty Pioneer Award 2003.

Peter Whates has been an adviser, writer and speaker on corporate social responsibility, cross-sector partnerships and business ethics since 1982. He has completed more than 50 strategic development projects for private, public and voluntary sector clients and also devised several award-winning cause-related marketing, employee volunteering and CSR recognition programmes. He has published extensively and is the co-author of *Communicating Corporate Social Responsibility*, to be published in April 2006. He is a member of the Board of Advisors of the CSR Association in Turkey and speaks regularly in the UK and Europe.

Introduction

Peter Whates

Business ethics is a fascinating topic and not just for the subject matter it covers, vital though this is for business, society and the individual.

To my mind, there is no other issue on the contemporary management agenda with greater resonance and relevance, nor one with greater capacity to both fascinate and bewilder in equal measure.

At the core of business ethics, after all, are deceptively simple, long-standing notions such as 'doing the right thing' that no reasonable person could possibly decry and no rational manager would wish to ignore.

Nor are the controversies sparked by how this is translated into the policies and processes of an organization particularly new. Campaigns on topics as diverse as the abolition of the slave trade and the adulteration of beer are rooted deep in the past.

What is different is the relatively recent emergence of a generalized ethical consciousness, not to say conscience. Notions of 'ethical business behaviour' are now embedded in the public consciousness and vocabulary, with arguments just as likely in the pub bar as the company boardroom.

While its form and character are undoubtedly still evolving, this new ethical landscape has already manifested itself in recent years in ways we now take for granted.

It has, for example, spawned a new breed of shareholder, the socially responsible investor. According to a recent survey quoted in the *Independent on Sunday* newspaper (Shaw, 2005), there are now more than 60 funds to choose from in the UK alone. The same report valued what they described as the 'green or ethical product' industry at £24.7 billion.

A process generically described as ethical tourism has also emerged to make travellers aware of the impact of their activities. This issue broke further new ground in the aftermath of the devastating tsunami in December 2004, when the focus switched away from the abstract 'tourism' product onto the tourist as an individual.

If the discomfort of individuals exposed to the unforeseen and not always subtle probing of 24 hour news crews was not enough, the 'ethics' of both staying and travelling to affected areas was subject to critical comment at different times and by different interests.

Some of this head-scratching confusion undoubtedly finds resonance inside organizations seeking a simplistic solutions-based approach to ethical issues. So undoubtedly does the more generally antagonistic view of business ethics expressed by television critic Tim Dowling (2005) with his self-penned characterization of the 'seven ethical dwarfs'.

His re-branding of the famous fairy tale characters came in the course of a review of a business reality TV show called *The Apprentice* fronted by Sir Alan Sugar, a well-known entrepreneur and chairman of major UK company Amstrad. Pouring scorn on the contestants, Mr Dowling suggested that the group reminded him of the seven ethical dwarfs 'Shallow, Unctuous, Transparent, Self-important, Pushy, Scheming and Smug'.

How ironic in the context of the general business ethics debate to find transparency listed as a vice.

Purpose

From even these limited examples it is self-evident that business ethics is a hot topic issue. But to make a valid contribution to the debate, this book requires a distinct purpose and myself a clear vision of how to deliver it.

The purpose is relatively simple. It is to 'dig below the surface' to first identify and then better understand the unique and sometimes perplexing conundrum that is business ethics and its impact on the modern organization.

The book is not designed to provide a forensic examination of the ethics process, however, so in the purest sense of the term is not a management textbook. Several widely and soundly researched theoretical books already exist and there is simply no merit in merely cloning them.

It is also consciously structured to provoke thought and debate rather than signpost seductive and at times illusory ready-made solutions. It is therefore not purely a management workbook, either. Several sources, including our own Institute of Business Ethics in the United Kingdom, have well-produced publications available to meet that need.

Perhaps, most importantly, the book is not a campaigning vehicle to promote one specific point of view. It does have many strongly expressed opinions and deeply held convictions, but these often reflect conflicting points of view as part of the ebb and flow of the debate. It also makes no attempt to promote any single sectional or business interest, particularly with regard to the role of the British Standards Institution as the National Standards body for the United Kingdom.

Personally, I have long held the belief that a robust system of international accreditation may provide a sensible compromise between the largely discredited reliance on free market self-regulation and the very real spectre of restrictive legislation that ultimately may damage legitimate enterprise.

Accreditation could actually even prove to be a valuable resource for the numerically huge mass of medium to small size enterprises that currently have ethics 'done to them', as much by major multinational companies as by any campaigning NGO. A respected system could also deliver significant cost savings for multinational corporations forced to devise their own monitoring and evaluation systems.

There was never a time when I intended to amplify on this personal perspective here, not least because it is a narrower debate than the broad scope I intend for this book. I am delighted to say there was never a time when the publisher even remotely hinted that I should reconsider.

Authors

The onus of delivering my vision for the book fell naturally on the authors, both as individuals and as a part of the wider writing team.

As a team, I wanted them to provide a wide-ranging brief on the nature of the interaction between the tenets of responsible business behaviour, the organization and its stakeholders. I also wanted the reader to gain an understanding of the different ways that business ethics issues can arise to challenge the modern manager.

To achieve this I set out to recruit contributors who could communicate lucidly and express views cogently without resorting to polemic. I was also looking for people with distinct opinions, whether or not they were fashionable.

As each individual contribution arrived, I considered it against a simple 'four Is' test. I wanted to read *informed* opinions based on experience, *insights* based on an ability to interpret events, the ability to describe the *impact* of business ethics on an organization and the skill to communicate this in a way that would *interest* the reader.

I also wanted an *international* dimension to be included wherever relevant and appropriate, in keeping with the universal reach of the subject across the globe.

One of the benefits of working in this area for many years is that I knew the majority of people I hoped would contribute before making the approach to them. In particular I had heard a number speak at two excellent conferences on the subject organized by Wilton Park.

It is not for me to judge how successfully the contributions collectively match the vision I had at the outset, although any gap between the two clearly derives from my failings as editor. I can only confirm that every author in the book was my identified choice.

Themes

Reading the contributions in this book has developed my general thinking and crystallized my views in some specific areas of the debate on responsible business behaviour. It made the editing job rewarding in the widest sense.

I will not be imposing my interpretation on the reader by stating the conclusions that I have drawn, however, for a reason rooted in my undergraduate past.

As a cash-strapped student forced to rely extensively on the university library, I grew to hate any prior reader who conveyed their judgement of what was important by underlining or similarly defacing the text.

In particular I grew to loathe the person who adopted a five star grading system, always in dark green ink, especially as they appeared to be the most diligent student on campus.

I intend instead to isolate four key themes that struck me as each contribution arrived and then again when reading the whole manuscript prior to submission.

The first concerns the future of regulation. The era of self-regulation within the firm, probably within an industry and perhaps even within an individual nation state, appears to be drawing inexorably to a close. The debate is crystallizing instead around what system, or set of mutually reinforcing systems, can best replace it and to whom can the regulatory burden best be entrusted.

This is a dynamic and fluid process with contrasting approaches already being taken at all levels including the individual firm, national legislators and international trade bodies. It is also a process into which external stakeholders including, but not limited to, NGOs have demanded the right to be involved as full participants.

Multinational companies in particular, it seems to me, now have little option other than to negotiate and then repeatedly renegotiate the terms of the global responsible business 'contract' in the manner of the annual wage round, only infinitely more frequently.

Agreeing the terms of the ethical licence to operate is a particularly high stakes game in finance, which is why I have devoted two chapters to it, but the outcome is growing in importance everywhere.

The second theme appears self-evident at first glance. Ethics is a modern day issue with genuinely global reach that impacts on every form of organization wherever it is domiciled, in whatever it trades and to however many (or few) shareholders it remits its dividends.

What is less self-evident, yet of considerable contemporary significance, is how deeply rooted and entwined are the bonds between the economic and political structures of many countries. I believe that in the UK, we often underestimate how much disruption the free market economic system elsewhere in Western Europe has faced from oppressive regimes, conflict and the like. The natural corollary is that we tend to underestimate its impact elsewhere in the world too.

My purpose in focusing on Latin America was to shed light on an often relatively neglected continent with both long and often complex traditions and several globally significant economies. What I learnt is that the ethics conundrum is just as flourishing, although in no sense can that be a cause for rejoicing.

That same unfortunate universality is clearly also much in evidence when looking at the impact of socio-political or pure militarily dominated conflicts on human and other rights. This fact was more a reconfirmation than a surprise to me, but none the less depressing for being so.

This brings me to the third clear theme to emerge, the current paucity of management education in responsible business behaviour of all descriptions.

On the one hand, a growing number of organizations do appear to have belatedly recognized that signing up to seductive mantras such as 'every employee is a reputation manager for the company' is the start of the journey rather than the destination. It does not as yet seem to be being translated into a systematic investment in programmes to equip staff with the tools to better understand and then manage responsible business behaviour, however, particularly something based on values rather than compliance.

A strong clue as to why training remains generally undervalued emerges in the shape of the current patchy international provision for teaching responsible business behaviour in MBA courses. In this highly competitive customer driven sector of education, a reluctance to deliver 'what the customer ought to want' is understandable. But if it is what the customer actually needs, and evidence continues to mount that it is, then the sooner the 'big hitters' of tomorrow see business ethics for the hard discipline it is, the better for all of us with pensions invested in under-prepared managers gambling with shareholder value.

The final theme snakes mostly silently through the book in the form of a ready-to-be-primed string of unknown length connected to an extremely destructive explosive charge. It concerns the emerging debate on just what constitutes 'responsible capitalism', whether society has a right to expect it and, perhaps most fundamentally, whether a profit-driven system has the capacity to even deliver it.

I approached Sir Geoffrey Chandler to address these issues because I knew he possessed the rare blend of experience, strategic vision and clarity of purpose to place the debate on business ethics in its widest context. It was a poignant moment, because 20 years ago, he had agreed to write the foreword to my first handbook on corporate community relations.

Fortunately he not only agreed, but placed only one, albeit telling, condition on his contribution. He would gladly author 'Towards a responsible capitalism?', but only if I removed the question mark from the title.

I will leave the reader to decide whether this optimism is in any sense misplaced. But relatively few business leaders seem willing as yet to fully champion the responsible business behaviour message and drive it deep into their corporate soul. Maybe they judge that with a market-based economy in the global ascendant there is no imperative to pay more than lip-service to the challenges posed by business ethics.

I hope this confidence survives the next global downturn when it comes without provoking serious social conflict. Nobody cheered more loudly when the Berlin Wall crumbled; indeed, I have a piece of it in my office. But we urgently need robust and sustainable paradigms for modern corporations that reach beyond merely seizing the profit-making opportunities that arose in its wake.

I would genuinely like to thank all the authors, who followed my brief far more closely than I had a right to reasonably expect while still delivering contributions of maximum interest that required minimal editing. When I did suggest changes, they considered them always with good humour and grace.

Finally, it's back to my university days to briefly reflect how greatly technology has lightened not only the editor's load, but that too of the previously long suffering colleague now spared laborious reams of retyping.

For this book, however, I dreamt up a subtly different tyranny instead, that of 'second reader to a deadline', to inflict on my long-suffering partner, Zchina Dowlatshahi.

Not only did she give me an informed MBA perspective on several chapters, but also managed to stay resolutely cheerful and read each slightly different version of this piece as if it was totally new and fresh to her. Her enthusiasm was both infectious and inspiring, even when I ignored her sensible advice. Thanks so much.

References

Dowling, Tim (2005) The fools of the trade *Guardian* 31 March
Shaw, Esther (2005) Ethical funds hit the target with investors *Independent on Sunday* 10 April

1

The Role and Limits of Ethics Legislation – The US Experience

Phil Rudolph

Introduction

The title of this chapter suggests a survey and analysis of the vast history of American regulation of business ethics. Such a task, however, is not without its difficulties because, stated simply, until very recently the United States has had no real experience in legislating business ethics. It has had abundant experience legislating business conduct, but legislating conduct is not the same as legislating for ethics.

Legislating conduct is really no big deal – conduct has been regulated since the beginning of time ('don't eat that apple'). Such regulation has ranged from the biblical ('thou shalt not kill') to injunctions aimed at arguably more mundane activities ('thou shalt not spit on the sidewalk').

The United States does not even corner the market in the legislation of *business* conduct. Such regulation – which manifests itself in employment laws, consumer protection laws, environmental laws and the like – while generally not nearly as detailed or granular as comparable regulation in the US, exists in some form or another throughout much of the industrialized world.

The United States is, however, unique in its regulation of public companies, particularly in the context of the manner by which those businesses interact with their shareholders. The reasons for this flow largely from historical differences in the nature, and corresponding risks, of ownership of US companies, as contrasted with ownership and risk profiles of companies, for example, in Europe. These differences, in combination with the scandals and market crises that have interposed themselves to varying degrees during the course of the past 75 years, have prompted the evolution in the US of a comprehensive regulatory system governing the way businesses interact with their owners that is largely unrivaled – at least for the present – anywhere in the world.

While concerns over notions of fairness, equity, honesty and the like have deeply impacted its content and substance, this comprehensive regulatory system has not, until quite recently, explicitly incorporated ethics. It has embraced instead the legislation of business conduct ('thou shalt and shalt not') and it has enjoyed famously mixed success. Efforts to legislate ethics, on the other hand, are a recent phenomenon. These efforts are reflected specifically in aspects of the Corporate Responsibility Act of 2002 (the Sarbanes-Oxley Act) and in the 2004 amendments to the US Federal Sentencing Guidelines for Organizations (US Sentencing Commission, 2004). There is, as yet, no real track record by which to measure their success or failure.

So why write a chapter entitled 'The Role and Limits of Ethics Legislation: The US Experience'? Because by evaluating US efforts during the past 75 years to craft a system of rules governing the manner by which companies interact with their owners, and by assessing the drivers behind recent US efforts to weave ethics explicitly into this regulatory fabric, much can be learned about both the need for, and the potential effectiveness of, business ethics legislation.

This chapter begins with a discussion of the history of investor protection legislation in the United States and of the structural and market circumstances that prompted it. It then addresses the limitations of such legislation, both in theory and in the specific context of the business scandals of the past. Consequent US regulatory efforts to incorporate notions of ethics and values explicitly into the laws governing business conduct are then discussed. Finally, the chapter will turn to the question of whether non-regulatory factors are likely to plug the gaps inherent in traditional conduct-focused legislative programs.

The intention is to offer a narrative on the limitations of rules-based regimes as mechanisms to promote ethical business conduct, through a retrospective assessment of US securities regulation. The goal of the chapter is not to suggest an alternative or better system, but rather to inspire a lively debate and discussion about how societies might best employ rules as one of a toolbox full of instruments to promote and maximize ethical behaviour.

US regulation of business conduct towards shareholders – a brief history

US regulation of business behaviour has been prevalent for well over a century, tracing its roots to the first US federal regulatory agency – the Interstate Commerce Commission (the ICC). The US Congress created the ICC in 1887 to oversee and monitor the activities of the railroads and their owners, colourfully nicknamed 'robber barons'. Similarly, the late 19th century predations of the oil industry (the 'oil barons') and other business trusts resulted in the enactment in 1890 of the Sherman Act and related federal statutes to protect the public against anticompetitive acts of businesses.

The United States Congress over the years has also wrestled with the challenges of protecting the integrity of business and the financial markets. The following anecdote has particular contemporary resonance and should trigger immediate recognition:

> 'As Congress investigated the collapse of a high-profile energy company, it faced a daunting challenge. One Senator said.that to understand the huge company's shocking failure, lawmakers must consider the regulatory and legal missteps that led to its downfall. How, he wondered, could Congress restore investors' confidence in the financial system? By repealing old laws? Enacting new ones?
>
> One of his colleagues answered by recounting an old joke: A man gets a message that his mother-in-law has died. "Shall we embalm, cremate or bury?" it asks. Replies the man, "Embalm, cremate and bury. Take no chances".' (Smith, 2002)

During the evolving course of this same investigation, the Senate released the following findings:

- 'self-dealing and outright fraud (not the least of which involved a gigantic, rapidly growing energy operation) have become associated with erosion of the stock market', and
- 'leading Wall Street investment banks are under fire for their lending and investing practices, including transactions designed to allow companies to misstate their financial results' (Brown, 2004).

The investigation from which the above events and findings are derived occurred in 1932, not 2002, as the US Senate evaluated the factors that contributed to the collapse of the stock market in 1929. The energy company whose actions precipitated the market's collapse was not Enron, but Middle West Utilities, and the fellow running the show was not Ken Lay, but Samuel Insull, the former business partner of Thomas Edison. The outcome of this Congressional investigation was not the Corporate Responsibility Act of 2002 (more commonly known as the Sarbanes-Oxley Act (2002)), but the passage of an array of similarly focused laws – including the Securities Act of 1933 and the Securities Exchange Act of 1934 – and the erection of comprehensive regulatory structures administered and overseen by the newly created Securities Exchange Commission (the SEC). This regime – which regulates business conduct but has until recently not pretended to regulate business ethics – has served as the platform for US securities oversight for the past 70 years. Its *raison d'etre* is and has always been to oversee the activities of public companies in order to protect investors specifically and, more generally, to protect the integrity of the financial markets in the United States[1].

In the years since the establishment of this regulatory regime in the 1930s, Congress has amended the securities laws and the SEC has adopted voluminous and comprehensive regulations aimed at tightening, strengthening and improving upon the original legislation. Notably, for example, the insider trading and junk bond scandals that made household names of the likes of Ivan Boesky and Michael Milken prompted a reassessment of regulations governing the activities for which those gentlemen were incarcerated. Messrs Milken and Boesky, in turn, seem like rank amateurs, and their antics like child's play, when measured against the activities of the more contemporary industrial 'robber barons' of the late 20th and early 21st centuries. These latter activities, in turn, prompted perhaps the most sweeping reassessment of US securities regulation – as embodied in Sarbanes-Oxley and related legislation – since such regulation came into existence.

Sarbanes-Oxley was the product of the market dislocation, economic turmoil and public outrage that resulted from the unravelling of Enron and from other corporate fraud scandals that began to emerge in the early days of the 21st century. With a heavy focus on governance, Sarbanes-Oxley rests upon the platform of the original securities legislation of the 1930s and is itself overseen by the SEC. It reflects the need, perceived by Congress and (presumably) the American people, to plug the gaps and fill the holes that enabled our contemporary manifestations of Middle West Utilities and Samuel Insull to, as in that instance, bring the capital market to its knees.

But the very need for Sarbanes-Oxley, the amended insider trading rules of the 1980s and other amendments and modifications to the US securities laws since the 1930s underscores the limits of regulation, or at least the limits of the specific types of regulation that have thus far been relied upon to guide corporate behaviour in the United States. Indeed, despite a comprehensive and longstanding regulatory regime created with the specific intent of addressing almost precisely identical forms of corporate malfeasance, the abuses of Enron, WorldCom, Tyco and other well-known companies were all too common throughout the latter part of the 1990s. Moreover, the negative impacts of these events upon investors and on overall confidence in the capital markets has been – in its own way – just as profound as the market collapse of 1929.

This is not to suggest that regulation of business conduct is wholly ineffective or is a bad idea. Rather, it is to suggest that regulation alone is not a silver bullet and should not be thought of as such. As stated (perhaps overstated) by the CEO of Hanover Mortgage in an April 2004 speech at the Carlson School of Management, 'Regulation is at best a "pain-killer"; it does nothing to solve the deeper systemic problems' (Lapin, 2004). All of which leads to the obvious question: is there a better approach?

To begin to answer this question, it is important to understand why US regulation of business is as rules-laden as it is in comparison with other jurisdictions. To a great extent, the proliferation of rules and regulations governing the manner by which US public companies interact with the investing public flows out of the nature of ownership of US businesses. Unlike European markets, for example, in which capital has historically been raised through government-run banks and through investment of retained earnings, US public companies have historically raised funds through the public issuances of stocks and bonds (see, in general, Hurst, 2004, p 44). Even Americans who do not own stocks directly have a vested interest in the activities of US businesses, given the extensive investments by pension funds in the US debt and equity markets (Hurst, 2004, p 44).

In this context, the crash of the stock market in 1929 had a true, tangible and dramatically negative effect on a vast collection of individuals, including particularly vulnerable individuals (the 'widows and orphans' for whom Congress expressed great concern) whose nest eggs and futures were heavily invested in US business. The extensive regulatory scheme embodied in the Securities Act of 1933 and the Securities Exchange Act of 1934 was occasioned by the urgent need to restore the faith of the investing public in the credibility and viability of the capital marketplace, since private investment was the principal financial engine for public companies.

European corporate and accounting regulations, by contrast, have historically provided fewer shareholder protections and mandated less financial disclosure, because there has historically been less public ownership, and because pensions generally are guaranteed by the state (Hurst, 2004, p 44). In essence, fewer conduct-focused regulatory protections of vulnerable shareholders exist throughout Europe because structurally, as opposed to behaviourally, fewer have historically been needed.

This is beginning to change. As Europe evolves towards a more US-style economy, as privatization and capital market financing replaces government ownership, and as the governments assume a lesser role in cushioning investors from the vagaries of the marketplace, increased risks have driven a push for increased regulation in what has hereto-fore been a bastion of the 'values-based' culture of Europe. Indeed, the EC has introduced an array of governance reforms in response to its recent scandals and is exploring revisions to the more values-based IASB accounting standards as well (see, in general, Hurst, 2004, pp 47–48). For the past 70 years, however, the US has largely cornered the market in rules-focused approaches to managing corporate behaviour.

The limitations of rules

Society needs rules to influence behaviour in tangible ways; it creates its system of rules to incentivize those behaviours it seeks to encourage and to disincentivize those behaviours it seeks to discourage. But there are limits to what rules alone can achieve. In a hypothetically perfect regulatory world, well-designed systems would be calibrated to inspire risk–reward calculations in which rational actors behave themselves. Punishment for murder would vastly exceed that for spitting on the sidewalk and the resources devoted to identifying murderers would similarly exceed those aimed at apprehending spitters. In such a world, the risk–reward calculation associated with committing a murder should, if properly calibrated by well-drafted and effectively enforced rules, reduce to zero one's incentives to commit murder. Yet murder is still a sad and constant reality of daily life, even in societies with the most draconian rules aimed at its prevention.

Clearly then, as the history of United States business legislation has taught us, misconduct will not be prevented by rules alone. Sometimes factors motivating or incentivizing unlawful behaviour will simply overpower the sanctions intended to discourage such behaviour. Moreover, while rules attempt to define the boundaries of conduct, these boundaries themselves are often squishy and ill-defined. They may be difficult to discern. Sometimes they shift and occasionally they disappear completely. Volumes can be written regarding the principal weaknesses of rules-focused regimes, but I will limit my discussion to a small handful of key factors derived, in some measure, from the recent spate of US corporate scandals and the regulatory response to them.

In the first place, because rules drive risk–reward calculations, rational profit-maximizing beings – in the absence of independent ethical constraints – will attempt to fiddle with the equation in order to reduce the risk and enhance the reward[2]. Often this takes the form of seeking out loopholes and exceptions, and of pushing hard against the boundaries that are presumably created by the rules. As evidence of this, one need only look to recent history; many of the scandals of the new millennium appear to have been impelled by a desire on the part of companies and their management to meet and exceed quarterly and annual earnings targets, so that they might, perhaps artificially, drive up the value of their company stock and their personal stock options portfolios. Loopholes, exceptions and hyper-technical interpretations of rules governing companies and their accountants provided the enablers for activities to occur that certainly violated the spirit, if not always the letter, of the law[3].

The traditional US approach to dealing with the loophole conundrum has been to enact more rules to plug loopholes, thus swinging the risk–reward pendulum back to the risk side of the ledger. This approach is not necessarily wrong but it is, at best, a temporary fix – every system of rules enacted to plug holes in existing systems of rules will itself contain holes that will eventually themselves be exploited, and consequently need to be plugged[4]. And this, of course, underscores a major challenge of rules-focused systems. Rules beget loopholes. Loopholes beget rules. Lawyers get rich. But ethical lapses persevere[5].

There is no question that the need exists to continually refine and improve upon regulatory regimes. Even accepting this, however, it is far from clear that the proper approach to the loophole problem would be to engage in the ad infinitum exercise of enacting rule upon rule to address all manner of malfeasance. As former US Supreme Court Justice William O. Douglas said during his tenure as Chairman of the SEC, 'By and large, governments can operate satisfactorily only by proscription that leaves untouched large areas of conduct and activity, some of it susceptible to government regulation but in fact too minute for satis-factory control; some of it lying beyond the periphery of law in the realm of ethics and morality.' (see Atkins, 2003). Justice Douglas's point is fairly compelling. Even if Congress could enact laws to address every manner of malfeasance, no matter how *de minimis*, it is doubtful that such a regime would be even remotely effective, and it would probably collapse of its own weight or perish from neglect.

In addition to the dilemma of the hole that can never be filled, a slavish reliance exclusively upon rules to drive behaviours is flawed for other reasons. These flaws have been exposed through the recent corporate and accounting scandals that have rocked the United States during the past few years. One of the key flaws is that myopically rules-focused systems run the very real risk of creating a forest/trees situation, in which those responsible for compliance with rules lose sight of the rationale underlying them in the first instance. This can, in fact, breed behaviour that is technically compliant but is either wholly illogical, focuses unduly on low hanging fruit at the exclusion of broader systemic challenges, or is ultimately at odds with the spirit of the rules themselves. One might argue that this fetish for literality drove many of the abuses of Enron, insofar as an attitude appears to have pervaded the company in which the question being asked of the accountants and others – either implicitly or explicitly – was 'tell me where it says I can't do this'. As noted by one business ethics practitioner in the USA, '[i]n their pursuit of their dreams or schemes, people focused on what they legally could do, and forgot about what they should have done' (Seidman, 2004, p 3).

The US passion for litigation almost certainly has not helped matters. The primacy of rules-based governance systems has evolved as the US legal system evolved. For reasons flowing from the availability of contingent fees, punitive damages, class action mechanisms, civil juries and the absence of a loser-pays system in the US courts, litigation has become a popular tool for redressing and resolving real or perceived wrongs in American society. The litigation culture that pervades US society drives people to focus rigorously on what is and is not explicitly permitted, mandated or prohibited, because literal compliance – and evi-dence of efforts to achieve literal compliance – has historically minimized legal risk and exposure. Although US business leaders abhor regulation, they nevertheless value certainty. It makes decision-making easier.

This forest/trees dilemma has explicitly been identified as a subject of concern in connection with the regulatory requirements of Sarbanes-Oxley. An article published in the November 2004 issue of *Compliance*

Week quoted the testimony of the Chief Financial Officer of Eli Lilly and Co. before a US Senate committee hearing on the impact of Sarbanes-Oxley as follows: 'I don't think a lot of companies are focusing on overall risks. They are focused on getting documentation completed and the mechanics of documentation cleaned up in time for the audit review. They haven't stepped back and looked at the risk profile of the business.' (Sammer, 2004, p 1). This same gentleman further noted that auditors often want companies to document who was in a particular meeting but do not focus on the substance of the meeting (Sammer, 2004, p 1)[6], adding, 'there has developed what seems to be an overemphasis on certain additional or duplicative levels of documentation, with declining value in terms of how much that additional documentation would add to the effectiveness of internal control' (Sammer, 2004, p 1).

A closely-related weakness of a purely rules-based approach to managing behaviour is that such an approach promotes a certification – or 'check-the-box' – mentality that encourages entities to do the minimum necessary to meet expectations. While this might drive literal compliance, it may nevertheless inhibit corporate actors from evaluating a broader array of behaviours that are not covered by the checklist of rules, and thereby might collide with the broader goals that regulations are intended to promote.

Ethics help mitigate these concerns. At the broadest and most intangible level, ethics help people make the 'right choices' when rules either do not exist, are unclear in their application or do not address the particular situation for which guidance is needed. Ethical frameworks rewire the risk–reward calculations that make rules-based systems so vulnerable. Because ethical systems are premised on a conception of social welfare driven by a set of shared values and principles rather than unvarnished self-interest, in a truly ethical business culture selfish motivation should take a back seat to a defined greater good[7]. Moreover, a culture of ethics helps eliminate the forest/trees problem by making an assessment of the forest an ever-present element of decisions and actions, regardless of how finite these decisions and actions may be. And while it is certainly the case that unethical activity occurs even within the most ethical of business cultures, the strength of the culture will minimize the likelihood that such activities will either permeate or threaten the existence of an organization. As one author has observed:

'[C]urrent research and experience ... suggest that the principal predictor of success in any compliance and ethics program is the culture of the organization itself. ... [S]cholarship [also] suggests that, with rare exceptions, effective programs must strike an appropriate balance between rules, values, and meeting reasonable stakeholder expectations: that an emphasis on compliance alone is often a self-defeating approach to preventing and detecting violations of law.' (Johnson, 2004)

Some businesses have long recognized this and have tried to inculcate their cultures with values and principles that transcend mere literal compliance with rules and regulations. An oft-cited example is Johnson & Johnson, whose seemingly instantaneous decision to pull its Tylenol product off of the store shelves during the tainting scandal of the 1980s was more than the legal system would necessarily have demanded. Although that decision had a dramatically negative immediate impact on the bottom line of the company, it was completely consistent with the long-established credo that had undergirded the company's culture for decades.

For every Johnson & Johnson, however, there have always been companies for whom codes of conduct, and rules and regulations, have been viewed as burdensome necessities and inconvenient obstacles to meeting earnings targets and beating the competition. These are companies that have checked the boxes, and have behaved (hopefully) within the literal boundaries of what the laws required, but that were ever-willing to push those boundaries – to engage in an aggressive form of the risk–reward calculation discussed earlier. These are the companies that, in so doing, have sorely tested the efficacy of the rules-focused system that has pervaded US regulation of business for the past century.

Recognizing, therefore, that legislation of conduct is ultimately imperfect, the obvious questions follow: whether society can better promote and encourage ethical business behaviour, and if so, how? A gradually evolving response to this question has begun to emerge in some out-of-the-ordinary US efforts to legislate business ethics itself. While the US government has danced around the edges of ethics legislation for some time, the scandals in the early days of the 21st century have made such initiatives far more explicitly ethics focused and have pushed them to the forefront.

US efforts to legislate ethics

In June 1986, 32 major US defence contractors pledged to adopt and implement a set of principles of business ethics and conduct that were intended to address procurement abuses in government contracting. The Defense Industry Initiative (DII) grew out of the recommendation of a blue ribbon commission appointed by President Reagan to address scandals that had plagued the defence industry. Specifically, the commission recommended that 'to assure that their houses are in order, defense contractors must promulgate and vigilantly enforce codes of ethics that address the unique problems and procedures incident to defense procurement. They must also develop and implement internal controls to monitor these codes of ethics and sensitive aspects of contract compliance' (see Defense Industry Initiative on Business Ethics and Conduct, 2000; Krawiec, 2003). These recommendations, and the consequent implementation of the DII, resulted in the emergence of a small group of executives who had specific responsibility for creating and managing internal ethics and compliance programmes for their respective businesses.

Their numbers would grow. In November 1991, the United States Sentencing Commission[8] promulgated the Federal Sentencing Guidelines for Organizations (FSGO) (2004). These guidelines came four years after the original Sentencing Guidelines for individuals took effect and were intended to address the difficult issues associated with imposing sentences on corporations convicted of federal criminal offenses – issues that were left untouched in the original guidelines. The FSGO incorporated input from the business community seeking to moderate the punishment (the stick) for businesses that violated the federal laws with some form of 'reward' (the carrot) for those that took steps to comply with such laws. Specifically, under the original FSGO, if a criminally culpable company had in place an 'effective program for preventing and detecting' criminal wrongdoing and cooperated with investigating authorities, its criminal fine could be reduced significantly. The benchmark for an 'effective' programme was largely derived from the DII.

Notably, despite the fact that the trade association formed in large measure to understand and address the implications of the original FSGO named itself the 'Ethics Officers Association' (Ethics Officers Association, 1992), the FSGO did not itself address the concept of ethics, *per se*. It spoke, instead, about the need for businesses to establish 'effective programs to prevent and detect violations of law', and repeatedly trumpeted the need for 'compliance standards and procedures'. In short, legal compliance, not ethics, was the focus of the FSGO.

In the wake of promulgation of the FSGO, companies began to implement internal compliance programmes with increasing enthusiasm. Subsequent judicial activity at both the state and federal level underscored and enhanced the risks associated with failing to build such programmes, and compliance activity grew like topsy. In 1992 the Ethics Officers Association had 12 members; today it boasts in excess of 1,000.

Among the myriad companies that enacted 'codes of ethics' in the wake of the promulgation of the FSGO was an upstart Houston-based energy company called Enron. There was little question that Enron had a programme of standards and procedures; indeed, Enron's voluminous code had been highly praised throughout the business community. But it is equally clear that Enron's award-winning programme was not effective. For example, though provisions of Enron's code would have precluded a number of the activities that have since become the stuff of notorious legend, management and the board routinely waived these provisions – either out of nefarious motives of their own or out of the naive belief that the waivers were necessary and appropriate to achieve legitimate business objectives. In all events, neither the laws and regulations governing Enron, nor those governing Enron's accountants, were sufficient to prevent activities that produced the governance and financial meltdown that occurred. Those activities, in turn, were impervious to an ethics code – and more importantly, an ethics culture – that was porous in its application.

In no small measure it was the failure of Enron's management and board to adhere to the proscriptions of its existing compliance standards – its code of 'ethics' – that produced the wave of regulatory initiatives designed to plug the ethical gaps through which Enron's leadership plunged. In fact, in the wake of Enron and the array of other scandals that roiled the business and financial communities in the early days of the new millennium, US regulators have endeavoured in earnest to build true ethical trip-wires into the regulatory regimes governing the activities of companies. Section 406 of the Sarbanes-Oxley Act requires public companies to disclose (a) whether they have codes of ethics (specifically denominated codes of 'ethics' as opposed to codes of 'conduct'), (b) whether these codes apply to their key executives, (c) any waivers of their codes of ethics for these individuals and (d) any changes to these codes (Sarbanes-Oxley Act, 2002). Moreover, if a company does not have ethics codes, it must disclose this fact and explain why it has not adopted one[9].

Section 406 defines a code of ethics as:

'Written standards that are reasonably designed to deter wrong-doing and to promote:

1. Honest and ethical conduct, including the ethical handling of actual or apparent conflicts of interest between personal and professional relationships;
2. Full, fair, accurate, timely, and understandable disclosure in reports and documents that a company files with, or submits to, the [SEC] and in other public communications made by the [company];
3. Compliance with applicable governmental laws, rules and regulations;
4. The prompt internal reporting of violations of the code to an appropriate person or persons identified in the code; and,
5. Accountability for adherence to the code.' (Sarbanes-Oxley Act, 2002)

Compliance with applicable laws, rules and regulations is but one of the criteria subsumed within this definition.

Of further note, Section 805 of Sarbanes-Oxley directed the US Sentencing Commission to review and amend the FSGO and related policy statements to ensure that they are sufficient to deter and punish business misconduct (Sarbanes-Oxley Act, 2002). This mandate coincided with a multi-year review of the FSGO that had been undertaken on the 10th anniversary of the guidelines in 2001. After a two-year study that included public comment and testimony, the Sentencing Commission submitted amended guidelines to Congress in April 2004, and the guidelines took effect on 1 November 2004[10].

The amended guidelines are noteworthy for several reasons. Perhaps most notably, the term 'ethics', which was absent from the original FSGO, has achieved a position of prominence in the amended guidelines. These guidelines note that an 'effective compliance and ethics program' is one of the mitigating factors that can reduce an organization's punishment for criminal misconduct (see *US Sentencing Guidelines Manual*, 2004, §882.1). The amended guidelines retain the language from the original FSGO, requiring that a business exercise due diligence to prevent and detect criminal conduct, but add the requirement that business 'otherwise promote an organizational culture that encourages ethical conduct and a commitment to compliance with the law' (see *US Sentencing Guidelines Manual*, 2004, §882.1(a)(2)). The Sentencing Commission notes that 'this addition is intended to reflect the emphasis on ethical conduct and values incorporated into recent legislative and regulatory reforms, such as those provided by the [Sarbanes-Oxley] Act' (US Sentencing Commission, 2004). The amended guidelines also prescribe seven minimum requirements considered 'the hallmarks of an effective program that encourages compliance with the law and ethical conduct' (US Sentencing Commission, 2004).

Although the guidelines are voluntary, failure to comply can have dramatic negative consequences for a company beyond merely those associated with heightened criminal sanctions for misconduct. The degree to which businesses have embraced the FSGO recommendations for compliance programmes has, in the past, affected such issues as whether the company's board itself could be charged with failure of oversight[11], and whether a company is behaving in accordance with business norms for the purposes of assessing liability in civil litigation.

In combination with Sarbanes-Oxley, the amended sentencing guidelines aim explicitly at the recognized need for businesses to do more than merely 'check the box' in creating compliance programmes. These new rules require the development by businesses of programmes tailored to the specific ethical challenges and risks that they face. In the event of ethical lapses, the adequacy and effectiveness of such programmes will be assessed after the fact by judges and juries – an admittedly imperfect system – but the goal of the guidelines is to force business leaders to bake ethics, rather than merely rote compliance, into their companies' day-to-day operations. As one author has noted:

> 'These new guidelines address the root cause of many of the corporate failures of recent years – ethical laxity among corporate executives. They are meant to address the real deficit that confronts corporate America – the trust deficit, the substantial loss of trust in corporations and their executives by the public and investors.' (Brown, 2004, note 2)

Will US ethics legislation meet the test?

As the legislation that would become Sarbanes-Oxley was being debated in the United States Congress, some of my European friends took great delight in mocking the penchant of the United States to enact voluminous rules and regulations to address society's ills. They noted in somewhat superior tones that companies in Europe, subject to far less prescriptive and granular systems of regulation, had somehow managed to avoid the ethical sinkhole into which – despite this country's legislative horn of plenty – the US business and accounting community had sunk.

At the time of these self-congratulatory harangues, Royal Ahold, Parmalat and other high-profile corporate scandals in Europe had not yet emerged. In fairness, their subsequent emergence proves nothing one way or the other, except insofar as it proves that people of all cultures and regulatory regimes are imperfect creatures who will, when presented with opportunities that seemingly outweigh risks, often make bad choices. What remains uncertain is whether the rules-based culture of the US makes its businesses more or less prone to ethical meltdowns. The Parmalat and Royal Ahold debacles (as well as other European business scandals of the more distant past) support a conclusion that US business is neither more nor less susceptible to these problems.

Indeed, at least one author has suggested that the evolution of Europe towards a US-style economy betokens a dramatic ethical crisis unless Europe also embraces a US-style regulatory regime governing businesses and accountants:

> '[T]here is a dangerous disconnect between the new reality of the European business world and the outdated rules that still govern it. "What we see in Europe is a push toward more capital market financing, and that requires changes in oversight," says Christian Leuz, a professor at the University of Pennsylvania's Wharton School. ... Among other things, Europe needs stronger securities oversight, shareholder protections, and, above all, uniform enforcement – if not an actual policing body akin to the SEC. Even tough regulations that could have ousted Parmalat earlier would have done little good in Italy, where current enforcement mechanisms are weak. "The US got securities regulation, including the SEC, after the 1929 crash. No European country did," [citation omitted]. "What Europe needs most urgently are securities laws that protect investors – not to mention enforceable corporate governance and accounting rules."' [12]

As noted earlier, the European Commission has begun to take steps in this direction, and is using Sarbanes-Oxley as a guide for doing so (see Hurst, 2004, p 47).

Still untested is the question whether true ethics legislation – if such a beast can even be said to exist – can or will make a difference. This is a question that only time will answer. Every prominent business scandal in the USA has been followed by a period of intense regulatory activity, then relative quiescence often of considerable duration, after which new scandals emerge and the process begins anew. Regardless of how seemingly airtight the new US ethics legislation is, this pattern is likely to persist. It remains to be seen, however, what these unknown and unknowable future scandals will tell us about the effectiveness of the ethics provisions of the new legislation.

At a certain level, regulation – even regulation of ethics – can only do so much. What US regulators have thus far not entirely grasped is the role that market forces will play in driving compliance with these rules. Many of the scandals of the Enron era were driven by the ever-increasing expectations of the US financial markets, whose companies and executives were and continue to be assessed – and very publicly assessed – every three months. The need to meet quarterly targets drives a short-term mentality that all but eliminates strategic action and that relegates issues like compliance and ethics to the category of annoying afterthought. The new rules force compliance and ethics into a more prominent position in the minds of corporate executives, but they are certainly not perceived as being any less annoying. Indeed, they appear to be perceived by many as a necessary evil.

The same market forces that drive 'quarterly earnings' thinking in business today, however, should increasingly drive ethical thinking in the future. The gutting of retirement funds and pension plans that occurred as Enron sank into the Gulf of Mexico has dramatically raised public awareness of the importance of corporate ethics to the 'average American', and to their sainted widows and orphans. And the ubiquity of 24-hour business news, the Internet, technologically-savvy private watchdog organizations and socially-responsible investor organizations and fund managers has effectively eliminated the ability of companies to keep their constituencies in the dark about anything. Thus, corporate stakeholders may increasingly demand ethical accountability as a prerequisite to investing in, or patronizing, a company and its products or services. One prominent practitioner in the field of corporate ethics has aptly noted in this regard, 'In this world where nothing stays hidden, companies must conduct themselves as though they have nothing to hide.' (Seidman, 2004, p 3)

As intangibles such as goodwill and reputational value make up an increasingly large percentage of the value of companies, ethical leadership will therefore assume a correspondingly greater role in the activities of these companies. 'Regulation can only go so far to curb corporate scandal. There will always be greedy individuals out there, but if a majority of citizens stop buying a company's stock and product, executives will think twice about stepping out of line.' (Hurst, 2004, note 5, p 4). Viewed in this light, then, the Johnson & Johnsons of the world should, over time, become more the rule than the exception, because a failure to undertake such leadership should, again over time, negatively impact the willingness of shareholders and fund managers to do business with companies who come up short. '[I]n this new world – where accusations of impropriety, rumor and innuendo have cost companies billions in market capitalization, even before guilt is established – companies are increasingly focusing on protecting and strengthening their reputations which, in turn, focuses them on ethics.' (Seidman, 2004, p 3)

Conclusion

Ethics legislation in the US is a noble experiment. It will arguably strengthen the latticework of governance laws and regulations that has existed for the past 75 years. The concept itself, however, is somewhat pregnant with irony in the context of the broader 'values-based system vs rules-based system' debate, insofar as it is entirely uncertain into which category the legislation of ethics would properly fit. In the end, while purists might consider it the unholy spawn of both, this highlights the folly of the entire debate. Both the 'rules-based' US regulatory system and the 'values-based' systems that exist outside of the United States have sizable strengths and notable flaws. Some form of meaningful, substantive ethics regulation is certainly necessary, but is, with equal certainty, not likely to be sufficient.

Ultimately, whatever regulatory systems are implemented to manage the conduct and the ethics of business, they will only be as effective as whatever equally or more compelling non-regulatory forces drive, and have always driven, day-to-day business decisions. This is a balance that is ever in flux, and will ever be so. All of which suggests that, after 75-plus years of the regulation of business conduct, and a far more recent effort to craft regulation specifically aimed at ethics, the United States is not yet able to truly assess the role and limits of its ethics legislation – the question implicit in the title of this chapter. In this context, it is particularly appropriate to recall the famous quote attributed to Mao Tse Tung who, when asked in 1949 to describe what he believed were the most significant lessons of the French Revolution, responded that 'it is too soon to tell'.

Notes

1 Each of the 50 states also has laws aimed at the same goals. The focus of this chapter, however, is on the federal regulatory regime.

2 We must always remember that incentives drive conduct. As the American author Upton Sinclair has been quoted as saying, 'It is difficult to get a man to understand something when his salary depends on his not understanding it.'

3 As one author has noted: 'Something that is not immediately apparent when you trawl through the media coverage of Enron ... [is that the] majority of off-balance sheet partnerships that Enron set up were legal. . . . They may have strained some of the rules of accounting, but they did not break these rules.' (Saunders, 2003).

4 In this light, reliance on rules alone to prevent misconduct becomes a Sysaphisian task, or a real world variant of Zeno's paradox, in which an arrow shot at a target – by virtue of its need to infinitely traverse a distance halfway to the target – will in theory never actually reach it.

5 'Focusing on informed acquiescence often obtains the opposite result, producing ever-increasing bureaucracies designed to enforce compliance with multiplying legal and regulatory requirements. Moreover, these bureaucracies are often met by cynicism and by the clever employees who attempt to game the system. Their violations lead to more bureaucracy, and this vicious cycle continues.' (Seidman, 2004)

6 Underscoring the point that an overly technical focus on compliance can detract from the broader goals of regulation, this executive stated: 'Make no mistake about it, documentation for documentation's sake will not deter financial fraud.' (Sammer, 2004, p 26).

7 This is, of course, a generalization that ignores, for example, the principle of ethical egoism, which posits that each person should do whatever promotes their own best interest, and should make moral choices based on this analysis. In the context of business organizations, such ethical doctrines seem misplaced.

8 The Sentencing Commission is an independent agency that resides within the judicial branch of the US government. It was given life in the Sentencing Reform Act provisions of the Comprehensive Crime Control Act of 1984, and is charged with the ongoing responsibilities of evaluating the effects of the sentencing guidelines on the criminal justice system, recommending to Congress appropriate modifications of substantive criminal law and sentencing procedures, and establishing a research and development programme on sentencing issues.

9 This new regulatory mandate is supplemented by ethics code expectations contained in new listing requirements for both the New York Stock Exchange and the NASDAQ.

10 The United States Supreme Court struck down as unconstitutional the theretofore mandatory application of the guidelines on 12 January 2005 [United States v. Booker, 125 S. Ct. 738 (2005)]. However, it is widely believed that the guidelines will continue to play an important advisory role for judges, and it is further expected that Congressional revisions intended to address the Supreme Court's concerns will retain, with respect to the Sentencing Guidelines for Organizations, the newly-minted focus on ethics.

11 See, for example, Caremark Int'l Inc. (1996) (suggesting that directors who fail to ensure that their companies have effective programmes may be deemed to have violated their fiduciary duties).

12 Hurst (2004, note 5, p 45). The author added, in the context of the wave of European financial scandals, 'the gap between regulatory philosophy and economic reality dwarfs anything in the US, and it was only a matter of time before greedy corporate types started exploiting it'.

References

Atkins, Paul S (2003) Speech by SEC Commissioner: "The Sarbanes-Oxley Act of 2002: goals, content, and status of implementation". *International Financial Legal Review* Mar. 25. Available at: http://www.sec.gov/news/speech/spch 032503psa.htm

Brown, Gary M (2004) Resisting temptation: new sentencing guidelines prod companies to take ethics more seriously. *Legal Times*, Nov. 15. Available at: http://www.law.com/jsp/dc/PubArticleDC.jsp?id=1100137007370

Caremark Int'l Inc. (1996) *Derivatives Litigation* 698 A2d 959 (Del Ch. 1996)

Comprehensive Crime Control Act of 1984. Available at: http://usinfo.state.gov/ usa/infousa/society/crime/crimegun1.pdf

Defense Industry Initiative on Business Ethics and Conduct (2000) *Annual Report* 1–2

Ethics Officers Association (1992) About the EOA. Available at: http://www. eoa.org/AboutEOA.asp

Hurst, Nathan F. (2004) *Corporate Ethics, Governance and Social Responsibility: Comparing European Business Practices to those in the United States.* Study conducted for the Business and Organizational Ethics Partnership, Markkula Center for Applied Ethics, Santa Clara University (Spring)

Johnson, Kenneth W (2004) *Federal Sentencing Guidelines: Key Points and Profound Changes* Ethics Resource Center (Sept.). Available at: http://www. ethics.org/resources/article_detail.cfm?ID=861

Krawiec, Kimberly D (2003) Cosmetic compliance and the failure of negotiated governance. *Washington University Legal Quarterly* 81:29 487, 497

Lapin, David (2004) *David Lapin, CEO, Hanover Mortgage, Governance Alone Cannot Create an Ethic.* Address to the Ethics in the Financial Services Industry after Sarbanes-Oxley Conference, Carlson School of Management, Apr. 16. Available at: http://www.strategic-ethics.com/paper10.htm

Sammer, Joanne (2004) Companies migrating from SOX 'myopia' to risk management. *Compliance Week* Nov.

Sarbanes-Oxley Act (2002) Available at: http://www.sec.gov/about/laws/soa2002. pdf. See also: http://www.sec.gov/spotlight/sarbanes-oxley.htm

Saunders, Chris (2003) *What Can We Learn From The Enron Affair?* Lancaster University Management School, Jan. 7. Available at: http://www.lums.lancs.ac. uk/news/accounting/2002-12-18/

Securities Act of 1933 (1933) 15 USC §77. Available at: http://www.law.uc.edu/ CCL/33Act/

Securities Exchange Act of 1934 (1934) 15 USC §78. Available at: http://www.sec.gov/divisions/corpfin/34act/index1934.shtml

Seidman, Dov (2004) The essential union of law and ethics. *Ethics Matters* Aug. Available at: http://ecampus.bentley.edu/dept/cbe/research/newsletter/newsletter_collection/2004Aug_newsletter/2004Aug_newsletter.html

Smith, Rebecca W (2002) Enron's rise and fall gives some scholars a sense of déjà vu – decades ago, a big power trust likewise pushed its luck – and earned a place in infamy. *Wall Street Journal* Feb. 4, A1

US Federal Sentencing Guidelines for Organizations (2004) 18 U.S.C. §3553(a). Available at: http://www.ussc.gov/orgguide.HTM

US Sentencing Guidelines Manual (2004). Available at: http://www.ussc.gov/GUIDELIN.HTM

US Sentencing Commission (2004) *Amended Organizational Guidelines* 13 (Apr. 30). Available at: http://www.lrn.com/library/whitepapers/ussc_guide_print.pdf

2

Beyond the Limitations of a Written Code of Ethics[1]

Alyson Warhurst and Kevin Franklin

The last 10 years have seen a significant increase in reported cases of corporate malpractice, fraud, scandal and corruption. This has negatively affected the share prices of businesses involved, impacted customer confidence and contributed to the gradual erosion of societal trust in business. It is partly because of such incidents that governments, investors and other stakeholders are increasingly holding companies accountable for their actions – both in terms of conformance with international best practice ethics standards and in terms of reporting on performance and associated business ethics 'risks'.

This chapter explores the potential and limitations of a written code of ethics as a means of safeguarding business reputation, building stakeholder trust and informing the risk assessment process – as well as educating and empowering managers to make more responsible decisions. We draw principally on a values-based approach to business ethics with roots in international human rights law and standards. In doing so we focus in particular on business ethics as being about how business might contribute to the protection of human rights – advancing the civil, political, economic, social and cultural rights that continue to inform the advancement of the sustainable development agenda, as presented in the United Nations Global Compact (United Nations, 2000a). These same issues are also presented as forming the basis of an 'ideal' code of ethics that might be tailored to suit an individual business through an inclusive process to embed these values in business behaviour.

Having identified the content and rationale for a code of ethics, we discuss briefly why just having a written code of ethics is not enough to instil ethical conduct in business. This in turn leads us to explore further opportunities and the potential value that might be obtained from a written code of ethics. We do this by suggesting a code of ethics 'process' and a set of tools that might be used to drive continual improvement in learning about and embedding both the code of ethics itself and instilling ethical conduct as an integral part of the way a business works. We close with a set of conclusions and recommendations for what a business might do to begin the code of ethics embedding process.

A values-based approach to business ethics

This section introduces the concept of a code of ethics as an integral part of a human rights or values-based approach to business responsibility. Taking a human rights or values-based approach is about doing the right thing because it is ethical and responsible and not because it is obviously beneficial to business *per se*. We view this as being fundamentally different from a corporate social responsibility argument, which is often about constructing a financial or risk management business case for social responsibility. A values-based approach to business ethics is about how business as an organ of society interprets and addresses its responsibility to safeguard these fundamental human rights (values). It is about how business embeds the protection of these rights and associated freedoms as an integral part of the way it works, in business processes, functions and in relationships with internal and external stakeholders (Warhurst, 2001).

At the core of the business ethics or values-based approach is the obligation and commitment as a corporate citizen to uphold and respect the fundamental rights and freedoms of individuals as enshrined in the Universal Declaration of Human Rights (UDHR). The UDHR (United Nations, 1948) specifically declares that 'every individual and every organ of society ... shall strive by teaching and education to promote respect for these (fundamental) rights and freedoms'. This includes business.

Whilst the responsibility for protecting individual human rights has traditionally been borne by governments (who ratify treaties and conventions), as business becomes progressively more powerful in the global economy, it is increasingly regarded as responsible for upholding those human rights and freedoms within its 'sphere of influence' (Addo, 1999; OECD, 2000) – including those applicable to employees, host communities and supply chain partners. Business is no longer seen as a neutral participant in the human rights agenda (Amnesty International, 2002). Instead there exists a potential for business to be considered complicit in human rights and ethics infringements that occur within in its sphere of influence. Voluntary initiatives such as the Global Compact (United Nations, 2000a) provide a context for companies to address these issues – thus reducing the risk of alleged complicity in human rights infringements. Developing bespoke codes of ethics or business principles can even further reduce the risk of alleged complicity, especially when formalized as part of a code of ethics process, as we will discuss below.

A typology of business ethics based on human rights

Human rights are the rights individuals have as human beings. They include civil and political, economic, social, cultural and development rights and should be enjoyed equally by all persons. Human rights as we understand them today are based on an international framework of law, which builds on the UDHR, the International Covenant on Civil and Political Rights (United Nations, 1966a) and the International Covenant on Economic, Social and Cultural Rights (United Nations, 1966b). Together these three instruments comprise the International Bill of Rights. The UDHR and the International Bill of Rights have set the direction for all subsequent work in the field of human rights and have provided the basic philosophy for many legally-binding international instruments designed to protect the rights and freedoms of individuals and groups. Together these instruments also provide the basis for the three 'generations' or categories of human rights initially identified by Karel Vasak in the late 1900s (see Weston, 2002).

Civil and political rights

First-generation civil and political rights relate to an individual's entitlement to liberty (the right to life, freedom from oppression and political participation). These rights are incorporated in Articles 2–21 of the UDHR and the International Covenant on Civil and Political Rights. First-generation discussions tend to talk of human rights in largely negative terms ('freedom from') rather than positive ('right to'). Examples include freedom from forced and bonded labour, freedom from discrimination, freedom from political oppression, freedom from arbitrary arrest and detention and freedom from interference in privacy and correspondence. What is constant in this first-generation conception is the notion of liberty as a shield that safeguards the individual against the abuse of political authority. This is the core sentiment of first-generation rights.

Economic, social and cultural rights

Second-generation economic, social and cultural rights are group rights that relate to equality (and the right to subsistence). These rights are embodied in Articles 22–27 of the UDHR and the International Covenant on Economic, Social and Cultural Rights. Second-generation discussions tend to talk of human rights in largely positive terms ('right to') rather than negative ('freedom from') as opposed to first-generation rights. They include the right to social security, the right to work, the right to rest and leisure, the right to education and the right to form and to join trade unions. Second-generation rights are fundamentally claims to social equity – many of which are embedded in the core standards and conventions of the International Labour Organization (ILO). Some authors (Weston, 2002) suggest that, as the social inequities created by globalization and capitalism become more evident over time, the demand for second-generation rights will grow and mature. This makes second-generation rights increasingly applicable to multinational business associated with the globalization process.

Solidarity or development rights

Third-generation solidarity rights acknowledge people's right to peace and to live in a safe and healthy environment as well as the collective right to environmental, cultural and economic development, i.e. development rights. The content of these rights has recently been elaborated in the Declaration on the Right to Development (United Nations, 1986), the Rio Declaration (United Nations, 1992) and the Vienna Declaration (United Nations, 1993). Three of the third-generation rights – the right to peace, the right to a healthy and sustainable environment and the right to humanitarian disaster relief – suggest the impotence or inefficiency of the nation-state in certain critical respects (Weston, 2002). The ongoing challenge faced by governments to deliver such rights makes the role of business and other 'organs of society' additionally critical in securing the advancement of development rights (Davis, 1973). This is especially relevant with respect to developing countries and the high levels of poverty, disease and economic malaise present in such nations (Maplecroft, 2005).

Both the Declaration on the Right to Development (1986) and Vienna Declaration (1993) make specific statements linking the human rights agenda to sustainable development. The Declaration on the Right to Development considers 'the right to development ... (as being) an inalienable human right'. And the Vienna Declaration echoes the intra- and inter-generational sentiment of the Brundtland definition of sustainable development (Bruntland, 1987) by recognizing 'the right to development should be fulfilled so as to meet equitably the developmental and environmental needs of present and future generations'. Upholding these rights cannot be realized by the action of one party alone, but requires cooperative international action between and amongst all organs of society – including business. This same sentiment is recognized in both the Millennium Development Goals (United Nations, 2000b) and the United Nations Global Compact (2000a), both of which are fundamentally allied to international human rights standards and sustainable development goals (Figure 2.1).

The content of an ideal 'code of ethics'

The Global Compact builds on the need for collective action by encouraging business to work in partnership with other social actors as part of the solution to the challenges of globalization and sustainable development. The Compact was introduced in July 2000 by UN Secretary-General Kofi Annan. It is a voluntary corporate citizenship initiative that brings companies together with UN agencies, labour, non-governmental organizations and other civil-society actors to foster action and partnerships in the pursuit of a more sustainable and inclusive global economy.

The Compact is based on 10 principles in the areas of human rights, labour, environment and anti-corruption – each of which can be linked to the human rights agenda noted previously (Figure 2.1). The 10 principles are derived from near-universal consensus in the UDHR, the ILO's Declaration on Fundamental Principles and Rights at Work (ILO, 1998), the Rio Declaration (United Nations,1992) and the more recent Convention Against Corruption (United Nations, 2003). Together these principles constitute what we consider to be a best practice code of (business) ethics.

The Compact specifically asks business to integrate the promotion of human rights, compliance with labour standards and environmental protection into its core business operations and to pursue projects and corporate activities that advance these principles. The Compact is not a regulatory instrument – it does not 'police' or enforce the behaviour

Code of ethics

[informed by the principles of the UN Global Compact]

Human rights	Labour standards	Environment	Anti-corruption
Principle 1 Businesses should support and respect the protection of…human rights within their sphere of influence	**Principle 3** Businesses should uphold freedom of association and recognition of the right to collective bargaining	**Principle 7** Businesses should support a precautionary approach to environmental challenges	**Principle 10** Businesses should work to counter all forms of corruption, including extortion and bribery
Principle 2 Businesses should make sure that they are not complicit in human rights abuses	**Principle 4** Businesses should eliminate all forms of forced and compulsory labour	**Principle 8** Businesses should undertake initiatives to promote greater environmental responsibility	NOTE A best practice code of ethics would also include additional 'economic' elements relating to – customer satisfaction, ethics supply chains, governance and financial responsibility, conflict and security
	Principle 5 Businesses should strive for the effective abolition of child labour	**Principle 9** Businesses should encourage the development and diffusion of environmentally friendly technologies	
	Principle 6 Businesses should end discrimination in respect of employment and occupation		
International Covenant on Civil and Political Rights (1966a) and the International Covenant on Economic, Social and Cultural Rights (1966b)	ILO Declaration on Fundamental Principles and Rights at Work (1998) and ILO Conventions (1930–1999)	Declaration on the Right to Development (1986) and the Rio Declaration (1992)	The United Nations Convention against Corruption (2003)

Relevant international human rights standards

[Universal Declaration of Human Rights (1948)]

Figure 2.1 The scope of business ethics and international standards

or actions of companies. Emphasis is instead on bringing about corporate change through the use of a learning approach that facilitates discussion between different groups in society and builds new relationships for future projects. For this reason the Compact has introduced policy dialogues and a learning forum to support the 10 principles. More recently, signatories have been required to report publicly on their progress in implementing the principles.

Reporting on such principles ideally requires participating businesses to think beyond the issue of reporting *per se*. It requires business to understand how its core products or services, business processes and ways of working compliment and advance the values of the Compact by contributing to human rights and sustainable development. For many companies, attaining this level of understanding begins by interpreting the universal principles of the Compact in a way that suits the products and services, goals, organizational culture and ethical position of the business – oft-times in a bespoke set of business principles or a code of ethics.

Beyond the limitations of a written code of ethics

The *Shorter Oxford English Dictionary* (2002) defines a code as a 'systematic collection of statutes' or a 'systematic collection of digests or laws (a set of rules on any subject)'. A code of ethics or set of business principles is more than a series of aspirational statements. It provides the high-level overview of a company's ethics or corporate responsibility commitments. Codes are value driven and sit at the governance level of an organization, closely allied to the business mission and vision. They provide employees and other stakeholders with an authoritative and easily accessible insight into the 'rules of engagement'. Codes or business principles challenge a company to translate its values into daily practice. They can also help generate trust and loyalty amongst internal and external stakeholders by providing a neat and succinct set of commitments stakeholders can gauge performance against. This section explores briefly some of the limitations associated with the written code of ethics before expanding the ideal structure of a code – as the basis for our code of ethics process discussion.

The limitations of a written code of ethics

A written code of ethics alone is not enough to ensure the commitments or 'rules of engagement' it sets forth are adhered to in the day-to-day activities of employees and in relationships with stakeholders. Codes or principles need to be actively cascaded down the different levels of management and into core business practices in a way that builds understanding, awareness and ownership – empowering individuals to enact and 'live' the commitments as an integral part of the way they work.

Traditionally, codes of ethics and business principles have been conceived as static documents purely to inform employees and interested parties about the beliefs and commitments of the business. They were often imposed 'top down' on managers and employees, devised by consultants and owned only by the top management. Once developed, they were frequently left to languish on the intranet or Internet – comforting only the few individuals or organizations that read them. But the numerous corporate scandals of the late 1990s and 2000s have made society more sceptical. Customers, investors, non-governmental organizations and other stakeholders now expect to see the commitments made in codes of ethics and business principles demonstrated and reported on in a systematic and transparent manner. They expect greater accountability and disclosure about risks and activities across the economic, social and environmental domains of business ethics[2]. This means finding ways and means of implementing and measuring the commitments made in a code of ethics throughout the business. It means breathing life and dynamism into the written code by sharing it with individuals who will own, enact and review its commitments on an ongoing basis.

Breathing life into a written code of ethics can also be constrained by any lack of internal 'ownership' or responsibility. The significance and cross-cutting nature of issues addressed mean that codes should be the responsibility of both a senior management representative and the board. Codes of ethics that are the responsibility of other departments such as human resources, external affairs or communications may be rendered inactive or weak in their enforcement ability, as such departments infrequently have the requisite technical understanding, management or leadership capacity to implement economic, social and environmental commitments across the business. The member of senior management or organizational body tasked with implementing the code should be sufficiently empowered to build awareness and capacity across different departments – translating the articles or clauses of the code into a meaningful set of implementation requirements and practical tools that fit within existing ways of working. The basis for this type of empowering and learning environment lies in the content (Figure 2.1) and structure of the code itself.

The structure of an ideal code of ethics

Preparing the ground for an effective code of ethics process begins by identifying the most appropriate content and structure of the code itself. The code of ethics should include articles and clauses relating not only to ethics and human rights issues themselves but also to the manner in which they will be implemented and who will 'own' them internally. This sets the context for business accountability by delimiting clearly what and how stakeholders might expect to see performance evaluated and reported on and who they should engage with to share their concerns or comments. A well-structured code of ethics will also better equip a business to cascade its commitments through to other management tools such as policies, guidance materials, procedures and audit programmes.

A code of ethics or set of business principles should include at least the following types of information.

- *A set of commitments* that oblige the company and its employees to behave in a particular way. Articles or clauses in the code might include an introductory commitment complimented by a set of sub-commitments or explanatory statements grounded in international best practice. These commitments and statements should be written such that they are equally relevant to the products and services, organizational culture and mission of the business in question.
- *An explicit obligation to legal compliance and reference to relevant standards.* It is considered best practice for codes to cite what treaties, conventions and initiatives have influenced its content – such as the UDHR and other best practice standards – across the economic, social and environmental domains of sustainable development. Reference to such standards may equally be presented in the preamble or associated guidance material if not cited in the code itself.
- *An explanation of scope.* The code of ethics itself or associated text, such as the preamble, should include a discussion of what parts of the business it applies to. This is especially applicable for multinational companies or corporates with separate legal operating companies. A best practice scope statement would also note the applicability of the code to business partners (suppliers, subcontractors and joint-ventures) and how it relates to other instruments or processes in the business.
- *A series of implementation statements that explain how commitments will be met.* The preamble or other appropriate section of

the code might also include information about relevant senior management or board responsibility. Functional ownership of the code may be designated to an advisory committee of both internal (cross-departmental) and external experts and stakeholders. Ideally such codes would be managed by a sub-board committee reporting to the relevant board member, chairman or chief executive.

- A *discussion of communication and awareness-building* about the code of ethics. This might include a brief description of what types of activities or forms of communication and awareness-building will be used to increase people's understanding of the issues, what they mean to the business and how they are being managed. This section should also include a business commitment to train and develop employee capacity to ensure the relevant people understand the code and the implications of not keeping to it. It is important to empower people sufficiently to make knowledgeable and informed decisions about business ethics and not simply to require they abide by a set of 'rules' (Nonaka and Takeuchi, 1995).

- A *management framework covering monitoring and evaluation.* This section will detail what mechanisms are in place to gauge how effectively the code of ethics has been understood and implemented against a set of predetermined targets. The code of ethics might also make a specific commitment to involve a third party specialist organization in the monitoring and auditing of performance – thus ensuring greater objectivity in the ongoing appraisal and review process. Ideally the code of ethics would also make a commitment to external disclosure through reporting and ongoing stakeholder engagement as part of the commitment to continual improvement.

Implementing and being fully accountable to the articles and commitments of the code will require a business to establish a systematic management framework and process that, together, provide the appropriate tools and process to make the code of ethics an integral part of the business fabric.

A code of ethics management framework

Implementing and embedding the commitments made within a code of ethics requires more than the code of ethics itself. It requires the cascading of articles and commitments through business policies, guidance materials and procedures and practical tools including audit and monitoring instruments – as presented in Figure 2.2 (Warhurst, 2003).

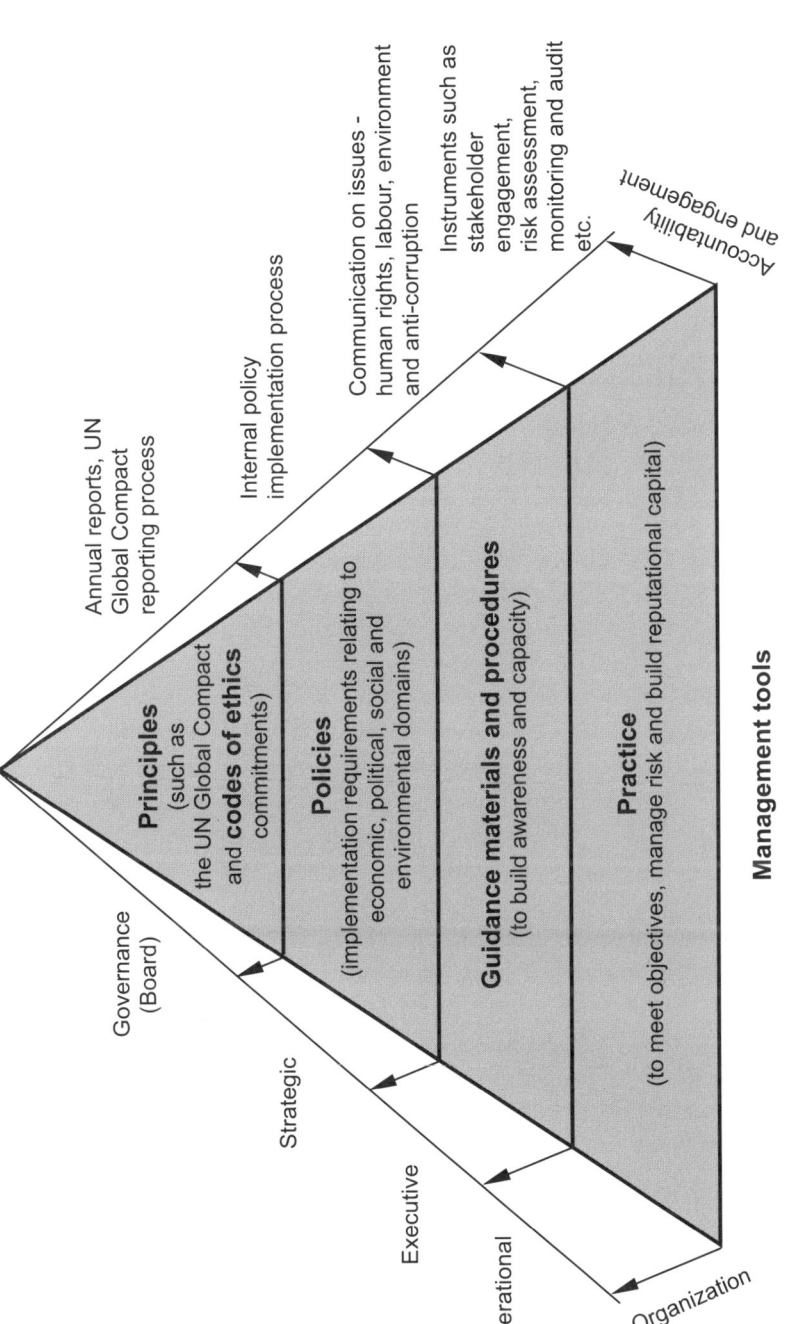

Management tools

Annual reports, UN Global Compact reporting process

Internal policy implementation process

Communication on issues - human rights, labour, environment and anti-corruption

Instruments such as stakeholder engagement, risk assessment, monitoring and audit etc.

Accountability and engagement

Principles
(such as the UN Global Compact and **codes of ethics** commitments)

Policies
(implementation requirements relating to economic, political, social and environmental domains)

Guidance materials and procedures
(to build awareness and capacity)

Practice
(to meet objectives, manage risk and build reputational capital)

Governance (Board)

Strategic

Executive

Operational

Organization

Figure 2.2 A business ethics framework

Each of these tools is relevant at different levels of the business and to different internal (and external) stakeholders. Together they form a management framework.

The code of ethics or set of business principles provides a high-level insight into a company's business ethics or corporate responsibility commitments. The code of ethics is value driven and sits at the governance level of an organization. Policies expand on the commitments made in the code of ethics or principles by providing further information about how they will be implemented and managed and what parts of the business they apply to. Ideally, policies will be designed to cascade or 'roll-out' from the separate articles or clauses in the code of ethics – providing the necessary direction for a company to discretely but confidently achieve its business goals. Policies relating to the code of ethics would traditionally cover the full range of human rights or sustainable development issues listed in Figure 2.1 across the economic, political, social and environment domains. Policies are generally 'owned' by managers located at the strategic level of the business.

Guidance materials and procedures expand on the policies (often short one or two page documents) and facilitate implementation. Procedures or guidance materials explain the content of the policies in more detail in simple, clear and unambiguous language – or even as a set of questions and answers. They can be derived to provide country-specific guidance about complex business ethics issues (Donaldson and Dunfee, 1999) or be the platform for rolling-out systematic 'ways of working'. This is especially the case when a business is working to implement well-known international standards such as ISO 9000:2000, ISO 14001:2004 or even SA 8000 (2001). Guidance materials sit at the executive level in an organization and are intended for use by middle management. Guidance materials should also be intimately linked to a set of practical tools that directly integrate articles or commitments from the code of ethics into part of the way employees work. Tools can be similar to procedures [as in ISO 14001:2004 and SA 8000 (2001)] but tend to be more specific and of immediate and obvious value. Examples include audit workbooks, user guides, stakeholder mapping and dialogue tools, and even impact or risk assessment instruments (as detailed in the next section).

Businesses should seek to ensure there is direct traceability from the commitments present in the code of ethics to the clauses present in policies and guidance materials, and to the content present in monitoring and audit questions and corrective action plans. When this degree of traceability (or transparency) is established in the management tools, then internal managers and other stakeholders will find it easier to measure and report on performance and explain business accountability with respect to the code of ethics commitments.

Formulating a code of ethics 'process'

Just as the existence of a written code of ethics alone is not enough to live the ethics commitments made by a business, neither is a cascaded suite of written management tools enough. They need to be actively used as part of a code of ethics (management) process (Figure 2.3). Indeed the process of implementing and evaluating the code of ethics is at least as valuable and important as the written code itself. The more internal and external stakeholder engagement the more robust a code becomes and the more employees and officers of the company view it as a living document to guide their decision-making rather than a dusty set of papers on a bookshelf. A code of ethics process should include the following types of tools or work streams – all inextricably bound together through in a continual improvement cycle based on the results of performance review and ongoing stakeholder engagement.

Risk assessment

The concept of risk assessment is an integral part of a robust code of ethics process, because it provides the vehicle for identifying and prioritizing what issues are managed. The risk assessment process not only enables a business to identify or scope existing ethics issues or concerns, it also empowers the business to develop mitigating and monitoring strategies to minimize anticipated or unforeseen negative impacts and gauge management proficiency with respect to dealing with business ethics risks and opportunities – such as reporting in line with the Global Compact and best practice sustainability guidelines like those presented by the Global Reporting Initiative (2002).

Issues and indicators

In a world where there is a widening sea of data but in comparison a desert of information, businesses are under increasing pressure to develop key performance indicators (KPIs) as a means of packaging usable information about complex phenomena such as a code of ethics or a particular set of stakeholder derived issues. Information obtained from indicators can then be used to inform business decision-making. Indicators also prompt businesses to identify verifiable targets and

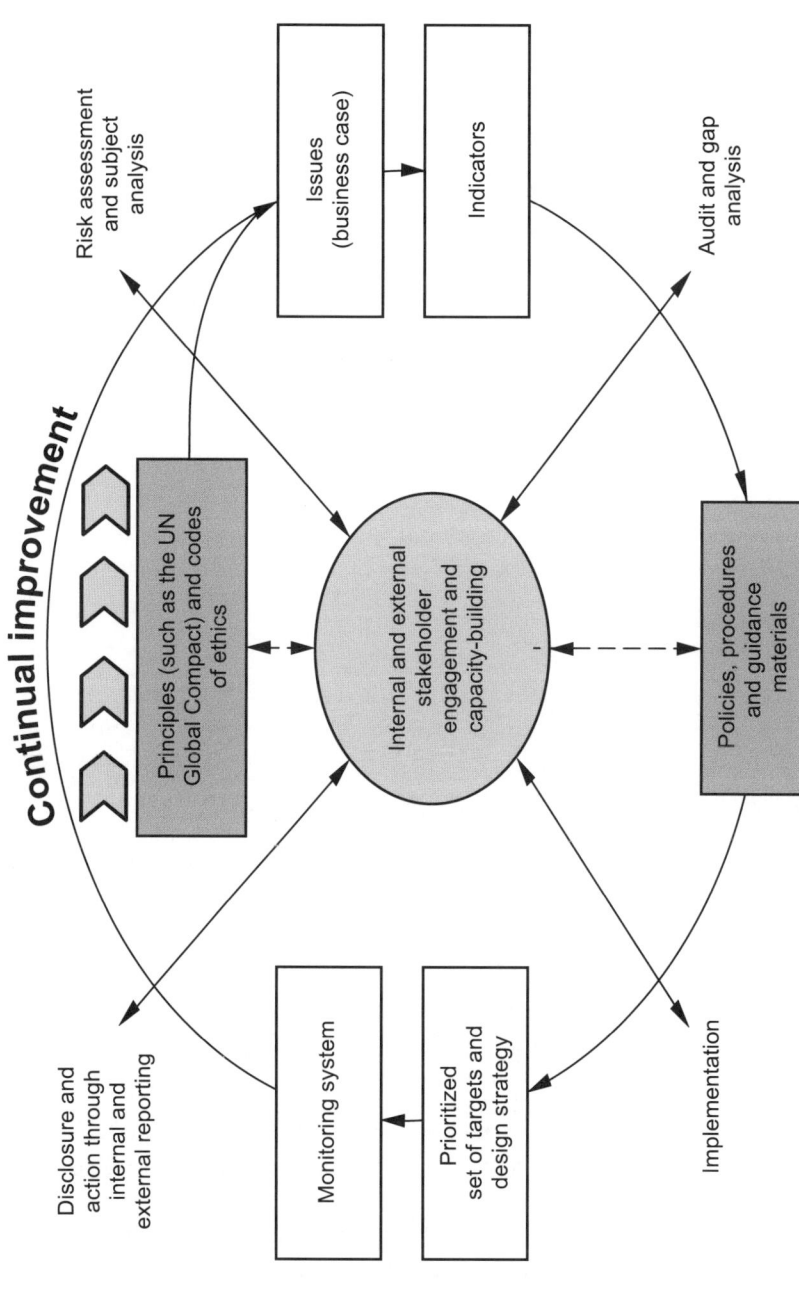

Figure 2.3 The business ethics 'process'

measure progress towards stated goals, thus helping fulfil the social purpose(s) of communication and awareness-raising, stakeholder engagement, reporting and accountability.

Gap analysis and auditing

Once a business has identified an appropriate set of issues and indicators, it should aim to determine the relative performance of its operations with respect to implementing the code of ethics. This can be achieved through the gap analysis (benchmarking) or audit processes. An audit is an examination of the policies, procedures, systems and records of an organization, together with its stated claims of performance. Audits can be internal or can be undertaken by external social or environmental auditors with a view to providing certification to a best practice standard (such as ISO 9000:2000, ISO 14001:2004 or SA 8000:2001) or assurance about the quality and meaningfulness of what the business is doing. Audits are also often completed as part of the reporting process to verify that information disclosed is correct or assure the quality of performance – as part of a company's commitment to transparency.

Capacity building

Capacity building is the process of developing individual or organizational capabilities such that the ability to innovate and bring about change is improved. Capacity building is an integral part of any code of ethics process because many ethics and human rights issues and instruments will be new and unknown to those tasked with management and implementation. To overcome these barriers, opportunities need to be created for learning and sharing experiences – through an experiential learning cycle. Building individual and organizational capacities about ethics issues, stakeholder perspectives and business processes will enhance a business's ability to identify and achieve its code of ethics targets. It will also create the knowledge and experience needed to solve problems and implement change in the future – as part of a continual improvement process.

Monitoring performance

Monitoring is similar to auditing, in that it is about obtaining information about and gauging business performance, but is often completed on a larger scale. Monitoring the implementation of a code of ethics might be completed through a targeted questionnaire sent to all business units or operating companies. Data collected as a result of monitoring can be analysed using statistical tools to identify 'hidden' trends or flaws in the code of ethics framework or implementation strategy – such as a persistent lack of policy implementation or new high risk operating countries or regions. The results of this process can also be combined with the more qualitative data obtained from auditing to further inform (a) the ongoing risks review process, (b) corporate reporting on performance and (c) future implementation programmes.

Reporting on progress

Reporting is a means of demonstrating performance or compliance with the code of ethics and associated policies. Reporting is also the starting point for listening, learning and responding to the views and concerns of customers and other stakeholders – because it enables others to 'see' and understand what companies are doing. Reporting is no longer a public relations exercise (Warhurst, 2003): stakeholders expect to see a simple and meaningful discussion of performance with respect to written codes, principles, policies and the implementation process. As a result it is increasingly important for companies to think strategically about what and how they report. Companies need to ensure that what they report is based on accurate, clear and well-managed information and actions, and that there is a logical goal-oriented 'system' behind their actions. It is partly for this reason that having a robust code of ethics process is so important.

Stakeholder engagement

Stakeholder engagement is arguably the most important instrument or work stream in the management process. Stakeholder engagement is important because it promotes dialogue and understanding between the organization and those impacted by it (Freeman, 1984; Donaldson and Preston, 1995). This enables the entity to understand the effects its activities have on different members of society, to prevent negative impacts, form productive partnerships and capture a range of different opinions and perspectives that can be used to maximize returns to employees, investors and society. Stakeholder engagement is about initiating open, two-way dialogue that seeks to build understanding and solutions to issues of mutual concern to both the company and its stakeholders. This is especially vital when dealing with sensitive or high risk issues present in a code of ethics. The engagement process also provides opportunities to further align internal business practices, to capture societal needs and concerns in future iterations of the code of ethics process, and to build trust-based relationships that contribute to long-term shareholder value.

It is the process of using and continually learning about the appropriateness and effectiveness of these management tools that finally breathes life into them – that makes them 'living' tools and not just static documents or constructs. It is the process of using and evaluating the effectiveness of these tools that enables one to better understand how well the code of ethics is being implemented, and to obtain the information needed to report to stakeholders on performance with respect to the code of ethics.

Conclusions and recommendations

This chapter introduced the rational and potential scope of a best practice code of ethics – based largely on the ethical obligations of business as an organ in society to further fundamental human rights and freedoms. As part of this discussion it looked in particular at the relationship between human rights and the right to sustainable development as part of the third-generational solidarity or development rights. These discussions went beyond the written code of ethics as an ineffective mechanism of delivering business sustainable development obligations. They explored the structure of an ideal code of ethics and presented a framework for how this structure might be cascaded to different management tools – by explaining what the code means for different levels and organizational departments. This led us to suggest a code of ethics process that brings this systematic series of written documents to life by embedding them in a cycle of implementation, performance review and continual improvement. Ongoing stakeholder engagement and capacity-building are vital parts of this code of ethics process.

Businesses looking to embrace the code of ethics process as part of the way they work should seek to go beyond the concept of stakeholder engagement *per se* to building partnerships – with both internal and external stakeholders. Partnerships involve people working together to achieve shared goals, in this case ethical business conduct and the advancement of human rights and sustainable development. They provide opportunities for sharing information, learning and generating solutions to problems that one actor alone cannot solve. Partnerships also enrich the communication and awareness-raising process building real, sustained knowledge that participants can pass on to colleagues, apply in different contexts and share in subsequent iterations and incarnations of the code of ethics process.

Notes

1   This chapter builds on the research and teachings of Professor Alyson Warhurst and Dr Kevin Franklin through 1995–2005.
2   Accountability is the duty of an organization to 'account' for its actions and impacts across the environmental, social, economic and ethical areas of its activities. In the past this term referred mainly to a company's financial performance and the board's responsibility to report on this performance and disclose financial information to a company's shareholders (Churchill, 1974). Now the meaning is broader and the groups of people who are considered to have a legitimate interest in understanding these impacts are considered to be more numerous – including both employees and external communities. To account for something is to explain or justify the acts and omissions, for which one is responsible, to people with a legitimate interest, i.e. being open or transparent. Accountability also implies a broader obligation of responsiveness and disclosure.

References

Addo, M (1999) Human rights standards and transnational corporations. In: Addo, M (ed) (1999) *Human Rights Standards and the Responsibility of Transnational Corporations*. London: Kluwer Law International

Amnesty International (2002) *Human Rights are Everybody's Business*. Available at: http://web.amnesty.org/library/pdf/POL340082002ENGLISH/$File/POL3400 802.pdf

Bruntland, G (ed) (1987) *Our Common Future: The World Commission on Environment and Development*. Oxford: Oxford University Press

BS EN ISO 9000:2000 (2000) *Quality Management Systems – Fundamentals and Vocabulary*. London: British Standards Institution

BS EN ISO 14001:2004 (2004) *Environmental Management Systems – Requirements with Guidance for Use*. London: British Standards Institution

Churchill, N C (1974) Toward a theory for social accounting. *Sloan Management Review*. Spring 1–17

Davis, K (1973) The case for and against business assumption of social responsibilities. *Academy of Management Review* 6:2 312–322

Donaldson, T and Dunfee, T (1999) When ethics travel: the promise and peril of global business ethics. *California Management Review* 41:4 45–63

Donaldson, T and Preston, L E (1995) The stakeholder theory of the corporation: concepts, evidence and implications. *Academy of Management Review* 20:1 65–91

Freeman, R E (1984) *Strategic Management: A Stakeholder Approach*. Boston: Pitman

Global Reporting Initiative (2002) *Sustainability Reporting Guidelines*. Available at: http://www.globalreporting.org

International Labour Organization (1998) *Declaration on Fundamental Principles and Rights at Work*. Available at: http://www.ilo.org/dyn/declaris/DECLARATIONWEB.INDEXPAGE

Maplecroft (2005) *Global Maps of Risk and Opportunity*. Available at: http://maps.maplecroft.com

Nonaka, I and Takeuchi, H (1995) *The Knowledge Creating Company*. New York: Oxford University Press

Organisation for Economic Cooperation and Development (2000) *OECD Guidelines for Multinational Enterprises*. Available at: http://www.oecd.org/document/28/0,2340,en_2649_34889_2397532_1_1_1_1,00.html

SA 8000:2001 (2001) *Social Accountability 8000*. New York: Social Accountability Int.

Shorter Oxford English Dictionary (2002) 5th edn. Oxford: Oxford University Press

United Nations (1948) *Universal Declaration of Human Rights*. Available at: http://www.ohchr.org/english/law/index.htm

United Nations (1966a) *International Covenant on Civil and Political Rights*. Available at: http://www.ohchr.org/english/law/index.htm

United Nations (1966b) *International Covenant on Economic, Social and Cultural Rights*. Available at: http://www.ohchr.org/english/law/index.htm

United Nations (1986) *Declaration on the Right to Development*. Available at: http://www.unhchr.ch/html/menu3/b/74.htm

United Nations (1992) *The Rio Declaration*. Available at: http://www.un.org/documents/ga/conf151/aconf15126–1annex1.htm

United Nations (1993) *Vienna Declaration and Programme of Action*. Available at: http://www.unhchr.ch/huridocda/huridoca.nsf/(Symbol)/A.CONF.157.23.En?OpenDocument

United Nations (2000a) *The Global Compact: Corporate Citizenship in the World Economy*. Available at: http://www.unglobalcompact.org/content/AboutTheGC/EssentialReadings/brochure_master.pdf

United Nations (2000b) *Millennium Development Goals*. Available at: http://www.un.org/millenniumgoals

United Nations (2003) *United Nations Convention against Corruption*. Available at: http://www.unodc.org/unodc/en/crime_convention_corruption.html

Warhurst, A (2001) Corporate citizenship and sustainable development. *Journal of Corporate Citizenship* 1 1–17

Warhurst, A (2003) *Working Paper: Imperatives of Corporate Citizenship*. Corporate Citizenship Training Materials. Warwick Business School

Weston, B H (2002) Human rights. *Encyclopaedia Britannica*, 15th revised edn. Available at: http://www.britannica.com/eb/article?eu=109242&tocid=0&query=human%20rights

3

Recruiting Ethics – Citigroup, Corporate Governance and the Institutionalization of Compliance

Justin O'Brien

In November 2004 Citigroup, the largest financial services conglomerate in the world, placed an advertisement on its website for the position of Director of Ethics. The proposed appointment came as the corporation crisis-managed the fallout from a range of ethical failures across its global operations that began with an investigation by the New York Attorney General, Eliot Spitzer, into systemic conflicts of interest on Wall Street in 2002 (O'Brien, 2003; O'Brien 2005a). Since then, Citigroup's business model and, in particular, its ethical framework, has come under sustained criticism.

Powerful and integral business units have been shown to be intricately involved in the design and marketing of aggressive financial engineering products in New York (GAO, 2003), allegedly complicit in the collapse of Parmalat through due diligence failures and accused of sharp practice in the manipulation of the Eurobond market through its London operation. To add insult to the reputational damage, Citigroup suffered the ignominy of having its prestigious private banking arm unceremoniously thrown out of Japan in November, accused of market abuse. Citigroup clearly has a global image problem.

Given Citigroup's global dominance, defects in its ethical structure have profound implications for the governance of finance markets generally, a responsibility acknowledged in public corporate communications (Citigroup, 2004a) and its internal Code of Conduct (Citigroup,

2004b). Bearing public witness to the need for a sound ethical grounding, the company proclaims the need to capture the high moral ground: 'We live by our values and expect all who work for us to live by them as well' (Citigroup, 2004b).

Announced with considerable fanfare, the Code of Conduct has been redesigned to highlight three key corporate aspirations. It strives to be a company with the highest standards of ethical conduct; an organization that people can trust; and dedicated to community service. Within the conglomerate, the Code establishes codified limits of acceptable behaviour, offers guidance to concerned employees, provides hotlines and emphasizes the need for both professional integrity and personal responsibility. Rooted in a cultural framework that emphasizes the importance of compliance, it serves to demonstrate to employees and regulators that credible risk management structures have been put in place. In large respect, the Code is a paragon of industry best-practice.

To be effective, however, a code of ethics requires what Schwartz (2002, p 40) terms 'penetration' across 'policies, processes, programs, structures, systems, and objectives'. In order to assess the efficacy of the Citigroup approach, it is therefore imperative to distinguish between 'form', 'implementation' and 'administration', both in terms of design and ultimate purpose. Immediately apparent from the cases sketched in the previous paragraphs and given more granular expression below is the demonstrable and continued failure within Citigroup to institutionalize ethical restraint. This can be traced to the absence or misapplication of normative ethical terms of reference *outside* or more accurately capable of *overriding* the restrictive confines of 'a business context'.

Explicitly, the Code makes clear that employees should 'determine when fiduciary duties arise and keep in mind that a fiduciary has a legal duty to act in the best interests of its clients – putting its clients' interests ahead of its own interests, or the interests of its affiliates or employees' (Citigroup, 2004b, p 8). A preliminary investigation by the Japanese Financial Services Authority found evidence of widespread misselling of financial products designed to buttress profits. The situation was made even more problematic because of the failure, in some cases, to even identify the clients it was offering complex derivative-based solutions, leaving the firm susceptible to charges that it could have abetted, if inadvertently, money laundering.

Appearing before a parliamentary investigation in Tokyo in November 2004, the head of operations in Japan, Douglas Peterson, could only manage a contrite apology. 'There was an aggressive sales culture whereby attention was not paid to the rules, even if those

involved knew what the rules were. We acknowledge there was a fundamental flaw in our organisation involving a weak culture of compliance
and internal controls' (*Financial Times*, 2004).

These failures did not just apply in the far-flung corners of the global
empire but also infected operations across Manhattan, as revealed in the
conflicts of interest investigation on analyst research, which destroyed
the career of Smith Barney's chief analyst, Jack Grubman, tarnished the
standing of the corporation's chief executive, Sanford Weill, and thor-
oughly undermined the credibility of the early warning systems deployed
within Citigroup to monitor ethical lapses (O'Brien, 2003, pp 276–277;
Galbraith, 2004).

The Code notes that 'any attempt by a Citigroup representative to
manipulate or tamper with the markets or the prices of securities,
options, futures or other financial instruments will not be tolerated'
(Citigroup, 2004b, p 16). Yet this is precisely the allegation muttered
sotto voce by concerned central bankers over the manipulation of the
Eurobond market in August 2004, two years after the passage of stringent corporate liability legislation in the United States designed to limit
ethical failure. In a trading coup mounted over multiple markets
conducted simultaneously across diverse trading platforms, the corporation netted millions of dollars while simultaneously destroying the
credibility of the market. As much as 70 per cent of the platforms used
belonged to MTS, which is owned by a consortium of banks, including
Citigroup. One trader quoted in the *Sunday Times* likened the raid to
'stealing a car in the street because its doors are open and the keys
are in the ignition' (*Sunday Times*, 2004). It is exceptionally hard to
square this practice with the corporation's 2003 annual report, which
states, in part, 'importantly, in 2003 we continued our thorough re-
examination of the way we do business, with an eye toward developing
standards that are not merely "common industry practice" or "letter
of the law" but the best practices in a given area. We need to be clear
about this subject: Because of our size and scope, because of our position of business leadership, we are held to a higher standard. We accept
this responsibility' (Citigroup, 2004a, p 6).

In the section dealing with the structured finance mechanisms that
facilitated the deception within Enron, the impetus within the compliance model articulated by Citigroup is for the clients to properly
account for their activities. 'Each of our clients must commit to disclose
promptly to the public the net effect of any financing transaction proposed to be executed by Citigroup that is material to the client and not
intended to be accounted for as debt in the client's financial statements.

If a client does not commit to make the disclosures required by our policy, Citigroup will not execute the covered transaction' (Citigroup, 2004b, p 18). Arguably, this formulation, designed to separate cause and effect, can be justified on the grounds that malfeasance by a third party should not be used to tar the reputation of a service provider of a service that is technically compliant with legislation. It also, however, transfers responsibility outside the corporation, absolving the financial designers of misfeasance or moral side-restraints by situating the creative accounting of structured finance within acceptable rules of the game. Within this narrow prism, the deception or fraud is not in the design of an aggressive and, if misapplied, potentially fraudulent instrument, but rather its inappropriate application. Within Citigroup, corporate ethics are placed, therefore, within a libertarian normative context (*Wall Street Journal*, 2005a).

The appointment of a Director of Ethics represented tangible evidence of a public determination by Charles Prince, the chief executive of Citigroup, that his tenure should be judged by improvements in the corporation's ethical standards. Set against this, the wording of the advertisement is instructive. The candidate would 'help ensure business activities are consistent with ethics policies'. According to the criteria, it was essential that applicants should understand 'regulatory guidelines, applicable laws and ethics in a business context'. While the position underscores the critical importance that ethics now places in the management of reputation, therefore, the terms of reference subjugates it to merely the appropriate application of reactive policies designed to comply with legal and regulatory instruments. This subservience is further underlined by the need to contextualize ethical behaviour within a distinct operating environment.

There is no evidence to suggest that the current leadership of Citigroup is less than sincere in its stated objectives to improve the ethical performance of the corporation. The critical question is why the framework developed to advance these objectives has proved so spectacularly unsuccessful. As the Japanese case demonstrates, the malaise continued despite knowledge of specific guidelines. This chapter argues that central to the failure is a gaming of the system facilitated by paradigmatic flaws within the wider terms of Anglo-American corporate governance in both its 'rules' and 'principle' based forms. These shortcomings have been further institutionalized by the passage of legislation or articulation of principles that deal only tangentially with the root cause of malfeasance and misfeasance: the elevation of short-term profit maximization to meet financial market metrics (Chandler and Strine, 2002)[1].

The investment banking model is at the very vortex of corporate malfeasance. The asymmetrical informational advantage given to financial intermediaries is exponentially enhanced given advances in technology. It is therefore a corporate and public policy priority to ensure transparent and accountable markets by redressing a cost–benefit calculus that is tipped in favour of the simultaneous elevation of misfeasance by default.

In the first section of this chapter, I trace and apply within the context of financial market governance the transformative model of ethical management developed by Rossouw and van Vuuren (2003), a heuristic framework designed to inculcate normative improvements. Second, I critically assess the legislative, regulatory and judicial enforcement environment in the United States and demonstrate how its dynamics negatively influences the integration of ethics within the corporate governance paradigm. Third, I highlight how the emphasis on form over function stymies rather than encourages movement towards the higher levels of moral development identified in the Rossouw and van Vuuren model. Finally, this chapter offers some tentative conclusions about how the concept of enforced self-regulation can provide an escape from a position of barren legalism.

A model for managing ethics

As a consequence of systemic failings in the corporate model, the management of ethics has moved from the periphery of organizational decision-making. A recent survey (Business Roundtable Institute for Corporate Ethics, 2004) identified five imperatives: the need to regain trust; manage investor expectations; ensure the integrity of financial reporting; impose restrictions on executive compensation; and develop an ethical tone at the highest levels of the organization. Integrating ethics into effective decision-making was cited by 57 per cent of those polled as the single most important strategic challenge.

As the Citigroup advertisement for a Director of Ethics makes clear, situating ethics within a distinct environment is exceptionally problematic. The capacity of the corporation to act as a moral agent is as contested as the debate over its public function (Wheeler, 2002), which, in turn, allows for a situational subservience of acceptable behaviour to the 'rules of the game'. Given the propensity to game both prescriptive and principle-based regulatory systems (O'Brien, 2005b), it is clearly impossible to legislate for ethics. It is possible, however, to change the risk–benefit calculus involved in the calibration of ethical decision-making within a business context.

Rossouw and van Vuuren (2003, p 390) suggest that a corporation's cognitive development and societal responsibility is informed by 'a group dynamic process in which individuals with different personalities, minds and levels of moral development participate'. For Rossouw and van Vuuren, changes in moral behaviour are causally linked to the objectives and priorities that the board and executive management set and the strategies deployed to operationalize these strategies. Using a heuristic device to manage 'corporate morality', they trace five key modal stages: 'immoral; reactive; compliance; integrity; and totally aligned'.

Movement from one mode to another is predicated by the confluence of internal and external factors. Change is driven, in part, by the failure of existing strategies and the need to retain existing privilege by staving off external oversight (McChesney, 1997). For contemporary executives there remains much potency in the advice provided by the Count to his ambitious nephew in *The Leopard*, di Lampedusa's (1958) classic account of 19th century Sicily, that if one wants things to stay the same one has to change. Thus, the shift to a reactive model can be triggered by the threatened or actual enforcement of corporate governance regulation or the need to minimize extant or future litigation exposure. It is often characterized by the design of corporate codes of ethics, the effectiveness of which are hampered by their symbolic rather than integral purpose. Irrespective of intrinsic design quality, this top-down unilateralism has enormous implications for the application and implementation criteria identified by Schwartz (2002). Reactive organizations remain susceptible to scandal precisely because immoral managers can exploit loopholes in design, monitoring or implementation. The dissonance between stated objectives and corporate reality also create public relations problems, leaving the corporation vulnerable to damaging leaks from disgruntled employees.

Public, media or legislative censure, in turn, drives the dynamic towards compliance mode, where the code becomes the standard against which the company measures its own ethical performance. This mode is informed by a conscious public decision to regulate ethics and eradicate unethical behaviour. This can be achieved through high-profile sackings and public pronouncements of the centrality of ethics to organizational decision-making. It is typically accompanied by training, individual signature validation and the formal induction of all new employees. Within the compliance mode, ethics takes on a distinctly transactional character. Rules are designed to be enforced rather than necessarily act as the foundation stone for the development of a structure based on the embrace and entrenchment of ethical values.

As with all rules-based solutions, it can breed creative compliance (Whelan and McBarnet, 1999; Lowenstein, 2004; McDonough, 2005; O'Brien, 2005b), with interested parties transacting their way around explicitly internally sanctioned or illegal activities. Within investment banking, in particular, this is highly problematic (Partnoy, 2003). Legal and compliance departments are traditionally cost centres which have limited organizational power to compete with aggressive performance targets based on the design of innovative products for which no case law exists. In this context, locating the locus of moral control within a submissive cost centre with little corporate power merely provides the basis for transactional amorality that extends to the legal and accountancy professions (Carver, 2005; Walker 2005).

The 'integrity' approach attempts to deal with these problems by internalizing values and standards. Central to its potential success in changing corporate culture is horizontal and vertical dialogical exchange. This leads to both value formation and commitment. To be successful it requires deep strategic investigation into the existing ethical climate and a genuine dialogue with internal and external stakeholders. Systems for rewarding and evaluating ethical success – and punishing deviance – need to be introduced through material incentives and dis-incentives. In the final phase, 'totally aligned organizations' are characterized by the fact that the ethics function is dispersed across and between horizontal and vertical structures, with individual managers empowered 'on all levels to integrate ethics in their repertoire of managerial skills and actions' (Rossouw and van Vuuren, 2003, p 400).

The public policy and corporate challenge involves moving from visionary rhetoric to systemic change. To be effective this requires a transformation from what Edelman (1960, 1964) identified as the 'politics of symbolism'. The corporate and political response to the crisis within corporate America nicely demonstrates the abiding strength of the Edelman explanatory lens in relation to the politics of financial regulation. The presentation of the malaise as the result of corrupted actors – rather than a system which has been rendered susceptible to corruption as a consequence of flawed incentives – provides a reassuring balm while leaving the wider structural failings relatively intact. Despite a succession of high-profile cases and rebarbative testimony in court cases in New York and elsewhere, convictions on substantive issues have been minimal (O'Brien, 2004b). Likewise, in response to

increased traction, linked directly to legislative and regulatory requirements, disproportionate focus has been placed on the design of generic
codes of practice rather the crucial cultural dynamics underpinning the
efficacy or otherwise of their implementation and administration.

Politicizing ethics: the political determinants of corporate governance design

Ethical failure in some of the world's most powerful corporations
remains an intractable issue, a consequence of the coalescence of motive,
opportunity, socially constructed norms and politically inspired derelict-
ion of regulatory oversight. The problems are magnified by deficiencies
in the dominant corporate governance paradigm, which takes an unnec-
essarily restrictive view of the public duties of a corporation (Ireland,
2000). Crucially, it is informed by an inadequate appreciation of the
fiduciary responsibilities of the professionals who govern the markets in
which they operate through associational enfranchisement.

While corporate failure is a global phenomenon, the situation is
much more pronounced in countries in which equity markets dominate, making it both a corporate and public policy priority to design
effective control mechanisms that cover not only the corporation and
the market but also those fiduciary professionals in whom the market
relies, including accountants, lawyers and investment bankers (O'Brien,
2004a). Despite the surge in regulatory, legislative and juridical
activism, the underlying reactive premise that malfeasance and misfeasance originate primarily from corrupted actors locates and restricts
external intervention in the dynamic space between the reactive and
compliance stages identified in the Rossouw and van Vuuren (2003)
model.

In a telling speech, the Chairman of the Securities and Exchange
Commission, William Donaldson, warned that reformers were facing
'an uphill struggle', precisely because of the propensity of managers 'to
pursue questionable activity right up to technical conformity with the
letter of the law and some will step over the red line either directly, or
with crafty schemes and modern financial technology that facilitates
deception' (Donaldson, 2004). The timing of the speech was particularly significant. It occurred just as the New York State Attorney
General uncovered further systemic conflicts of interest in the mutual
fund and insurance industries, mainstays along with investment banking
in the financial markets (O'Brien, 2005b, 2005a, p 302).

While Donaldson is correct in highlighting the emergence of a concerted fightback that emphasizes the increased cost to business of compliance, he is silent on the inherent flaws of the regulatory design. Just after he nominated himself as Democratic candidate for the New York gubernatorial contest in 2006, Eliot Spitzer argued in an interview with the author that the problem lay primarily with the entire self-regulation paradigm. 'The whole idea should be placed in a box engraved "nice idea didn't work". The excesses have demonstrated serious flaws in the paradigm. I am not convinced it can ever work' (O'Brien, 2005b).

For Spitzer, the answer does not lie in more proscriptive regulation, which itself is susceptible to creative compliance, but rather a much more proactive and imaginative enforcement stratagem based on an acknowledgement that voluntary compliance and industry self-policing represents the triumph of an 'insidious form of industry capture'. There is considerable merit in Spitzer's argument (cf. Seligman 2003a, 2003b). By its very nature, governance changes the relationship between the economic market, the political market and civil society and curtails the capacity of the state. There is now growing recognition that inappropriate deregulatory strategies can themselves allow for the expansion of corruption, with agency capture arising not from excessive discretion but enforced structural inertia (Kaufmann, 2003).

A functioning ethical framework systematizes and rationalizes corporate thinking within a normalized rule structure. It offers a template to deal with all situations or moral hazards arising from excessive discretion. To be effective it must be situated within a matrix that gives due cognizance to the competing, and, at times, conflating imperatives of culture, law, ethics and accountability (Ayres and Braithwaite, 1992). The changes have failed to deliver on their stated objectives precisely because of an inordinate emphasis on the form of rules rather than their function. This has led not only to the reduction of the promise of governance, but has also provided intellectual ammunition for the critics of external oversight (Romano, 2004).

Form over substance: the theoretical limits of the paradigm

The contemporary debate on corporate governance design stems from two competing discourses, both of which have serious weaknesses associated with 'creative compliance' or enforceability. The first argues that corporations should be governed through a principles-based system, in which individual firms decide on how to implement 'best practice' guidelines on a 'comply or explain' basis. While offering the advantage of tailoring governance structures to the specific needs of an individual corporation, it lacks sufficient detail to act as an enforceable contract against which the corporation can be held to account.

The second approach, which has received tangible backing from the United States, is to mandate corporations, through both legislation [Sarbanes-Oxley Act (2002), Section 406] and listing requirements on the primary exchanges, to incorporate into their articles of association particular governance forms, including ethical codes of practice. This more prescriptive approach has the benefit of clarity but suffers from the possibility that self-interested actors will game the regulatory system by engaging in technical rather than full compliance. In both regimes, however, the primary mechanism driving change – greater granularity in the articulation of principles and ever more prescriptive rules – has been scandal occasioned by regulatory and self-policing failure. The question then becomes how to institutionalize credible restraints that can ensure against malefaction and protect the integrity of information provided to and acted on by the markets.

There are four primary means of ensuring control in publicly quoted corporations: the capital markets or banks, which provide corporate financing; the product market, in which a corporation operates; the regulatory environment; and the internal controls designed and ostensibly managed by the board of directors. At the beginning of the millennium each mechanism simultaneously failed, leading to a systemic crisis of confidence in the corporate model and its system of governance (Demirag and O'Brien, 2004).

The design, implementation and monitoring of effective internal and external controls to minimize the risk of fraud, misrepresentation and ethical failure is central to the study of corporate governance. Its capacity to engineer cultural change, however, is minimized by the limitation self-imposed by ideational terms of reference that privilege existing power relations (Nadel, 1975; Romano, 2004). While a distinction must be made between 'shareholder' and 'stakeholder' models of governance, the terms of reference in the construction of corporate governance codes of best practice and legislation centre primarily on the legal protection of shareholders (OECD, 2004). This has the effect of globally reinforcing a minimalist conception of the duties of the corporation in law and practice.

The problem is made much more difficult to resolve because of the way in which both approaches to corporate governance tend to focus exclusively on the interrelationship between the board, the management and the shareholders. Even when that relationship is extended to encompass the interests of stakeholders – including employees, the communities in which it operates (actualized through corporate social responsibility programmes) or wider society – there is a privileging of rights and concomitant ordering of legal priorities that shifts depending on the domicile of the corporation.

The contractual basis of much corporate governance theory – based on the illusory concept of shareholders as owners acting as the vanguard in a line of defence that is, in turn, predicated on a functioning market for corporate control (Galbraith, 2004) – views the governance of a corporation as an essentially private affair to be externally disciplined by market mechanisms best designed and implemented by professionals.

By focusing primarily on the direction and control of the key relationship between shareholders as owners, the board of directors they appoint to guard their interests and the management which is contracted by the board to run the corporate operations (Cadbury, 1992; OECD, 2004), the paradigm leaves little room for ethical concerns. Shareholder maximization retains its dominance despite the excessively narrow terms of reference and its logical privileging of a hierarchical form of organization that is not only in itself inherently problematic (Pound, 2000) but also bears little resemblance to the complexity of modern international corporations (Child and Rodriguez, 2003).

Meeting financial metrics are not necessarily an indication of the underlying health of the firm, as indicated to devastating effect by the spectacular collapse of Enron and other major enterprises. This simplistic model nevertheless continues to provide the intellectual foundations of the corporate governance movement in the United Kingdom and the United States. It argues that the introduction of a raft of improved procedural measures will solve the agency problem. Crucially, it rests on a theoretical premise based on the power of ideational certainty rather than economic rationality (Kirshner, 2003; Demirag and O'Brien, 2004; Galbraith, 2004). It serves, however, an acute ideological imperative, which is to limit both the scale of formal regulatory oversight and the range of policy response within an emasculated range (Edelman, 1960, 1964). An inevitable by-product of this myopia is the pre-ordination of future ethical lapses.

Conclusion

The board of directors of major corporations remain in the frontline in the defence against malefaction, its ranks augmented by the conscription of the accountancy profession, which, in the United States and the European Union, has seen its capacity to govern through self-regulation severely curtailed (Smith 2003; Zeff, 2003). There is a pressing need for the design of effective compliance programmes to which the corporation can be held publicly accountable. Here it is interesting to note that the off-balance sheet transactions formulated by the former chief financial officer of Enron, Andrew Fastow, required the board of directors to derogate twice from its own ethical framework. This derogation was not publicly announced, leading to a lack of transparency and, in effect, to its degradation as an effective control mechanism. Two of the most effective provisions within Sarbanes-Oxley (2002) specifically address that danger. The first calls on corporations to deposit a copy of its ethics programme with the Securities and Exchange Commission. The second mandates corporations to inform the SEC if they change or derogate from its provisions. This provides the regulators with an early warning system. The publication of the filings allows the market and other interested parties with access to crucial relevant information. This important reform represents a move from reporting to disclosure.

Voluntary and compulsory compliance programmes, if properly enforced, have the potential to minimize the risk of corporate corruption. They act as early warning systems, guarding against catastrophic damage to corporate reputation and provide the market with confidence that risk management systems are in place. Equally, flawed reform agendas can legitimize conflicts of interest. Behind the illusion of fundamental change lie control mechanisms that may be devoid of substance. This can lead to a sub-optimal allocation of resources in the fight against corporate malfeasance and misfeasance. It is imperative that the tone is set at the highest levels of the corporation and that appropriate structures are put in place in order to convince employees and the wider market that the corporation is governed within ethically defined parameters.

To be effective, an ethics programme must link cultural and organizational factors. Through weaving ethics into the corporate identity by aligning the programme with material incentives (and disincentives which will see the non-payment of bonuses, sacking for gross misconduct, etc., resulting from sharp practice), the basis of credible restraint is inculcated. Ethical programmes must be linked to material incentives in order to be effective. The obverse is also essential: any derogation from the ethics programme, even if financially lucrative, must be punishable by non-payment or claw-back of bonuses. Sharp practice that complies with the law but causes reputational damage should be penalized.

What has not happened in a structured manner, however, is any serious attempt to limit the self-regulatory environment of the legal profession or the investment banks. These sectors are governed by a rationale that remains based on the gradual implementation of voluntary best practice guidelines. Much of the excess that occurred in the major markets can be traced to changes to the legislative framework governing banking and financial services that deepened the securitization of the economy without simultaneously upgrading the regulatory environment to take into account a much more complex financial architecture (Stiglitz, 2003; Lowenstein, 2004). These changes increased dramatically the Aristolean 'chremestic' (Daly and Cobb, 1994) demands placed on all actors to abide by the short-term demands of the equities markets, which elevated the pre-eminence of share price, calculated according to a quarterly cycle. Meeting the expectations of the market became an industry in itself. Dominant players such as the major investment banks repeatedly failed to perform the due diligence component of their fiduciary role (GAO, 2003). Reform of corporate governance systems which does not give due cognizance to the need to control the operations of market professionals is of questionable value.

The structured involvement of financial professionals in the design of many of the practices that have brought the corporate model into disrepute, coupled with ineffective regulatory and political oversight, necessitate equal weight being placed on the political determinants of corporate governance and a pressing need to critically examine the interface between political and economic governance.

We are living in an age of global markets, governed by antiquated, inadequate and inappropriate national regulatory structures. This presents an opportunity and a challenge for corporations and regulators. A vibrant, well-administrated corporate sector is vital for economic development, social and political cohesion, and access to global sources of capital. While the specific concerns facing each national jurisdiction differ, underpinning all policy innovation is the need to enhance transparency and accountability within corporations and the markets in which they operate.

As Alan Greenspan (2004), the chairman of the Federal Reserve, has noted, 'rules are not a substitute for ethics'. Policymaking has, however, the potential through critical enforcement to re-calibrate the corporate response to ethical failures towards the intersection between the compliance and integrity mode through more imaginative and pro-active policing of the market. In this context, the most important investigations into Wall Street malfeasance from an ethical perspective were Eliot Spitzer's conflict of interest probe into systemic defects in the governance of research analysts which mandated a global settlement and a sidebar deal organized by the Department of Justice with Merrill Lynch. This ensures that ethical considerations are included, on the threat of immediate criminal guilt, in its future determination into whether or not to enter structured finance transactions (O'Brien, 2004b). Both offer a form of enforced self-regulation that necessitates meaningful change within the corporation itself.

Although the Merrill deal was only introduced to ward off a damaging criminal indictment, it does offer the possibility of internalizing ethical restraint. It is a model that the Director of Ethics at Citigroup would be well advised to entertain.

Notes

1   The Public Company Accounting Oversight and Investor Protection Act 2002 (Sarbanes-Oxley) serves four interlinked aims. It creates new structures to regulate both the audit process and the profession; increases the responsibilities and criminal liabilities of corporate boards to ensure against future malefaction; provides greater protection for 'whistleblowers'; and enhances the authority of the Securities and Exchange Commission to police the market. As such, the Sarbanes-Oxley Act, 2002 imposes new restrictions on the capacity of corporations seeking to raise finance on US capital markets. To secure access to the liquidity offered through listing on the primary exchanges, all corporations, irrespective of domicile, must follow the more restrictive provisions of the Act. They must also follow stricter listing requirements mandated by the exchanges under the guidance of a more assertive SEC. The interaction between legislation, forced changes to the self-regulating exchanges and greater federal oversight over the professions creates a powerful dynamic towards a global regime based on US norms.

In this context, it is particularly striking that the debate has moved towards testing the efficacy of the legislative reforms without sufficient analysis of the structural and ethical defects exposed as a consequence of the stock market collapse and Enron's implosion. Investors are encouraged to return to the marketplace, with the assurance that the conditions that led to the excesses of the past have been eradicated. Confidence is indeed gradually returning. Contrary to early claims that the legislation would lead to substantial delisting and capital flight, the American securities market netted $75 billion per month from foreign investors in the first seven months of 2004, an increase of 50 per cent on the same period last year (*Wall Street Journal*, 2005b). Whether the reforms warrant such confidence is a highly questionable assumption (see Chandler and Strine, 2002; O'Brien, 2003; Demirag and O'Brien, 2004).

References

Ayres, I and Braithwaite, J (1992) *Responsive Regulation: Transcending the Dereg-ulation Debate*. Oxford: Oxford University Press

Business Roundtable Institute for Corporate Ethics (2004) Mapping the Terrain. Details available at: www.darden.virginia.edu/corporate-ethics/news/map_060804.htm

Cadbury, A *et al.* (1992) *Report of the Committee on the Financial Aspects of Corporate Governance*. London: Gee and Co Ltd. Available at: http://www.ecgi.org/codes/documents/cadbury.pdf

Carver, Jeremy (2005) The Role of Lawyers. In: O'Brien, Justin (ed) *Governing the Corporation: Regulation and Corporate Governance in an Age of Scandal and Global Markets*. Chichester: John Wiley & Sons

Chandler, W and Strine, L (2002) The New Federalism of the American Corporate Governance System: Preliminary Reflections of Two Residents of One Small State. New York University Center for Law and Business. Working Paper no. CLB 03–01. Available at: http://papers.ssrn.com/abstract=367720

Citigroup (2004a) *2003 Annual Report*. Available at: http://www.citigroup.com

Citigroup (2004b) *Code of Conduct*. Available at: http://www.citigroup.com

Child, John and Rodriguez, S. (2003) Corporate Governance and New Organiza-tional Forms: Issues of Double and Multiple Agency. *Journal of Management and Governance* 7 337–360

Daly, H and Cobb, J (1994) *For the Common Good: Redirecting the Economy Toward Community, the Environment, and a Sustainable Future*. Boston: Beacon Press

Demirag, I and O'Brien, J (2004) Conflicting and Conflating Interests in the Regulation and Governance of the Financial Markets in the United States. *The Journal of Corporate Citizenship* Autumn: 15

Donaldson, W (2004) Chairman of the Securities and Exchange Commission Speech to Business Roundtable, Washington, DC, 14 October. Available at: www.sec.gov/news/speech/spch101404whd.htm

Edelman, M (1960) Symbols and political quiescence. *The American Political Science Review* 54:3 (Sept.) 695–704

Edelman, M (1964) *The Symbolic Uses of Politics*. Urbana, IL: University of Illinois Press

Financial Times (2004) Citigroup promises to compensate Japanese clients. 1 Dec.

Galbraith, John Kenneth (2004) *The Economics of Innocent Fraud: Truth for Our Time*. London: Allen Lane

General Accounting Office (2003) *Investment Banks, The Role of Firms and Their Analysts with Enron and Global Crossing*. GAO-03–511, Mar.

Greenspan, A (2004) Capitalizing reputation. Remarks at the 2004 Financial Markets Conference of the Federal Reserve Bank of Atlanta, Sea Island, Georgia, 16 April. Available at: http://www.federalreserve.gov/boarddocs/speeches/2004/

Ireland, Paddy (2000) Defending the *Rentier*: Corporate Theory and the Repriva-
    tization of the Public Company. In: Parkinson, John, Gamble, Andrew and
    Kelly, Gavin (eds) *The Political Economy of the Company*. Oxford: Hart
    Publishing

Kaufmann, D (2003) *Rethinking Governance: Empirical Lessons Challenge
    Orthodoxy*. Available at: http://www.worldbank.org/wbi/governance/wp-
    governance.html

Kirshner, Jonathan (2003) The Inescapable Politics of Money. In: Kirshner,
    Jonathan (ed) *Monetary Orders: Ambiguous Economics, Ubiquitous Politics*.
    Ithaca, NY: Cornell University Press

di Lampedusa, G T (1958) *The Leopard*. Milan: G Feltrinelli

Lowenstein, R (2004) *Origins of the Crash: The Great Bubble and Its Undoing*.
    New York: Penguin Press

McChesney, F (1997) *Money For Nothing: Politicians, Rent Extraction, and
    Political Extortion*. Cambridge, MA: Harvard University Press

McDonough, William (2005) Accountability in an Age of Global Markets. In:
    O'Brien, Justin (ed) *Governing the Corporation: Regulation and Corporate
    Governance in an Age of Scandal and Global Markets*. Chichester: John Wiley
    & Sons

Nadel, M (1975) The hidden dimension of public policy: private governments and
    the policy-making process. *Journal of Politics* 37:1 (Feb.) 2–34

O'Brien, J (2003) *Wall Street on Trial: A Corrupted State?*. Chichester: John Wiley
    & Sons

O'Brien, J (2004a) Ethics, probity and the changing governance of Wall Street,
    cure or remission. *Public Integrity* 7:1 (Winter) 43–54

O'Brien, J (2004b) Beyond compliance: testing the limits of reforming the gover-
    nance of Wall Street. *International Journal of Business Governance and Ethics*
    1:2/3 162–174

O'Brien, J (2005a) Redesigning Financial Regulation: Eliot Spitzer, State-Federal
    Relations and the Battle for Corporate Control. In: O'Brien, Justin (ed)
    *Governing the Corporation: Regulation and Corporate Governance in an Age
    of Scandal and Global Markets*. Chichester: John Wiley & Sons

O'Brien, J (2005b) Governing the Corporation: Regulation and Corporate
    Governance in an Age of Scandal and Global Markets. In: O'Brien, Justin (ed)
    *Governing the Corporation: Regulation and Corporate Governance in an Age
    of Scandal and Global Markets*. Chichester: John Wiley & Sons

OECD (2004) *OECD Principles of Corporate Governance*. OECD: Paris. Available
    at: www.oecd.org

Partnoy, F (2003) *Infectious Greed: Enron and Beyond – The Story Behind Enron
    and Its Wider Implications*. London: Profile Books

Pound, John (2000) The Promise of the Governed Corporation. In: *Harvard
    Business Review on Corporate Governance*. Boston: Harvard Business School
    Press

Romano, R (2004) The Sarbanes-Oxley Act and the Making of Quack Corporate
    Governance. European Corporate Governance Institute Finance Working
    Paper, no. 52/2004

Rossouw, G and van Vuuren, L (2003) Modes of Managing Morality: a Descriptive
    Model of Strategies for Managing Ethics. *Journal of Business Ethics* 46:4 389

Sarbanes-Oxley Act (2002) Pub. L. No. 107–204, 116 Stat. 745. Available at: http://www.sec.gov/about/laws/soa2002.pdf. See also: http://www.sec.gov/spotlight/sarbanes-oxley.htm

Schwartz, M (2002) A Code of Ethics for Corporate Codes of Ethics. *Journal of Business Ethics* **41**:1/2 27

Seligman, J (2003a) Cautious evolution or perennial irresolution: self-regulation and market structure during the first 70 years of the Securities and Exchange Commission. Paper presented at *The Duke Global Capital Markets Center-NYSE Conference on Current Issues in Institutional Equity Trading, West Palm Beach, 13 December.* Available at: http://www.fuqua.duke.edu/conference/dei/nyse/

Seligman, J (2003b) *The Transformation of Wall Street: A History of the Securities and Exchange Commission and Modern Corporate Finance.* New York: Aspen.

Smith, L (2003) A Fresh Look at Accounting Ethics. *Accounting Horizons* **17**:1 (Mar.) 47–49

Stiglitz, J (2003) *The Roaring Nineties: A New History of the World's Most Prosperous Decade.* New York: Norton

Sunday Times (2004) Bond raiders. 15 Aug.

Walker, David (2005) Restoring Trust After Recent Accountability Failures. In: O'Brien, Justin (ed) *Governing the Corporation: Regulation and Corporate Governance in an Age of Scandal and Global Markets.* Chichester: John Wiley & Sons.

Wall Street Journal (2005a) Citigroup CEO pursues culture of ethics. 2 March

Wall Street Journal (2005b) Foreign investors boost purchases of US securities. 17 Aug.

Whelan, Chris and McBarnet, Doreen (1999) *Creative Accounting and the Cross-Eyed Javelin Thrower.* Chichester: John Wiley & Sons

Wheeler, S 2002. *Corporations and the Third Way.* Oxford: Hart Publishing

Zeff, S (2003) How the US accounting profession got where it is today. *Accounting Horizons* **17**:4 (Dec.) 267–286

4

The Role of NGOs in Creating an Ethical Climate for International Business

John Sayer

Much is said of the growing power and influence of corporations, attributed in part to a relative decline in government willingness and ability to regulate economic activity in an era of economic liberalization and globalization. There is, however, a second sector of society that is also growing in size and influence – the non-governmental organizations. They have, in some ways, stepped into the space left by small government.

The engagement of companies and NGOs on questions of equitable and sustainable development carries profound significance for the ethics of business, and for the character of the development process as a whole. Public expectations of the role and responsibility of business, and the degree to which these can be met voluntarily or will be subject to mandatory controls, will also emerge from the NGO–business debate.

This chapter examines the relationship between NGOs and corporations, and the impact of this on business policies and practices. It will identify the principal forms of interaction and the factors motivating both parties to undertake these relationships. The chapter will discuss the impact of this encounter on corporate behaviour. Finally, it will examine some of the trends, challenges and possibilities that exist for business–NGO relationships.

The nature of NGOs

Trade unions have the longest record and the most experience at engaging the private sector with regard to its policies. For more than a century, the labour movement has confronted business on a number of issues beyond the immediate protection of its members' interests, voicing concern about the broader impact of business in society. On trade issues, trade unions have worked actively against exploitative conditions of production in developing countries. They have sometimes been accused of highlighting poor labour conditions in developing countries in order to make the case for controlling imports from those countries and protecting their current members' jobs. The unions counter that these calls are combined with a great deal of work to help workers organize and improve working conditions and labour rights in the developing world.

This chapter will focus on NGOs as organizations that are independent, not-for-profit and not self-serving in aims and related values in membership organizations such as farmers' associations or trade unions (Ball and Dunn, 1995). NGOs working on international development are at the forefront of civil society debates on the impact of business on development, in terms of the economic and social impact of trade, investment and financial policies. Green groups are very involved with issues of corporate conduct where it has impact on the environment and sustainability. Human rights and women's groups are also involved where these issues have bearing on their areas of concern.

Civil society has grown significantly since the 1980s. Although definitions of NGOs vary, the United Nations estimated the number of NGOs grew from about 29,000 in 1993 to more than 100,000 in 1999 (Edwards and Hulme, 1996). Some 35,000 NGO workers attended the Fourth World Conference on Women in Beijing in 1995 (Paul, 2000). The Union of International Organizations holds profiles of over 58,500 international NGOs on its database (Union of International Organizations, 2004).

NGO interaction with the corporate sector

Companies and NGOs have been interacting for more than a century. Civic and business organizations may be very different today from their 19th century counterparts. Reform groups seeking an end to slavery and votes for women in the 19th century clearly interacted with companies and received both supportive and critical responses. The Anti-Slavery Society, founded in 1839, continues its work to this day (Anti-Slavery Society, 1839).

Early examples of corporate social responsibility also exist. The forward-thinking chocolate-making families, including those owned by the Cadbury and Rowntree families, gave attention to the wellbeing of their workforces and the wider community around their factories (although less is recorded about their concern for the conditions of those producing the cocoa beans in developing countries). The Cadbury and Rowntree descendants fund a range of social programmes through trusts and foundations. But the rise in corporate concern with social responsibility programmes, and the engagement of NGOs in the process, emerged on a significant scale in the 1990s.

Many of the earliest relationships between NGOs and companies took the form of cash and material donations from business in support of the charitable activities of the NGOs. This relationship reflected the prevailing ethos of the development NGOs of the time, most of which began their work involved in post-war reconstruction, famine and disaster relief. Those involved with poverty alleviation viewed this work in terms of the charitable provision of welfare (Smillie 1995; Sogge, 1996).

For many NGOs the principal (often the only) relationship with corporations remains that of a recipient of corporate donations. In addition to straightforward charitable donations, NGOs and corporations have developed a number of marketing relationships in which the charity stands to gain revenue in exchange for providing direct publicity for the corporation. This can take the form of well-publicized sponsorship of the charity's events, or the charity's endorsement of a particular product in exchange for a donation, or cause-related marketing, in which the charity receives a share of income from the sales of certain goods or services. A common example would be 'affinity' credit cards. Carrying its logo, the charity receives a small sum from every transaction charged to the card (Sogge and Zadek, 1996; Heap, 1998).

As NGO welfare programmes progressed into more sophisticated development and livelihood programmes, including efforts to help poor people demand better opportunities to help themselves, NGOs rapidly became aware of the power structures depriving poor people of equal opportunities. An examination of the economic systems that perpetuated poverty inevitably led NGOs to speak out against unequal levels of economic and political power, restrictive control of resources and the role private business played in this system.

Among early examples of NGO campaigns are criticisms of companies benefiting from business in apartheid South Africa and Pinochet's Chile. Another campaign which continues to this day called for an end to the aggressive and misleading marketing of powdered baby milk in developing countries (Fowler and Biekart, 1996).

In recent years, NGO campaigns targeting the conduct of the private sector have multiplied, with the more notable examples including the following.

- Calls for pricing, research and copyright policies by pharmaceutical companies which take account of the lower capacities to pay and the pressing needs in developing countries.
- Criticism of the aggressive marketing of tobacco in developing countries where health awareness, health warnings and advertising restrictions are not as developed.
- Campaigns to ban the trade in certain types of weapons, such as landmines and small arms, particularly to repressive regimes and areas of civil war.
- Marketing of milk powder for babies in ways that imply it is preferable to breastfeeding in countries where clean water and washing facilities are scarce.
- The selling of agricultural products subsidized in rich countries, such as sugar, cotton or milk, to developing countries, damaging the livelihoods of local producers and creating dependency.
- Control and depression of world prices by a small group of international trading companies on agricultural commodities such as coffee, vital to the survival of small producers.
- The use of child and prison labour in the manufacturing of carpets, furniture, footballs, sports goods, etc.
- Labour rights, health and safety and child labour issues in the shoe, toy, electronics, textiles and garment industries.
- Campaigns targeting major retailers, brands and trading companies calling for them to take responsibility for the social, environmental and labour conditions under which the goods they source in developing countries are produced.
- Seeking prior, informed consent from communities affected by the activities of mining companies to take account of traditional and formal land rights, environmental impact, royalty payments, economic impact, etc.
- Financial transparency on the part of all companies doing business in developing countries, to reduce corruption and offer clearer pictures of their impact on livelihoods.

Critical campaigning sits rather uneasily alongside any funding relationship. Campaigning often involves high-profile public actions and media exposure, leaving corporate public relations departments scrambling to generate an appropriate and credible response and corporate bosses fuming. Many NGOs are investing increased resources in both the media and communications capacity necessary to broadcast an effective message, and also developing their capacity to generate research and policy documents which add authority and credibility to their slogans (Anderson, 2000).

Within the context of advocacy, NGOs need to decide whether they should concentrate on lobbying the wealthy and influential in the corridors of power, or engage in high-profile critical actions to publicize their demands. These don't always sit comfortably. Street activists will look critically at 'insider', closed-door discussions between NGO leaders and politicians or business leaders. On the other hand, political and corporate heads may choose not to engage with NGOs that have sought high-profile opportunities to publicly condemn them.

The emergence of engagement

In a climate of close scrutiny and growing pressure on corporations from consumers, investors, local communities and the regulatory authorities, it is inevitable that some companies subject to critical campaigns and reports by NGOs and the media will respond to the criticism positively, admitting that some problems exist and expressing a desire to improve. This has led to some companies approaching their NGO critics for advice and cooperation in programmes of change. While not all NGOs are willing or equipped to assist in this way, a third area of interaction has emerged. This involves forms of NGO–business cooperation designed to assist corporations in their efforts to clean up bad practices and have a more positive social and environmental impact (Crane, 2000).

After trade unions, environmental groups were the first to develop strategies and policies for interaction with companies. Initially these were mostly critical but an increasing number grew to be cooperative. Awareness of environmental issues is sufficiently high among both the public and politicians that the green movement has shifted from purely critical activity, signalling environmental problems, and has moved to working on practical solutions with business and government. NGOs working on poverty, on the other hand, still believe they have work to do to raise public concern and political will on the issue to a sufficiently critical level. They need to convince corporations of the importance of addressing global social justice issues. This, they believe, must be more developed before they can shift from problem-focused to solution-focused advocacy (Heap, 2000).

In programme cooperation with corporations, NGOs are often seen as intermediaries, building bridges between corporations and a variety of stakeholders including affected communities, local NGOs, potential customers and others who wish to voice their opinions about the impact of the company's activities on their lives (Waddell, 2000).

The spread of corporate codes of conduct and industry standards on social and environmental issues indicates the recognition on the part of many international corporations that addressing these issues, or being seen to address these issues, has become essential. In designing and developing these codes and standards, companies have frequently sought to involve NGOs, including their most vociferous critics. In a number of cases, collaborative work has resulted, going beyond the initial creation of the codes to include NGO participation in their implementation, monitoring, evaluation and remediation (Heap, 2000).

NGOs believe that supporting the establishment of corporate codes of conduct can bring improvements in corporate purchasing and investment practices in ways which bring faster benefits to working conditions and environmental performance than campaigning for public policy and legislative change. They also contend that working with NGOs on the issues required in codes of conduct can lead companies to become more aware of international labour and environmental standards (Kearney, 1999; Heap, 2000).

A large number of criticisms of voluntary codes of conduct, and NGO involvement in their design and implementation, have arisen from NGOs as well as trade unions, academics and others. Critics note that most NGOs lack the capacity, authority and legitimacy to design or monitor corporate standards on labour, environmental and social issues (Bendell and Murphy, 2000). Supply chains can involve several levels and thousands of small factories, workshops, pieceworkers and home-workers. Problems with devising effective systems for monitoring and compliance seem to be a principal weakness in codes of conduct in general. Where monitoring plans exist, NGOs and unions are often excluded (Ferguson, 1998; Picciotto and Mayne, 1999).

By helping companies design, implement, monitor and evaluate codes of conduct, critics argue that NGOs are playing the role of legislator, police force, judge and jury, which is both unsatisfactory and unsustainable. The sceptics would suggest that it is more important for NGOs to use their scarce resources to retain pressure on corporations through adversarial lobbying and public campaigns (Fowler and Heap, 2000). Some NGOs will take payment from corporations for work on codes of conduct and some NGOs have been set up simply to bid for such work. This raises issues of co-option and conflict of interest between maintaining critical objectivity and seeking further paid work from the companies they are criticizing (Heap, 2000, pp 124–125).

Workers and others in the developing countries which many codes of conduct purport to benefit are often the least involved in their design and implementation. Lack of workers' participation in the monitoring of codes of conduct is seen by labour organizations as their biggest weakness (Asia Monitor Resource Centre, 2001). Related to their origin, codes can impose a northern consumer agenda. They can give a higher priority to ending child labour than to the more basic issues of freedom of association or wage levels (Ferguson, 1998). The cost of compliance is often passed to the sub-contractors, who are still under pressure from the purchasing departments of the same companies to offer the lowest prices. Additional costs for high social and environmental standards are sometimes taken from the wage packets of the workers (Kearney, 1999).

NGOs working on livelihoods for poor people see a danger that the poorest and most vulnerable producers, ironically those people who codes of conduct were established to protect, can become excluded from the production system when strong codes are put in place. Meeting the standards of comprehensive codes can be complex and involve costly investment. There are also economies of scale in the expensive process of monitoring compliance which favour larger-scale producers. Both these factors can lead to a concentration of production in larger factories or farms, away from homeworkers, pieceworkers or smallholders, who are usually poorer and often women-headed households (Newbold, 2002).

There is still a large group of NGOs who believe they should apply most of their energy to calls for stronger national and international legislation mandating standards of corporate conduct. This includes some NGOs that have spent time engaging with corporations and been disappointed by the pace and degree of change emerging from the experience.

Against this backdrop, the Fair Trade movement is having a significant impact on the trading practices of mainstream business. The roots of the Fair Trade movement lie in development NGOs seeking ways of improving livelihoods and realizing how international trading systems, and big corporate cartels, could leave poor producers exploited and vulnerable. Thus, Fair Trade activities frequently began with heavy subsidies and institutional support from NGOs. Today the movement combines some organizations that survive through trading fair trade goods and others which still resemble NGOs, and concentrates on promoting the concept of fair trade and the issues that underlie it, both among consumers in the north and through assisting producers in developing countries.

The Fair Trade movement has done a great deal in the past two decades to raise consumer awareness about injustices and inequalities within the conventional trading system. It has also spearheaded a theoretical debate and a practical choice of fairer alternatives. Fair trade businesses have carved out their own market share to the point where these are competing with mainstream private sector companies in certain products, such as coffee and chocolate.

In response to the successes of fair trade (in terms of both sales and messaging) some companies have developed their own codes of conduct and product traceability programmes. In addition many food retailers have begun to develop their own name-brand products with fair trade accreditation.

A number of garment, food and sports goods retailers, including some who were attacked in critical campaigns of the past, are involved in initiatives with trade unions and NGOs to look at ways to make their trading more ethical. These are often described as 'ethical trade' programmes, to distinguish them from fair trade. As with fair trade, they aim to improve the labour rights of workers in the supply chain and improve the environmental and social impact of international trading activities. As this is an attempt to change the practices of major mainstream players, rather than build up an alternative, ethical trade initiatives usually involve aspirational targets and transition plans. The approach is one of taking account of the current pressures and real conditions confronting the major commercial companies, and charting a course from where they currently stand to where they could or should be in terms of acceptable and sustainable social and environment trade practices.

Factors encouraging business engagement with NGOs

Much is written elsewhere in this book about the growing power of the international corporation relative to national governments. But civil society has stepped into some of the space created by retreating government intervention in the market. Protesters, consumer activists, lobbyists and socially concerned investors are increasing pressure on companies concerning environmental, social and labour issues. This oppositional force can be just as transnational as the corporations they are facing. Many believe NGOs are building a new form of 'civil regulation' or 'social licensing' for economic activity. International NGOs are critical players in the creation of new global norms and standards of acceptable corporate behaviour and this is emerging as a kind of informal governance (Bendell 2000; Newell, 2000; Warhurst 2001).

The Rio Earth Summit of 1992, for example, recognized that governments should not be the sole adjudicators of their citizens' interests on the international stage. The Rio conference recognized the role of 'major groups', a range of NGOs, unions and organizations representing youth, women, indigenous peoples and industry, and declared that these should be consulted and included in decision-making (Mabey, 1999).

The collapse of Enron and WorldCom due to financial dishonesty, and shareholder revolts in Britain against exorbitant executive pay packages, have focused attention on the ethics and social responsibility of major international corporations. Some of the most high profile protests are now focused on multilateral bodies such as the World Trade Organization, the World Bank and the G8. Critics claim that these organizations are dominated by representatives in thrall to big business and use their global authority primarily in the interest of big business (Juniper, 1999; Newell, 2000).

Concern with corporate power is not restricted to the ranks of balaclava clad street protesters. More moderate critics have emerged, some of them close to the companies. Alongside the growth in critical activism there has developed a broadening of the definition of the responsibility of companies to their stakeholders. Primary stakeholders are no longer only the company's shareholders and employees; they also include customers and suppliers. Companies are also coming to accept the need to account to a broader group of stakeholders including neighbouring communities, NGOs, the general public and the people and governments of the many countries where the company invests and trades (Nelson, 1996; Rogers, 2000).

Investors are no longer a small number of avaricious millionaires. In large public companies, many shareholders are pension fund and mutual fund managers – representing and taking instruction from employees, trade union members and small investors. They are increasingly concerned about the ethical as well as the financial performance of the companies in which they have invested. (Simpson, 2002).

NGOs have realized that institutional investors are an important pressure point in corporate lobbying. Activists have increasingly begun to confront investment banks and major investors directly regarding the impact of those companies in which they invest (Bendell and Lake, 2000).

Arguably the greatest business case for good environmental and social conduct is risk reduction. Many business leaders consider the damage to their companies of being seen as bad is far more significant than the advantages to business of being seen as doing good. Thus reducing the negative takes precedence over heightening the positive (Hilton and Gibbons, 2002). Campaigning NGOs are all too aware of this and have become adept at targeting public opinion in their campaigns.

NGOs can be useful allies for companies seeking to reduce risk through genuine change. Relationships with NGOs can enable a company to gain better knowledge of how it is viewed from a variety of sources and to better understand any current or potential criticisms. NGO contacts, networks and alliances can inform companies of issues and concerns they might otherwise miss and provide early warning of potential problems. NGOs can facilitate inclusive and transparent consultation, dialogue and negotiation with groups affected by corporate activities, and company codes and standards can be more locally appropriate, created in processes which leave them popularly supported (Waddell, 2000).

The power of the brand has become a principal asset of more and more companies as a greater proportion of costs go towards marketing and support functions while actual production is sub-contracted to anonymous factories in the developing world. Many factories also produce goods sold by the brand's major competitors. The principal work of many clothes, shoes, accessories and sports goods companies is to create and market an image, so that the clothes and shoes can be sold at a premium (Klein, 2000).

As the brand becomes a company's principal asset, threats to that brand caused by a poor record on social, environmental or labour standards become a potent new kind of business risk, representing a threat to 'reputational capital' and a new corporate Achilles' heel (Bendell, 2000). Campaigners against corporate abuses have not been slow in realizing the vulnerability represented by the brand. Many campaigns specifically directed at a brand have proved effective at forcing their corporate targets to alter their policies and practices.

Reputation also affects the internal health of a company. Staff motivation and morale, plus the ability to recruit and retain more talented staff, is greater in companies with favourable public reputations and strong social programmes (Draper, 2002).

The revolution in information technology has also put an additional spotlight on corporations. The public can now hear of corporate misconduct more directly than ever before. People affected by corporate activity can communicate more easily and effectively with a company's stakeholders. Through the Internet, communities displaced by mining companies, or garment workers forced to work overtime in dangerous conditions, for example, can explain their grievances to developed-world customers or fellow workers at the head office more quickly and convincingly than was ever possible before. NGOs often help play an intermediary role in facilitating such communication (Elkington, 1997; Bray, 2000; Heap, 2000).

Major international companies dwarf not only all NGOs, but also the majority of the world's nation states in terms of economic power. But new information technology is no respecter of economic might. It has created a very level playing field when it comes to disseminating information to the media and the public. The Internet's capacity to democratize both the receipt and dissemination of information has helped change the balance of power between companies, NGOs and consumers. A small impoverished NGO can reach exactly the same number of people with the messages on its website as a vast Fortune 500 company.

Much of the intense scrutiny of corporate behaviour is a response to consumer concern in the developed world. The same level of scrutiny is seldom applied to intermediate and non-export industries which sell neither consumer goods directly to the public, nor are engaged in agriculture or mineral extraction with direct impact on communities (Mayne, 1999). Manufacturers of industrial equipment, components and other materials for industry, as well as financial institutions, may not be subject to the same type of consumer and community activism (Bello, 2001). Transnational companies based in developing countries such as Indonesian mining operations and Malaysian logging companies, also avoid the same level of critical examination as those companies headquartered in countries with a larger body of critical NGOs.

Many executives now see both short-term and long-term enlightened self-interest in an ethical stance for the company and the more general wellbeing of society. Companies with the capacity to predict a tightening of regulations on social or environmental conduct can take early action and gain 'first mover advantage' over those companies forced to take remedial action at the last minute (Hutton and Cowe, 2002).

Companies working well with NGOs can benefit through the identification of new markets and in the development of products suitable
for such markets, and the opportunities presented by political, social,
cultural and environmental conditions (Waddell, 2000).

As pressure grows on corporations to pay attention to social and
environmental issues, companies are also responding to criticism and
approaching NGOs and other parts of civil society seeking remedial
advice, ideas and cooperation. Because much of the pressure for
improvement emanated from NGOs to begin with, it is sometimes difficult for them to refuse to get involved. NGOs can be criticized for
condemning economic practices without presenting credible alternatives
(Edwards, 2002).

Accepting the importance of the structural issues underlying poverty
and inequality, development agencies have become more concerned
with the impact of macro-economic events on poverty and equity such
as debt, trade, foreign investment and financial crises (Elkington and
Fennell, 2000; Newbold, 2002). They have also applied more resources
to policy research in recent years, attempting to better understand these
issues, and to lobby and campaign on these more complex economic
subjects with authority and credibility (Edwards and Hulme, 1996).
The decline of Marxism in international development debate and the
emergence of a single global economy has left most NGOs more focused
on understanding the economic forces at work and the levers for
reform, rather than on the pursuit of political change.

New models of cooperation and partnership

The move towards greater NGO–corporate engagement is seen by some
as part of a more general growth in the concept of partnership. Also
referred to as 'intersectoral collaboration' and 'multi-stakeholder partnership' the concept has grown in the aftermath of privatization and
deregulation (Nelson, 1996). In the welfare sector, so vital to the lives
of poor people, this is being encouraged in the form of 'public–private
partnership'. In development thinking, there is a great deal of discussion about partnerships for development, some of it stemming from
recognition at UN conferences in Rio and Copenhagen that government, business and civil society must work together if development
targets are to be met (Murphy and Coleman, 2000).

Further motivation for NGO engagement with the private sector is
brought about by the increasing role of corporations in the provision

of services at the heart of development and vital to the needs of poor people, such as health, education, social services and water supply. This is not without controversy, as many NGOs harbour a belief that neither they nor the companies should enable governments to escape their fundamental duty to ensure the delivery of basic social services to their poorest citizens.

NGOs also recognize the advantages of more professional standards in both the publicity and communication of their services, and in financial management, good governance, technical issues and higher standards of reporting to funders. In all these, NGOs recognize that lessons can be learned through closer cooperation with the private sector.

Measuring the impact of NGO interaction on corporations remains a challenge, whether this involves criticism or cooperation. While we cannot attribute all improved corporate behaviour to NGO activity, it is clear that public opinion, and civil society, catalysed, synthesized and represented by NGOs, either as consumers or investors, has had a large influence on changing private sector opinions of their need to pay attention to the threats related to poor social and environmental reputation.

It is very hard to dis-aggregate the efforts of NGOs to influence corporate behaviour from the efforts of government, media, the public and those people who believe their lives are being negatively affected by business. What we can say is that NGOs play an important part in the cauldron of opinion that brings issues to light and generates the pressure for change.

Development NGOs draw their initial inspiration from their understanding of the problems facing poor people as they encounter them in the villages, shanty towns, farms and factories. In a complex iterative process, as well as being informed by poor people, they also seek to inform them and to help to organize and articulate their demands, and interpret their problems in the context of macro-economic systems and power structures. Development NGOs bring concerns voiced by poor people to the attention of the media, and through them, to the public. As well as seeking to bring public and media pressure to bear on governments and corporations, they also lobby political and business leaders directly. But NGOs are only one of the influences on public opinion and public pressure. Whether consumers, investors or voters, the public is also motivated by direct experience, by the media and by political parties. The international NGOs are, in turn, influenced by the climate of opinion in their home countries, often in the developed world. These opinions are reflected in their membership, their governing bodies and their staff.

In summary, it is critically important for NGOs engaging corporations to find ways of measuring the impact of advocacy and engagement, and the opportunity cost of the time and money spent interacting with companies. While the work is vital, it is generally undeveloped (Nelson and Zadek, 2000).

Having said this, certain clear changes in the ways companies do business and trade are generally attributed in whole or in part to the advocacy efforts of non-governmental organizations. These include:

- The imposition of trade sanctions on apartheid South Africa and military-ruled Chile.
- A ban on trade in landmines and increased controls by many nation countries on arms exports.
- Creation of the Forestry Stewardship Council, accrediting furniture and wood products produced from sustainable forestry practices.
- Creation of the Marine Stewardship Council, accrediting marine products harvested sustainably.
- Creation of Rugmark, accrediting carpets made without exploiting child labour.
- The growth of fair trade items and their distribution by mainstream retailers.
- Establishment of Ethical Trading Initiative, Fair Labour Agreement, Global Reporting Initiative, the UN Global Compact and other multi-stakeholder initiatives working on codes, standards and ways of measuring responsible trade and investment practices.
- The creation of an international code of conduct for the marketing of baby milk.
- Establishment of an essential drugs list, and more flexibility on cheaper generic drug production.
- Loosening of trade barriers to garment imports from some of the least developed countries (Edwards, 2002).

One can even argue that all measures that seek to create a more ethical approach to trade have been influenced, directly or indirectly, by the campaigns and publicity work of NGOs exposing the negative consequences of some trading activities on the environment, the lives of poor people, labour rights, women's rights or human rights.

The ultimate battleground over international trade policy involves the WTO. Despite years of campaigning on GATT policy, which preceded the formation of the WTO, NGOs felt that the terms for the formation of the organization were dominated by powerful, developed country governments, acting in the interest of transnational corporations. However, in more recent rounds of WTO talks designed to broaden its reach into new areas, NGOs have found common cause with developing country representatives and have resourced, influenced and supported, through demonstrations, these delegates in refusing to acquiesce in the introduction of new WTO rules which would chiefly advantage powerful corporations from the north.

Britain's Ethical Trading Initiative brings together companies, NGOs and trade unions to develop joint labour, social and environmental codes in global supply chains, share practical ideas on improving practices and raise public awareness of the issues involved. In this, it is similar to the Fair Labor Agreement in the USA and the Canadian Taskforce on labour standards in the textiles and footwear sector. WTO rules prohibit discrimination against imports on the basis of the conditions of their production, but such multi-sector initiatives become a way of raising standards through consumer, NGO and company peer pressure (Kearney, 1999).

Future challenges and trends

The principal issue facing NGOs as they plan their engagement with the corporate sector is the choice between the pragmatic achievement of realistic short-term gains or adherence to basic beliefs that sustainable change needs to be more radical and far reaching. In practical terms, this becomes a choice between prioritizing engagement with companies on their voluntary programmes of internal change and social responsibility, or concentrating resources in critical advocacy and research calling for deeper changes in national and international regulatory frameworks and the international economic architecture.

It is very hard for the same NGO to play both the role of a critical advocate as well as constructive partner. An NGO doing both will risk charges that it is being used by one company to gain competitive advantage, or that its research and campaign materials are compromised by selective cooperation with individual companies. No less than commercial sports brands, the reputation of a campaigning NGO is a vital aspect of its effectiveness. The impact of the NGOs' message with public, media and government rests on the belief that the organization is impartial, professional and driven by ethics and principles alone. In this belief, public surveys throughout the world rate the public trust of NGOs above government, business and the media. Any suggestion that financial interest influences their advocacy message could devastate an NGO's reputation.

Only a large, financially independent NGO with expertly planned strategies and a finely-honed capacity for timing can credibly criticize and work with companies at the same time. For most NGOs, it is better to decide what form of engagement they are best equipped for, and to pursue that engagement alone.

Within the ranks of NGOs and beyond, there remain unwavering critics of the whole concept of engagement with the corporate sector to achieve change. They argue that NGOs should concentrate on campaigns for macro-economic changes, targeting national and international organizations. While they support continued critical activism against the corporate sector, they see this in terms of illustrating the need for regulation. These critics of cooperation suggest that working with TNCs consolidates corporate power, increases their standing in society, endorses their activities and strengthens their defences against attack from more critical NGOs (Heap, 2000). Instead, TNCs should be ceding that power as they are the underlying cause of social and environmental problems (Covey and Brown, 2001).

Critics of the market systems underlying all corporate activity cannot be easily characterized as a diminishing group of ageing Marxists stuck in the 1970s. They are joined by a youthful and growing anti-capitalist movement, which has caught the imagination of many young people beyond those who appear on the streets outside WTO or G8 meetings. The anti-capitalist movement may not have a well defined and unified ideology, but represents a broad church, combining ideas from feminism and environmentalism as well as socialism, and the decentralized participatory organizational techniques of anarchism. The movement sees economic growth as a false god in the quest for a just and sustainable society and asserts that any economic system dominated by market forces, growth and competition is inimical to the creation of a system of equity and justice.

While individual NGOs have to make choices as to where their resources are applied, different approaches are not necessarily in opposition. Voluntary measures to develop and implement standards play an important role in road testing realistic measures and set benchmarks which can inform future legislation and regulation.

Stock markets, national export guarantee schemes and other quasi-governmental incentives for business require adherence to certain voluntary codes of conduct as a prerequisite. While this does not represent mandatory legislation, companies wishing to take advantage of the benefits on offer must sign up to the social and environmental code. This illustrates the grey area between voluntary initiatives and binding legislation.

Companies that take the lead in developing and implementing higher environmental, labour and social standards do not want to see their prices undercut by free riders. Some believe that companies taking the most progressive action on corporate social responsibility will ultimately agree to join with NGOs to press for regulation, particularly if more scandals on the scale of Enron and WorldCom occur. If new controls are eventually introduced, those companies with robust policies on environmental and social issues will enjoy first mover advantage (Newell, 2000).

For NGOs engaging with the corporate sector, capacity is often a major challenge. The number of companies seeking dialogue with NGOs has grown a great deal while NGO resources have remained constant. Individuals within NGOs that are best equipped and most open to discussions with companies are often overwhelmed by invitations (Elkington and Fennell, 2000).

In many of their engagements with NGOs, companies express concerns about the confidentiality of information they share with organizations that may turn around and publicize problems if the relationship does not go well. Within the same NGOs, there may be those who wish to work with companies and those who would like to use the resulting intelligence for campaign work (Crane, 2000). This is also related to the habit of NGOs to extend the agenda of concern as work progresses. Companies that agree to work with an NGO on one area of concern may find that new issues are brought to the table as the relationship matures.

But inconsistency is not the sole preserve of NGOs. Company personnel responsible for community affairs or corporate social responsibility may seek the reassuring company of NGO associates, while other staff or departments may retain hostility or suspicion towards NGOs.

Co-option or compromise of an NGO through collaboration with a large and powerful corporation remains a live topic for debate within NGOs. The challenge of co-option remains whether it is real or simply perceived to be so by constituencies or others in the NGO community. While too much antagonism can reduce the effectiveness of NGO–business engagement, there is more to be gained in the relationship if both sides express their beliefs and principles robustly and respect diversity of opinion (Kalegaonkar and Brown, 2000).

What is clear is that for engagement to work, NGOs and companies working together must seek agreement from the outset on:

- the common concerns that bring them together to work, and also the differences that remain and the limitations of the engagement;
- agreement on roles, responsibilities and decision-making processes (Nelson 1996; BOND, 1999);
- the levels of transparency and communications strategies that will surround the cooperation (BOND, 1999);
- the involvement of other stakeholders by each party (Weir, 2000).

Efforts to identify and address power imbalances in the NGO–corporate relationship should be made. Related to this, financial dependency of one partner on the other is best avoided, or at the very least clarified and noted (Nelson, 1996; Kalegaonkar and Brown, 2000). A successful relationship requires the commitment of professional staff in the NGO and internal capacity on the part of the company. Leadership from senior management of both parties is essential (UNEP, 1994; Austin, 2000). Good preparatory research is required by the NGO.

Is business to be influenced?

The interaction between NGOs and corporations has grown in response to the increasing recognition by NGOs that corporations play a central role in shaping the development of nations and communities, and that they can do this in ways that have negative or positive outcomes. This is reinforced by recognition on the part of corporations of the risks of failing to respond to social criticism as well as the benefits of working with NGOs to become more socially responsible in matters of trade and investment. This growth in NGO–business contact has produced as increasingly complex range and style of relationships.

There is no 'one true path' for NGO interaction with the private sector. Those NGOs involved in high-profile confrontational campaigns are ensuring that the risk factor attached to poor ethical standards remains high. Thus the critical campaigners push companies into the arms of engaged NGOs. Those NGOs which engage companies in devising ways to improve performance are ensuring that benchmarks rise and practical solutions are tried and tested. NGOs can provide guidance to receptive companies about what conduct genuinely benefits local environments, employees and local people, and what behaviour is tokenistic, top down and superficial.

Those NGOs working with companies do not necessarily support the corporate arguments that voluntary codes are sufficient. Nor do they see a conflict of interest in working with companies in defining voluntary codes and standards. Leading edge voluntary initiatives can help define what desirable and feasible legislation might look like. NGOs hold the belief that progressive corporations will eventually join the call for co-competitive regulation in order to ensure that unprincipled freeloaders do not benefit from voluntary standards.

The resolution of the relationship between the private sector and NGOs will be critical to the shaping of popular and governmental attitudes about acceptable behaviour of corporations in society, the ethics of business and the values underlying the economic system as a whole. The exchange of ideas between civil society and the private sector will determine how international trade, investment and finance can be made to have more a positive impact on the environment and human rights for all people on the planet. More importantly, it will shape the contribution corporations make to the achievement of the millennium development goals, seeking to reduce poverty, disease, and illiteracy in the first 15 years of this century (Nelson and Prescott, 2003). For the poorest and most vulnerable, this is a life and death issue.

The long term consequence of NGO–company contacts is hard to predict. Two scenarios are sketched in the following paragraphs. The real future will lie somewhere between the two extremes. With hope, it will emerge closer to the best case.

The worst case is that there are increased attacks on the transparency, accountability and legitimacy of NGOs. Their motives, ethics and tactics are targeted by companies that decide that attack is the best form of defence. Tactics include expensive lawsuits against critical NGOs, attempts to have NGO assets frozen during protracted legal proceedings and media campaigns highlighting specific cases of mismanagement and poor research on the part of NGOs.

Corporations set up tame, well-funded NGOs and co-opt existing NGOs through divide and rule tactics supported with generous funding offers. This creates divisions in several areas of NGO debate, weakens effective coalitions, confuses the public and lowers popular respect for NGOs as a whole.

A global economic downturn with competition for resources and markets sees a reduction of corporate social responsibility programmes. The ease with which these are abandoned reveals how shallow and marginal many of them were. Harder economic times focus consumer interest back on cheap prices alone.

There is a revival of Milton Friedman's 40-year-old dictum that there is only one social responsibility of business – to increase its profits (Friedman, 2002).

Companies flourish, global output rises. Fabulous wealth is concentrated in well-defended enclaves. At the same time, the number of poor people grows. Their needs are not addressed by mainstream market forces and they are the first to suffer from the increased decay in the environment. While technology helps shield the rich from pollution, the weather begins to change in ways even they can no longer predict or control.

The best case, by contrast, is that as CSR deepens, flagship companies invest more and more in improving the social, labour and environmental impact of their core business activities. They prosper as a result and join with NGOs to propose the development of mandatory national and international social and environmental standards for corporations.

It becomes a universal social expectation that corporations apply good social and environmental practices in the same measure that they apply good financial practice.

Governments develop fair and co-competitive regulations and norms which end the externalization of the environmental and social costs of business activity.

For the first time, a corporation wins the Nobel Peace Prize.

References

Anderson, I (2000) Northern NGO advocacy: perceptions, reality, and the challenge. *Development in Practice* 10:3/4 (Aug.) 445–452

Anti-Slavery Society (1839). Available at: http://www.antislavery.org/homepage/antislavery/history.htm

Asia Monitor Resource Centre (2001) Credibility gap between codes and conduct. *Asian Labour Update* 37, Nov. 2000–Jan. 2001, Asia Monitor Resource Centre, Hong Kong, pp 1–8

Austin, J (2000) *The Collaborative Challenge: How Nonprofits and Business Succeed through Strategic Alliances*. Hoboken: Jossey-Bass Publishers

Ball, C and Dunn, L (1995) *Non-Governmental Organizations: Guidelines for Good Policy and Practice*. London: The Commonwealth Foundation

Bello, W (2001) *No Logo: A Brilliant but Flawed Portrait of Contemporary Capitalism*. Bangkok: Focus on the Global South

Bendell, J (ed) (2000) *Terms for Endearment: Business, NGOs and Sustainable Development*. Sheffield: Greenleaf Publishing

Bendell, J and Lake, R (2000) New frontiers: emerging NGO activities to strengthen transparency and accountability in business. In: Bendell, J (ed) *Terms for*

Endearment: Business, NGOs and Sustainable Development. Sheffield: Greenleaf Publishing, pp 226–238

Bendell, J and Murphy, D (2000) Planting the seeds of change: business-NGO relations on tropical deforestation. In: Bendell, J (ed) *Terms for Endearment: Business, NGOs and Sustainable Development*. Sheffield: Greenleaf Publishing, pp 65–78

BOND (British Overseas NGOs for Development) (1999) *The BOND Report: NGO Futures – Partnerships with the Private Sector*. Available at: http://www.mailbase.ac.uk/links/business-ngo-relations/files/bondreport.html

Bray, J (2000) Web wars: NGOs, companies and governments in an internet-connected world. In: Bendell, J (ed) *Terms for Endearment: Business, NGOs and Sustainable Development*. Sheffield: Greenleaf Publishing, pp 49–63

Covey, J and Brown, D (2001) *Critical Cooperation: An Alternative Form of Civil Society-Business Engagement*. IDR Reports, vol. 17, no. 1. Boston: Institute of Development Research

Crane, A (2000) Culture clash and mediation: exploring the cultural dynamics of business-NGO collaboration. In: Bendell, J (ed) *Terms for Endearment: Business, NGOs and Sustainable Development*. Sheffield: Greenleaf Publishing, pp 163–177

Draper, S (2002) Good work: employees as drivers and demonstrators of CSR. In: Cowe, R (ed) *No Scruples: Managing to be Responsible in a Turbulent World*. London: Spiro Press, pp 47–62

Edwards, M (2002) Does the doormat influence the boot: critical thoughts on UK NGOs and international advocacy. In: Eade, D (ed) *Development and Advocacy*. Oxford: Oxfam

Edwards, M and Hulme, D (1996) *Beyond the Magic Bullet: NGO Performance and Accountability in the Post-Cold War Period*. West Hartford: Kumarian Press

Elkington, J (1997) *Cannibals With Forks: The Triple Bottom Line of 21st Century Business*. Oxford: Capstone

Elkington, J and Fennell, S (2000) Partners for sustainability. In: Bendell, J (ed) *Terms for Endearment: Business, NGOs and Sustainable Development*. Sheffield: Greenleaf Publishing, pp 150–162

Ferguson, C (1998) *A Review of UK Company Codes of Conduct*. London: Department for International Development

Fowler, A and Biekart, K (1996) Do private aid agencies really make a difference? In: Sogge, D (ed) *Compassion and Calculation: The Business of Private Foreign Aid*. London: Pluto Press, pp 36–67

Fowler, P and Heap, S (2000) Bridging troubled waters: The Marine Stewardship Council. In: Bendell, J (ed) *Terms for Endearment: Business, NGOs and Sustainable Development*. Sheffield: Greenleaf Publishing, pp 135–148

Friedman, M (2002) *Capitalism and Freedom* 40th anniversary edn. Chigago: Chicago University Press

Heap, S (1998) *NGOs and the Private Sector: Potential for Partnerships?* Oxford: International NGO Training and Research Centre (INTRAC)

Heap, S (2000) *NGOs Engaging with Business*. Oxford: International NGO Training and Research Centre (INTRAC)

Hilton, S and Gibbons, G (2002) *Good Business: Your World Needs You*. London: Texere Publishing

Hutton, W and Cowe, R (2002) Beyond clean-up to product stewardship: the environmental agenda. In: Cowe, R (ed) *No Scruples: Managing to be Responsible in a Turbulent World*. London: Spiro Press, pp 81–94

Juniper, T (1999) Planet profit. *Guardian Weekly* 25 Nov., 12

Kalegaonkar, A and Brown, L (2000) *Intersectoral Cooperation: Lessons For Practice,* IDR Reports, vol. 16, no. 2. Boston: Institute for Development Research

Kearney, N (1999) Corporate codes of conduct: the privatized application of labour standards. In: Picciotto, S and Mayne, R (eds) *Regulating International Business: Beyond Liberalization*. London: Macmillan Press, pp 205–220

Klein, N (2000) *No Logo: Taking Aim at the Brand Bullies*. London: Flamingo

Mabey, N (1999) Defending the legacy of Rio: the Civil Society Campaign against the MAI. In: Picciotto, S and Mayne, R (eds) *Regulating International Business: Beyond Liberalization*. London: Macmillan Press, ch 4

Mayne, R (1999) Regulating TNCs: the role of voluntary and governmental approaches. In: Picciotto, S and Mayne, R (eds) *Regulating International Business: Beyond Liberalization*. London: Macmillan Press, pp 235–254

Murphy, D and Coleman, G (2000) Thinking partners: business, NGOs and the partnership concept. In: Bendell, J (ed) *Terms for Endearment: Business, NGOs and Sustainable Development*. Sheffield: Greenleaf Publishing/The New Academy of Business

Nelson, J (1996) *Business as Partners in Development: Creating Wealth for Countries, Companies and Communities*. London: The Prince of Wales Business Leaders Forum

Nelson, J and Prescott, D (2003) *Business and the Millennium Development Goals: A Framework for Action*. London: International Business Leaders Forum

Nelson, J and Zadek, S (2000) *Partnership Alchemy: New Social Partnerships in Europe*. Copenhagen: The Copenhagen Centre

Newbold, Y (2002) Out of sight, out of mind? Scruples in the supply chain. In: Cowe, R (ed) *No Scruples: Managing to be Responsible in a Turbulent World*. London: Spiro Press, pp 113–126

Newell, P (2000) Globalisation and the new politics of sustainable development. In: Bendell, J (ed) *Terms for Endearment: Business, NGOs and Sustainable Development*. Sheffield: Greenleaf Publishing, pp 31–39

Paul, J (2000) NGOs and global politics. *Global Policy Forum*. Available at: www.globalpolicy.org/ngos/analysis.anal00.htm

Picciotto, S and Mayne, R (eds) (1999) *Regulating International Business: Beyond Liberalization*. London: Macmillan Press

Rogers, C (2000) Making it legit: new ways of generating corporate legitimacy in a globalising world. In: Bendell, J (ed) *Terms for Endearment: Business, NGOs and Sustainable Development*. Sheffield: Greenleaf Publishing, pp 40–48

Simpson, A (2002) Money talks: the rise of socially responsible investors. In: Cowe, R (ed) *No Scruples: Managing to be Responsible in a Turbulent World*. London: Spiro Press, pp 21–31

Smillie, I (1995) *The Alms Bazaar: Altruism Under Fire – Non Profit Organizations and International Development*. London: IT Publications

Sogge, D (1996) Settings and choices. In: Sogge, D (ed) *Compassion and Calculation: The Business of Private Foreign Aid*. London: Pluto Press, pp 1–23

Sogge, D and Zadek, S (1996) 'Laws' of the market? In: Sogge, D (ed) *Compassion and Calculation: The Business of Private Foreign Aid*. London: Pluto Press, pp 68–96

Union of International Organizations (2004) *UIO Online Databases*. Available at: https://www.diversitas.org/db/x.php

United Nations Environmental Program (UNEP) (1994) *Partnerships for Sustainable Development*. Paris: UNEP

Waddell, S (2000) Complementary resources: the win-win rationale for partnerships with NGOs. In: Bendell, J (ed) *Terms for Endearment: Business, NGOs and Sustainable Development*. Sheffield: Greenleaf Publishing, pp 193–206

Warhurst, A (2001) Corporate citizenship and corporate social investment: drivers of tri-sector partnerships. *Journal of Corporate Citizenship* no. 1 (Spring) 57–73

Weir, A (2000) Meeting social and environmental objectives through partnership: the experience of Unilever. In: Bendell, J (ed) *Terms for Endearment: Business, NGOs and Sustainable Development*. Sheffield: Greenleaf Publishing, pp 118–124

5

Human Rights in Business: The Scope of Accountability – A New Horizon

James Oury

Commercial landscape

For over a decade, environmental and social concerns have been gaining prominence on the business agenda. Transnational corporations (TNCs) have become the driving agents of the global economy. Along with this economic influence and its globalization inevitably comes political influence, such is the nature of the beast. TNCs today have considerable political leverage and are under increasing pressure from a broad range of interests groups to use it wisely.

There is no doubt that foreign direct investment (FDI) can be a force for good, bringing with it as it does employment, capital and technology to developing countries. The flip side, however, is that often, instead of bringing the rights and values of the home country with it, a company can find it all too tempting to exploit the less strictly regulated host countries' practices in order to capitalize on profit. There are many levels at which a company may allow itself to instigate or become complicit in detrimental behaviours. This can range from failing to question their supply chain in far-away 'trouble spots', or allowing subsidiaries to carry on accepted practices under the guise of cultural differences, to supplying arms to para-military groups. At its worst, a company can be cited as an accomplice in crimes against humanity, as was the case regarding the supply of Zyklon B, the gas used by the Nazis for mass extermination, by a subsidiary of I.G. Farben, who claimed it was merely a delousing agent. The same company was involved in the construction of the slave labour factory at Auschwitz. At Nuremburg, three of its senior executives were convicted.

Debates surrounding the human rights obligations of businesses have intensified. The more prominent human rights issues and those that arise more frequently relate to the treatment of local communities living in the vicinity of natural resource operations and the protection in certain labour-intensive consumer goods industries (Mares, 2004). The experiences of companies such as Nike and Shell in the course of their respective operations have, among myriad examples, awakened businesses to the need to identify and manage risks presented by human rights issues. Nike's employment of labour in sweat shops throughout South-East Asia resulted in worldwide condemnation and, despite grand PR efforts, they have admitted that conditions for their factory workers are still very poor. Shell's weighty mistake was to stand by while several community representatives were subjected to extra-judicial execution in response to their criticism of the social and environmental impacts of oil exploitations. These instances provided the motivation necessary to focus minds on the impact that (previously reputable) corporations can have in their spheres of influence and the way in which they will be held responsible in the eyes of the world. The fact that, owing to globalization via technology, information regarding these debacles travelled at lightening speed around the world, means that little opportunity is left for damage limitation after the fact.

With the popularity of concepts such as corporate social responsibility and the triple bottom line (planet, people, profit), public perceptions are shifting and ethical investment and consumerism mean that a company can actually do very well by doing good. It is in this vein that adhering to human rights standards and voluntary codes can be a mutually beneficial approach. Shareholder value increases with improved reputation so profits rise while investment in local communities results in long-term economic growth for host countries. Unfortunately, it can take more than an encouraging word to convince a pressed managing director that this is in everybody's best interests. This is especially so owing to the traditional belief that profit and ethics are mutually exclusive. The increase in litigation against ever more visible and influential corporations for complicity in human rights abuses, however, seems to be very effective in focusing efforts on the task in hand.

Successive waves of mergers and acquisitions have given birth to corporate giants such as ExxonMobil whose net income peaked at a record $17.7 billion in 2000. Indeed, there are many more companies whose turnover and profits surpass the combined national income of several war-torn countries. In fact, 51 of the 100 largest economies in the world are companies. This combined with political instability and liberal economic reform (which has reduced state power) means that a greater responsibility is conferred on the private sector (Carbonnier, 2001). This responsibility is slowly being borne out by a response in the international legal community, which aims to make those firms accountable for their actions in the pursuit of profit.

Legal landscape

Insisting that companies behave in an appropriate way is nothing new. Regarding the environment and workers' rights, companies have long been subject to regulation by government and lobbying by non-governmental organizations (NGOs). What is new, however, is the degree to which such expectations are being recast in human rights terms and the extent to which new human rights claims are being advanced in relation to the private sector (International Council on Human Rights Policy, 2002).

It is in international law that detailed human rights rules have been developed in the last 50 years or so, placing obligations on states. International human rights law has its historical antecedents in a number of international legal doctrines and institutions. The most important of these are humanitarian intervention, state responsibility for injuries to aliens, protection of minorities, the League of Nations' Mandates and Minorities Systems and international humanitarian law. In recent years, however, the focus has shifted increasingly towards the liability of accomplices with the advent of the war crimes tribunal. From its early manifestations at Nuremburg and Tokyo to the contemporary tribunal, the focus has not been so much on the principal perpetrator but the complicity of peripheral actors. The net is being cast wider still, as a result of globalization, towards another category of 'non state' actor; the commercial corporation. Within days of the adoption of the Rome Statute of the International Criminal Court, the *Financial Times* published an article warning commercial lawyers that the Treaty's accomplice liability provision 'could create international criminal liability for employees, officers and directors of corporations' (Schabas, 2001, quoting Nyberg, 1998). While it is recognized that the ICC has no jurisdiction over 'legal persons' such as corporate entities, under Article 25.3, it can in fact assert jurisdiction over individual actors within the corporation, namely directors. Thus, the statute extends accomplice liability to an individual who in any way aids a criminal group, when that person knows the group ordinarily commits criminal acts. To this extent 'individual corporate executives of corporations who knowingly assist or deal with such groups who commit human rights violations may be prosecuted by the ICC' (American Non-Governmental Organizations Coalition for the International Criminal Court, 2004). Just how forcefully the ICC will go after accomplices in the boardrooms will depend on prosecutorial policy. Developing the law offers significant promise of holding violators of human rights and international humanitarian law to account, although vested financial and business interests may mean this is more problematic in practice. If businesses pause for reflection and adapt their practices accordingly, humanitarian law will have fulfilled its goal of deterrence (Schabas, 2001, p 456), and businesses can fulfil their objectives by staying ahead of the game.

Human rights instruments relevant to business

Many people believe it is necessary to bring multinational corporations under the authority of international human rights frameworks. Traditionally, international law conforms to a state-centric view of world politics. States are viewed as the primary actors in the international system, with international law acting to regulate relations between states. Challenges to the role and primacy of the state in world politics has, however, fundamentally altered the role and function of international law. International law has expanded, but is increasingly focused, through concerns about human rights, with the individual (Wells, 2003).

This strengthening of international legal commitments to human rights can be seen as another aspect of the multi-faceted nature of globalization. States have lost authority to supranational bodies at the same time as they have privatized many of their domestic functions. But it is economic globalization that is generally presented as the major challenge to state sovereignty. The challenge comes in particular from financial speculation in deregulated currency markets and the growing economic power of multinational corporations. States are more likely to attempt to attract international capital rather than to try to regulate it. In a globalized economy, firms (especially those in manufacturing) can move easily across borders and evade boycotts and sanctions. The diminishing centrality of the state in world politics is accompanied by the rise of multinational corporations (MNCs) as rival sources of power and influence in the world (Wells, 2003).

With intergovernmental aid now largely overtaken by foreign direct investment, the temptation for host countries to attract investors with minimal human rights standards is often difficult to resist. Human rights abuses can occur whether the outsourcing takes place via wholly or partly owned subsidiaries or through use of supply contracts. It is the ability of MNCs to operate across national borders and outside the effective supervision of domestic and international law that makes them important actors ripe for greater investigation under international law. MNCs often act in concert with host states in suppressing local populations, forcibly moving them or forcibly requiring their labour – this is known as 'militarized commerce'.

It is with this in mind that human rights law is increasingly being looked at from the perspective of the protection of individuals from corporate activity. Over the years, a body of international human rights law has grown up that echoes with experience evidencing the actions of states, and increasingly corporations, against the rights of the individual. Now those laws are being expanded upon by voluntary codes and instruments, which enable the world at large to oversee and apply pressure to individual actors in the corporate sphere and allow them to be held accountable for their actions under the umbrella of profit-making.

Universal Declaration on Human Rights

Human rights had already found expression in the Covenant of the League of Nations, which led, *inter alia*, to the creation of the International Labour Organisation when the proposal for a 'Declaration of the Essential Rights of Man' was put forward. On 10 December 1948, The General Assembly of the UN adopted and proclaimed the Universal Declaration on Human Rights as a common standard for all people and all nations, to the end that every individual and *every organ of society* would strive to promote respect for the enshrined rights and freedoms and by progressive measures, national and international, to secure their recognition and observance, both among the peoples of member states and among people of territories under their jurisdiction (United Nations, 1948). The Declaration was the first comprehensive human rights instrument to be proclaimed by a universal international organization. The Declaration proclaims two broad categories of rights: civil and political rights on the one hand, and economic and social rights on the other.

The Declaration's catalogue of civil and political rights which are relevant to business operations include the right to life, liberty and security of the person; the prohibition of slavery, of torture and cruel, inhuman or degrading treatment; the right not to be subjected to arbitrary arrest, detention or exile; the right to a fair trial in both civil and criminal matters, the presumption of innocence and the prohibition against the application of retrospective laws and penalties. The Declaration recognizes the right to privacy and the right to own property. It proclaims the right to freedom of speech, religion, assembly and freedom of movement. Perhaps more frequently relevant for business purposes are the catalogue of economic, social and cultural rights which are proclaimed to be indispensable for an individual's dignity and the free development of their personality. These include the right to social security, to work and to protection against unemployment, to equal pay for equal work, and to just and favourable remuneration ensuring for them and their family an existence worthy of human dignity, and supplemented, if necessary, by other means of social protection (Buergenthal, 1988). In situations where, for instance, an oil company builds a pipeline, which, as a consequence, inhibits the use of land by those who have been farming it for centuries, these rights are particularly poignant.

International Bill of Human Rights

It is from this foundation that assumptions about the rights and fundamental freedoms have been made and subsequent laws and conventions have built upon. On the back of the Declaration, the International Covenants on Economic, Social and Cultural Rights (United Nations, 1966a) and Civil and Political Rights (United Nations, 1966b) were adopted in 1966. The Covenant on Civil and Political Rights is drafted with greater juridicial specificity and lists more rights than the UDHR. Such additions include the right of a child to be accorded such measures of protection as are required by their status as a minor; this is highly relevant to the use of child labour in sweatshops in South-East Asia and the exploitation of child soldiers in Africa. The Covenant on Economic, Social and Cultural Rights contains a longer and much more comprehensive catalogue of rights than the Declaration. It recognizes the following: the right to work; the right to the enjoyment of just and favourable conditions at work; the right to form and join trade unions; the right to social security, including social insurance; the right to the protection of the family; the right to an adequate standard of living;

and the right to the enjoyment of the highest attainable standard of physical and mental health. As you can see, these are significant in the consideration of treatment to be afforded to workers in a wide range of circumstances, as is the right to the enjoyment of just and favourable conditions of work ensuring payment which provides workers with fair wages and equal remuneration for work of equal value (later recognized in various national anti-discrimination legislation), a decent living for themselves and their families, safe and healthy working conditions, equal opportunities in promotion, and rest, leisure and reasonable limitations on working hours and periodic holidays with pay, as well as remuneration for public holidays (Buergenthal, 1988, p 44). These provisions are particularly important considering the standards under which so many workers are expected to work today, even in relatively liberal and progressive Western democracies. Taken together the UDHR and the two covenants, including the two Optional Protocols, are known as the International Bill of Human Rights. The Bill provided the basis for subsequent Conventions, which have allowed human rights law to become a national as well as international concern, and this will hopefully translate into real protection for workers and others affected by the operations of businesses at both the micro and macro levels.

International Labour Organization

The first specialized UN agency to be set up was the International Labour Organization (ILO), which seeks the promotion of social justice and internationally recognized human and labour rights. It was founded in 1919 and is the only surviving major creation of the Treaty of Versailles. The ILO formulates international labour standards in the form of conventions and recommendations, setting minimum standards of basic labour rights: freedom of association, the right to organize, collective bargaining, abolition of forced labour, equality of opportunity and treatment, and other standards regulating conditions across the entire spectrum of work related issues. It promotes the development of independent employers' and workers' organizations and provides training and advisory services to those organizations. Within the UN system, the ILO has a unique tripartite structure, with workers and employers participating as equal partners with governments in the work of its governing organs (International Labour Organization, 1998). This approach no doubt adds legitimacy and positively enforces the opportunity for constructive debate and flexibility between different organs of society in the representation of their interests.

European Convention on Human Rights

The European Convention on Human Rights was ratified by all the Member States in 1950 and came into force three years later (Council of Europe, 1950). The decision to draft the European Convention was made after the UN adopted the UDHR. The rights guaranteed therein include; the right to life; the right not to be subjected to torture, inhuman or degrading treatment and punishment; freedom from slavery; the right to liberty, security of the person and due process of law; freedom from retrospective laws and punishment; the right to private and family life; freedom of thought and conscience; freedom of religion, of expression and of peaceful assembly; and the right to marry and found a family. In its preamble, the Convention cites the objective of enforcing the rights stated in the UDHR. To this end, the Convention established the European Commission of Human Rights and the European Court of Human Rights to ensure the observance of its provisions (Buergenthal, 1988, p 76). Owing to the legal supremacy of the European Community, member states have enacted enabling legislation or have interpreted domestic legislation in light of these developments, which give the rights a sense of immediacy and therefore legal persons within member states must be aware of their indirect impact.

WTO/World Bank

The World Trade Organization (WTO), dealing as it does with the rules of trade between nations, is in and has always been in a position to determine whether and how international trade law embraces human rights principles. In fact the GATT/WTO legal regime already adheres to non-discrimination, the development and extension of which being a matter that is of interest to corporations as the driver of international trade. It is therefore in their interests to be familiar with, and adept at the promotion of, developing such dimensions (Kinley, 2003).

The World Bank, through its activities and its renewed commitment to human rights, will play a key role in the promotion of human rights and in the building and strengthening of national human rights capacities in the countries in which it operates. Central to the Bank's work is the reduction of poverty. In promoting economic development, the Bank aims to create an environment for the enjoyment by individuals of all their human rights. Indeed, the right to development is all-encompassing, demanding the realization of civil, cultural, economic, political and social rights. This approach enhances the human dimension of World Bank strategies focusing on, among other aims, strengthening institutions of governance and democracy. From this perspective, the role of human rights as empowering individuals and communities is obvious (World Bank, 2005).

Geneva Conventions

Where there are exceptional circumstances, it is appropriate for a country to derogate from its responsibilities under the UN Conventions. Generally, these circumstances arise in times of war or emergency. It is at this point that humanitarian law comes into play. Prior to the 20th century, a civilian population caught up in hostilities was largely unprotected against the violence visited upon them by the armed forces. The adoption of the Geneva Convention in 1864 afforded victims of war some semblance of protection. The four Geneva Conventions of 1949 developed the concept of international humanitarian law. Of particular importance was the Geneva Convention IV 'Relative to the Protection of Civilian Persons in Time of War', which includes safe-guarding would-be victims against grave breaches committed during an armed conflict (Geneva Convention, 1949). Today, important parts of the Geneva Conventions are considered to have acquired the status of customary international laws, thus making them obligatory also for states that are not party to these instruments.

Nuremberg

At around the same time, the recognition and acceptance of inter-national courts as a means of prosecuting individuals for various humanitarian crimes became more than a possibility. The Nuremburg War Crimes Tribunal was established under the London Agreement and Charter. The trials commenced in 1945 and, for the first time, indi-viduals were held accountable, not only for specific war infringements contrary to international humanitarian law, but also for conduct amounting to crimes against humanity (de Than and Shorts, 2003, p 273). It was not until the early 1990s that the international com-munity again called for a judicial solution to the horrific humanitarian crimes being perpetrated, this time in the former Yugoslavia. Although there had been instances in the preceding years calling for such action, under the UN Charter, Art. 2(7), the United Nations was prevented from intervening in matters which essentially fell under the heading of domestic jurisdiction. However, with the break up of the Soviet Union, the UN Security Council was given more prominence and, being charged with the maintenance of international peace and security, could establish subsidiary organs with which to prosecute individuals who posed a threat to peace and security in violation of international law under the charter.

ICTY/ICTR

The jurisdiction and prosecutions under the Statute of the International Criminal Tribunal for the Former Yugoslavia (ICTY), Article 2, are restricted to 'grave breaches' of the 1949 Conventions, i.e. 'core crimes' such as genocide, crimes against humanity and war crimes. Under Article 7 of the Statute, those individuals who planned, instigated, ordered, committed or otherwise aided and abetted in the planning, preparation or execution of a crime were to be held criminally responsible. 'Aiding' is defined as giving assistance to someone, 'abetting' involves the facilitation of the commission of an act by being sympathetic thereto (de Than and Shorts, 2003, p 289). The International Criminal Court (ICC) is the first international court to be established by, and with the cooperation of, the world community (rather than by the major Allied Powers or the Security Council). The Rome Statute of the ICC goes one step further than that of the ICTY and imposes criminal liability upon an individual who '[f]or the purposes of facilitating the commission of such a crime, aids, abets or otherwise assists in its commission or its attempted commission, including providing the means for its commission.' (Schabas, 2001, p 442). These developments in policy represent a commitment to ensure that the commission of a crime covered by the Rome Statute will not be subject to the ambiguities of previous incarnations. The world community is demanding accountability as far as is possible and, although there will certainly be (and are already) hurdles in applying these sentiments, it is encouraging that such steps are finally being taken.

Developments in international law relating to corporations

Companies no longer wait to find themselves the subject of a class action before they familiarize themselves with the laws governing the areas in which they operate. As a tool in the management and limitation of risk, companies are becoming proactive in issues surrounding their accountability. Along with standards and other management tools, there are a number of initiatives that encourage firms to become the authors of their own destinies. It is in this vein that the following projects have been formulated.

The UN Global Compact

The United Nations Global Compact (United Nations, 2000) is a learning forum revolving around 10 principles derived from key international instruments focusing on human rights, labour standards, the environment and corruption. One of the Compact's founding premises is that, without the private sector's active involvement, there is a danger that universal principles will remain unimplemented. Consequently, the Global Compact seeks to underpin the global economy with universal values defined by international instruments. The first two principles of the Global Compact concern human rights. First, businesses should support and respect the protection of internationally proclaimed human rights, and second, businesses should make sure they are not complicit in abuses. The Global Compact is purely voluntary, though the rights it refers to are generally binding on states (Commission on Human Rights, 2005). In contrast with its contemporaries, however, the Global Compact doesn't have a monitoring mechanism.

UN Draft Norms

The United Nations Draft Norms on the Responsibilities of Transnational Corporations and other Business Enterprises with Regard to Human Rights (2003) ('The Norms') were intended for providing assistance to companies framing their human rights responsibilities. They were an attempt to assemble the plethora of international human rights instruments into a single legible document and as such constitute an authoritative business-related interpretation of the UDHR and subsequent human rights conventions. The UN sub-commission on human rights confirmed that, although the Norms have no legal status, a report was commissioned to identify options for strengthening standards on the responsibilities of businesses in human rights and possible means of implementation. In April 2005, the UN Human Rights Commission requested by resolution the appointment of a Special Representative on the issue of Human Rights, Transnational Corporations and Other Business Enterprises (Commission on Human Rights, 2005).

The OECD guidelines for multinational enterprises

These guidelines are recommendations to businesses from the 30 OECD member states and the eight adhering non-member states concerning conduct in many areas of business ethics. The recommendations cover a broad range of issues from compliance with local laws and regulations, safeguarding of consumer interests, abstaining from anti-competitive practices and meeting host countries' tax liabilities. A separate recommendation relates to human rights generally, asking business to 'respect the human rights of those affected by their activities consistent with the host government's international obligations and commitments'. Further, the commentary to the guidelines stresses the relevance of the UDHR. The guidelines also include recommendations in relation to workers' human rights, such as freedom of association, the right to collective bargaining, the effective abolition of child labour, the elimination of all forms of forced or compulsory labour and non-discrimination in employment and occupation. Whilst voluntary and without universal authority, the guidelines are proving widely influential with business managers of international companies (Commission on Human Rights, 2005).

ILO Tripartite Declaration of Principles

In comparison to the OECD guidelines, the ILO Declaration provides guidance to multinational enterprises as well as domestic business, governments and workers' organizations on labour-related aspects of corporate social responsibility (International Labour Organization, 1998). It covers several areas related to workers' human rights. Owing to the universal nature of the ILO and its tripartite structure, the geographical and company reach of the declaration is technically broader than that of the guidelines. The tripartite basis means that the declaration has the support of governments, employers and workers. However, it too is voluntary, save that the conventions it refers to are binding on state parties.

The Alien Tort Claims Act

This Act (US House of Representatives, Office of the Law Revision Counsel, 1992) grants jurisdiction to US Federal Courts over any civil action by an alien for a tort only, committed in violation of the law of nations or a treaty of the United States. The law, which was enacted in 1789, was revived following an action in 1980 by a Paraguayan man who successfully used the ATCA to sue the policeman who tortured his son to death in Paraguay (Birchall, 2004). Others have since filed suits against individuals, including Zimbabwe's Robert Mugabe, seeking compensation for damages resulting from breaches of international law. Recent efforts to use the Act to sue transnational corporations for violations of international law in countries outside the US mean that the ACTA could become a powerful tool to increase corporate accountability (Birchall, 2004). Indeed, a suit against Unocal Corp, an El Segundo-based energy company, accused the corporation of being responsible for forced labour, rapes and a murder allegedly carried out by soldiers along a natural gas pipeline route in Myanmar. It is alleged that the company knew or should have known that the Myanmar army committed human rights abuses while providing security for the $1.2 billion pipeline project. Unocal settled the landmark suit in 2005. The settlement bolsters other ACTA cases and signals to corporations that this law is applicable to them, and they are going to face major litigation (Lifsher, 2005). Other companies facing similar lawsuits include Exxon Mobil Corp in Nigeria; Occidental Petroleum Corp, British Petroleum, the coal miner Drummond Co. and Coca Cola in Colombia. A Human Rights Watch Representative said that this settlement allows the parameters of what is and is not acceptable for a company operating abroad to be set.

Principles of complicity are drawn mostly from criminal law and are generally based on proof of knowledge, something that has proved difficult in the development of corporate liability. The International Criminal Court, although it does not yet have jurisdiction over legal persons/corporations, only natural persons, is concerned with the most egregious of wrongful conduct: genocide, crimes against humanity, war crimes and aggression. It does not take too big a leap of imagination to extend international criminal law to multinationals. Corporate liability for crime has increasingly appeared on the agenda in many jurisdictions over the last 10 years. Additionally, it is not so difficult to conceive of a corporation as the subject of international law. While the mindset of the criminal lawyer is to think about individuals, that of the international lawyer was for a long time to think about states/a group entity, albeit of a special kind. But the ICC and other war crimes tribunals specifically address the crimes of individual human agents. Thus it might be said that national law is going corporate and international law is going individual. Indeed the Rome Statute contained in its draft form a clause extending jurisdiction over legal persons (Wells, 2003).

Owing to a failure to comprehensively deal with specific human rights, however, there is still a gap in understanding regarding what the international community expects of business when it comes to human rights. This does not, however, mean that they are not expected to adhere to them.

Conclusions: levels of responsibility

Commonly a classification system covering three types of involvement is used to describe corporate complicity with abusive states: direct, indirect and beneficiary complicity. Direct complicity would include cases of joint participation, for example if Unocal had supplied personnel to work with the Burmese military. Indirect complicity comprises those situations where the multinational corporation's activities help to maintain a regime's financial and commercial infrastructure. Beneficiary or third-order involvement describes the way that businesses silently exploit the regime, benefiting from lower wage costs because of poor conditions or discriminatory practices, for example. Human Rights Watch suggests that corporate complicity covers situations in which '[a] corporation facilitates or participates in government human rights violations. Facilitation includes the company's provision of material or financial support for states' security forces which then commit human rights violations that benefit the company.' One writer describes this as 'collapsing' the distinction between direct and indirect complicity (Wells, 2003).

However these actions and inactions are categorized, there is no escaping the fact that the world is changing, and with it so are the responsibilities of individuals, states, corporations and the international community. Care must be taken in assessing risk. No longer is it enough to consider our own interests or those of the company we work for and its shareholders. Even if the extra-territorial operations of transnational corporations are not substantially regulated by either domestic or international law with respect to human rights obligations at present, there is certainly a move towards such regulation. A company must be aware and willing to act in concert with international human rights law.

References

The American Non-Governmental Organizations Coalition for the International Criminal Court (2004) *Information Regarding the Possible Investigation by the ICC of the Situation in Ituri, Democratic Republic of the Congo.* Available at: http://www.amicc.org/docs/AMICC_DRC_Q&A.pdf

Birchall, Jonathan (2004) The questions over aiding and abetting: Alien Tort Statute. *Financial Times* 5 August. Available at: http://www.globalpolicy.org/intjustice/atca/2004/0802alien.htm

Buergenthal, Thomas (1988) *International Human Rights*. St Paul, MN: West Publishing

Carbonnier, Gilles (2001)Corporate responsibility and humanitarian action. *IRRC (International Review of the Red Cross)* 83:844 Dec.

Commission on Human Rights (2005) *Report of the Sub-commission on the Promotion and Protection of Human Rights*. 61st session, item 16 on the provisional agenda. Available at: http://www.un.org/News/Press/docs/2005/hrcn1109.doc.htm

Council of Europe (1950) *The European Convention on Human Rights*. Available at: http://www1.umn.edu/humanrts/instree/z17euroco.html

Geneva Convention (1949) *The Geneva Conventions of 12 August 1949*. Geneva: International Committee of the Red Cross, pp 153–221. Available at: http://www.icrc.org/ihl.nsf

International Council on Human Rights Policy (2002) *Beyond Voluntarism; Human Rights and the Developing International Legal Obligations of Companies*. Geneva: International Council on Human Rights Policy

International Labour Organization (1998). *Declaration on Fundamental Principles and Rights at Work*. Available at: http://www.ilo.org/dyn/declaris/DECLA-RATIONWEB.INDEXPAGE

Kinley, David (2003) Lawyers, corporations and international human rights. *Showcase Session on Corporate Social Responsiblity at International Bar Association Conference, San Francisco, 15–19 September*

Lifsher, Marc (2005) Unocal settles human rights lawsuit over alleged abuses at Myanmar pipeline. *Los Angeles Times*, 22 Mar. Available at: http://www.glocalpolicy.org/intjustice/atca/2005/0322unocalsettle.htm

Mares, Radu (ed) (2004) *Business and Human Rights: A Compilation of Documents*. Amsterdam: Martinus Nijhoff

Nyberg, Maurice (1998) At risk from complicity with crime. *Financial Times* 27 July

Schabas, William (2001) Enforcing international humanitarian law: catching the accomplices. *IRRC (International Review of the Red Cross)* **83**:842 (June)

de Than, Claire and Shorts, Edwin (2003) *International Criminal Law and Human Rights*. London: Thompson and Maxwell Publishing

United Nations (1948) *Universal Declaration on Human Rights*. Available at: http://www.un.org.Overview/rights.html

United Nations (1966a) *International Covenant on Economic, Social and Cultural Rights*. Available at: http://www.ohchr.org/english/law/index.htm

United Nations (1966b) *International Covenant on Civil and Political Rights*. Available at: http://www.ohchr.org/english/law/index.htm

United Nations (2000) *The Global Compact: Corporate Citizenship in the World Economy*. Available at: http://www.unglobalcompact.org/content/AboutTheGC/EssentialReadings/brochure_master.pdf

United Nations Draft Norms on the Responsibilities of Transnational Corporations and other Business Enterprises with Regard to Human Rights (2003). Available at: http://www1.umn.edu/humanrts/links/NormsApril2003.html

US House of Representatives, Office of the Law Revision Counsel. United States Alien Tort Claims Act 28 U.S.C.§1350. (1992) Available at: http://uscode.house.gov/

Wells, C (2003) Available at: http://www.ccels.cardiff.ac.uk/pubs/wellspaper.html

World Bank (2005) *Development and Human Rights: The Role Of The World Bank*. Available at: http://www.worldbank.org/html/extdr/rights

6

Inter-governmental Initiatives in Support of Appropriate Standards of Business Conduct – Are They Effective?[1]

Kathryn Gordon

Introduction

International trade and investment are widening and deepening the economic ties that bind the countries of the world together. Most people welcome these developments – there is a solid consensus that market economies, when accompanied by appropriate public and private governance, provide the most effective means for enhancing material, social and environmental well-being[2]. Binding laws, formal standards and informal norms for business conduct provide coordinating mechanisms so that all relevant actors can play their roles in enhancing well-being more effectively.

This chapter addresses the question of whether or not inter-governmental initiatives are effective in supporting the development and observance of appropriate standards of business conduct – that is, standards that have broad legitimacy and that contribute to a global economy that enhances the well-being (broadly defined) of all the world's people. In addressing this question, the chapter moves from the conceptual to the concrete, via the following sections.

1. *The need for coordination – humans as a social species.* In order to understand how law, formal standards and informal norms interact to influence business behaviour, one has to understand how

humans behave in groups. This section looks at the micro-level behaviours that support the human ability to cooperate. It shows how, in advanced societies, the gradual development of formal standards and binding law has supported ever more sophisticated forms of cooperation. It also notes the key role of the nation state in this process.

2. *International organizations and coordination in the world economy.* This section looks at the coordination challenges posed by today's global markets. Multinational enterprises are on the front lines in dealing with economic 'culture shock' that inevitability arises when business operations straddle numerous countries, cultures and legal jurisdictions. This section looks at the role of international organizations in setting standards for the global economy and describes the OECD's unique approach to international policy cooperation.

3. *The OECD definition of corporate responsibility and the OECD Guidelines for Multinational Enterprises.* The OECD perspective on corporate responsibility and its government-backed code of conduct for international business, the OECD Guidelines for Multinational Enterprises, are described (OECD, 2000). The section also reviews recent developments in adhering governments' follow up on the guidelines.

The need for coordination – human beings as a social species

Human beings are the ultimate social species (see, for example, Alexander, 1987)[3]. Throughout their history, their survival has depended on coordinated group action – humans have organized themselves into groups in order to secure access to resources and to defend themselves against other groups and other species. In advanced market economies, this collective aspect of human behaviour is as important as it was in earlier stages of human development. For example, the extreme division of labour seen in advanced market economies creates wide-ranging (indeed global) interdependence and a need for coordinating the actions of actors who are separated, both geographically and culturally. Economic history can be understood (in part) as a process of innovation leading to increasingly complex coordination mechanisms – mechanisms that allow coordination of transactions between individuals that are ever further removed from one another in a cultural and geographical sense. Formal standards are part of this ongoing process of innovation.

If standards are to be influential, then they must account for the complex array of behavioural patterns that have been built into the brain over hundreds of thousands of years of human and pre-human evolution. Humans have a strong inclination to cooperate in group activities, a need to 'belong' and a set of characteristic emotions, motivations and behavioural patterns that allow them to regulate activities within groups (see Jones, 2001)[4]. If standards, norms and formally codified law are to enhance the performance of societies and markets (e.g. to allow them to become more peaceful and secure, to produce higher material standards of living and to achieve other important goals), then they must deal effectively with micro-level behaviours – they must help humans capitalize on their more positive characteristics and to moderate their more negative ones.

These behavioural characteristics include:

1. *Complex self-interestedness.* Microeconomics is based on the view that individuals are self-interested (that is, rational, utility maximizers). However, for the highly social, group-dependent human species, the nature of self-interest is complex. Self-interest in humans includes concern for 'self' but also typically extends to members of an individual's immediate family and to members of the groups to which the individual belongs and on which their well-being depends (individual feelings of attachment and loyalty to groups might have been functional as human beings evolved as a group-dependent species).

2. *Altruism and social capital.* Altruism within families is a readily observable feature of all human societies, e.g. parents caring for and protecting their own children more than those of others. Altruism outside the family appears to weaken as the degree of relatedness between individuals weakens, but generalized altruism (that is, that benefits unrelated individuals) is common (see Stout, 2001)[5]. Generalized altruism may be due, at least in part, to an ingrained tendency among humans to act in ways that reflect the tight link between individual and group welfare that undoubtedly existed as the human species evolved. Unlike in modern societies, exclusion from the group in more primitive societies would have been tantamount to a death sentence. As a result, investments in general welfare can often be expected to pay off for the individual making them and it may have made sense (in human evolutionary terms) to build in a tendency toward general altruism (not something that is always present, but a definite pattern in human behaviour). This sum of all of these investments, the associated

behavioural norms and standards that support individual investments in general well-being has been called 'social capital' (see, for
example, Fukuyama, 1999).

3. *Emotion and motivation.* Many human emotions are used to regulate group activity – moral judgements about behaviour, anger,
spite, punishment, ostracism, loneliness, self-righteousness, encouragement, approval, loyalty, sociability and status seeking. When
looking at what motivates people, it is important to neither underestimate nor to exaggerate the importance of material punishments
and rewards. While material incentives are important, they are not
necessarily the most powerful influences on human behaviour. Once
basic material needs are met, people are often more motivated by
social, in-group dynamics – they will seek status and social recognition and try to avoid group punishments such as ostracism and
derision. Again, it is possible that this emotional basis for the regulation of individual behaviours in groups – an innate capacity for
self-regulation – was built into the human brain as the species
evolved in groups of hunter-gatherers. The importance of this for
thinking about standards and the enforcement of standards is that
it implies that soft, social forms of norms enforcement should not
be dismissed as meaningless. On the contrary, while they cannot
explain everything, they are critically important for understanding
the micro-basis of individual decisions to comply with (or not)
standards and with binding law.

4. *Deception and coercion.* The human species has a number of other
characteristics that are also relevant for the design and enforcement
of standards. The capacity for deception is well developed in human
beings (with their elaborate arsenal of deceitful behaviours and their
equally elaborate deception detection capabilities), as is the capacity
for (often violent) coercion. In addition, individuals often act in
groups to enhance the effectiveness of both deception and coercion
– thereby bringing all the emotional and cognitive capabilities to
bear on the problems of deceiving and coercing.

5. *Forging individual and group identities.* Humans are adept at relating individual identities to group identities – that is, at identifying
affiliations. Indeed, the idea of group affiliation is closely related to
norms because group affiliation is often associated with the ability
to show appropriate adherence to group norms, e.g. speaking a
language without an accent – that is, applying norms for pronun-
ciation in a faultless manner – is one way of demonstrating one
cultural or national affiliation. This capacity to forge group identities relies on the capacity to determine who is a member of the

group and who is not. This in turn draws on cross cutting signals relating to culture, race, language, gender, nationality, occupation and many other characteristics.

With the ingenuity that typifies it, the human species has increasingly managed to give complex institutional expressions to its basic capacities for cooperation within groups. In particular, humans have used their powers to communicate, formalize and record to create other ways of communicating expectations about behaviour. These have allowed humans to go beyond the constraints of (emotion-based) group regulation that depends on face-to-face contact. In particular, formalized standards and binding law are major institutional innovations that allow for impersonal coordination of group activity[6].

At the present time, the nation state dominates world affairs in the economic and political spheres. The nation state is the highest level of human organization in which binding law and formal private standards are made and implemented (sub-national groups are also important). In the present international standards-setting context, the nation state both dominates international political affairs and reveals its own (rather significant) limitations. Nation states' approaches to solving coordination problems are anchored in such national features as culture, institutional traditions and structural patterns in the economy – thus, social capital (the ultimate resource that makes behavioural control – including control of business conduct – effective) is largely local or national while policy challenges are increasingly multi-layered, involving global, national and local dimensions (see Bowles and Gintis, 2000)[7].

The next section will argue that the decision flexibility of the nation state has been undercut by global standards-setting activities. While the nation state is still very much the dominant actor in this international standards-setting exercise, it could be argued that the world has entered a new phase of institutional innovation – based on a highly decentralized, almost confederated, model of international governance – that may provide some of the international coordination needed to promote a more smoothly operating global economy.

International organizations and coordination in the global economy

The previous section suggests that one of the key challenges for the world economy lies in reconciling the growing internationalization of economic activity with the fact that international economic policy – the system of global rules – is largely a patchwork of policies made by nation states and by sub-national entities. In the early years of the 21st century, this picture is still largely valid, but it is growing less so. At the present time, nation states still make and enforce most laws, but they often do this subject to a growing framework of international principles and guidelines for good practice.

The globalization of economic activity combined with the ongoing national basis for most policy institutions gives rise to a sort of economic 'culture shock' – international trade and investment has created tensions and uncertainties as large number of actors are forced to deal with ethical questions that their locally or nationally based laws, private standards and informal norms cannot fully answer (indeed, many of them give contradictory signals to business). For example, withholding certain types of material information from investors is a common practice in some countries, while it is punishable as a crime in others. Consumer protection is carefully looked after in one country, whereas *caveat emptor* is *de facto* the reigning policy in others. Determining which behaviours are acceptable and which are not in such situations – that is, setting behavioural standards – is an important problem of economic coordination. Multinational enterprises – which often cover thousands of cultures and legal jurisdictions – are on the cutting edge of dealing with this culture shock. Indeed, seen from an evolutionary perspective, the strong emotions often observed when activities of multinational enterprises are discussed – moralistic aggression, righteous self-defence, anger, etc. – are the micro-behavioural signs that the world economy is operating with a shortfall of effective law, formal standards and shared informal norms.

Thus the world is searching for institutions that can reduce the tensions caused by global economic culture shock and that help enhance trust and cooperation among the different actors in the world economy. Like their counterparts at the national level, these international institutions must be able to deal with the challenges of bringing out the best (welfare enhancing) aspects of human behaviour while also minimizing the damage caused by other human behaviours (e.g. coercion, violence and deceit). However, while recognizing the need for further development of global institutions in support of the global market economy, it is also useful to acknowledge the significant progress that has already been made in building a framework for international coordination.

This framework is housed in the world's major international organizations including the OECD, the International Monetary Fund, the

World Bank, the United Nations system and the Bank for International Settlements. International policy guidelines cover an enormous range of issues, e.g. international bank supervision, competition policy, child labour, the fight against corruption, corporate governance, transparency of fiscal systems, protection of foreign investors' rights, rules for electronic commerce, guidelines for taxing international companies (to name but a few). Complementing these official institutions are private standards-setting organizations such as the International Organization for Standardization and its national affiliates.

Among the major international organizations, the OECD has a distinctive, club-like way of trying to influence national policies and practices. This arises from two closely related features. First, its membership is limited to 30 of the world's most affluent countries. Second, its decision processes are fully consensus-based – all decisions are taken on the basis of unanimity. Under OECD rules of procedure, member countries are considered 'peers' and, under these rules, one country's imposition of its will on another country would be procedurally impossible – in effect, all countries have veto power. These collegial rules of procedure are the OECD's principal strength and weakness – they make decisions slow and cumbersome, but they also contribute to credibility and 'buy in' once decisions are made.

The OECD has made important contributions to the international framework of behavioural norms – its Convention on Combating Bribery of Foreign Public Officials in International Business Transactions (which creates binding obligations on signatories) (OECD, 1998) and related anti-bribery instruments have established the OECD as the leading international forum in the fight against international corruption. Its work in the area of taxation has been influential on both public policy and on multinational enterprises' tax management. Likewise, the OECD Principles of Corporate Governance (OECD, 2004), The Forty Recommendations of the Financial Action Task Force on Money Laundering (1990) and its Guidelines on Managing Conflict of Interest in the Public Sector (OECD, 2003b) are the most influential standards in their areas.

The OECD typically backs up these standards with economic analysis, production of internationally comparable statistics and related peer reviews. During the peer reviews, public officials examine each others' policies – acting more like a peer advisory council than a jury. In this way, the basic concepts and principles written into OECD instruments can be looked at in their national or even local settings. The building up of consensus on concepts and principles in the international policy arena and subsequent provision of a soft, consensus-based follow-up mechanism presents definite advantages relative to some other international organizations' ways of influencing domestic policies and practices: 1) it makes it clear that national governments are in control of and responsible for their policy measures – OECD processes do not in any way remove responsibilities from member governments by authoritarian, coercive procedures; and 2) accounting for local 'colour' – national or local norms, institutions, structural characteristics and human capacities – are fundamental components of the OECD approach to international policy coordination (see Goodman and Jinks, 2004)[8].

The OECD's work on corporate responsibility is typical of this consensus-driven, non-authoritarian process. The OECD Guidelines for Multinational Enterprises (OECD, 2000) – a government-backed code of conduct for multinational enterprises – help to define what it means to be a member of the OECD (countries are *inter alia* reviewed with respect to their willingness and ability to adhere to and promote the guidelines). Subsequent sections of this chapter review OECD thinking about corporate responsibility and discuss recent developments in relation to the guidelines.

Corporate responsibility – definitions and emerging trends

The OECD's view is that the primary contribution of business – its core responsibility – is the conduct of business itself. The role of business in society is to develop promising investments opportunities so as to yield competitive returns to the suppliers of capital. In so doing, companies create jobs and produce goods and services that consumers want to buy. This perspective renders the OECD view on corporate responsibility compatible with its work on corporate governance. Indeed, the OECD Principles of Corporate Governance (OECD, 2004) – one of the most influential 'soft law' instruments ever issued by the OECD – are part of the backbone of the OECD approach to corporate responsibility.

While the OECD views value maximization as being the core function of the business sector, it also acknowledges that the business sector must respond to 'competing demands' from society. Companies are expected to obey the various laws that are applicable to them and, as a practical matter, must respond to societal expectations that are not written down in law books.

This might seem to be a conservative perspective – one that resembles Milton Friedman's views on corporate responsibility[9]. However, the OECD view differs in important respects from Friedman's perspective. In particular, Friedman fails to look closely at the deeper question of how legal and ethical compliance is accomplished in group settings and to recognize compliance for what it is – a very subtle process that goes to the heart of what companies are (groups of human beings working together) and of how companies position themselves in the broader societies in which they operate. Because of this lack of nuance, people advocating Friedman's perspective often dismiss the importance of corporate responsibility initiatives (see Henderson, 2001). In contrast, in the OECD view, these initiatives represent one of the most important international business trends of the last quarter century (see OECD, 2001).

Many companies have invested heavily in trying to meet the difficult challenges of legal and ethical compliance in a global economy. OECD research (OECD, 2001) shows that thousands of enterprises on at least four continents have participated in this trend. It also suggests that there are significant variations – by country and by sector of operation – in the issues companies choose to deal with and in their approaches to these issues. Broadly speaking, OECD research suggests that there has been movement toward the creation of international standards in many areas, but that the world is still a long way from having *de facto* standards in most areas of business conduct.

Examples of such divergences can be seen in Figures 6.1 and 6.2. Figure 6.1 shows that nearly all of the top 100 multinational enterprises publish policy statements on environment and health and safety while fewer than half deal publicly with the issue of corruption.

Figure 6.2 reveals large sectoral variations in the propensity of companies to publish policy statements on corruption. While such variations reflect the diversity of companies' individual business environments, they also reflect other differences such as the state of development of agreed norms for conduct in different issue areas and sectors. Understanding these differences and encouraging convergence towards good practice are among the main objectives of the OECD guidelines.

Private initiatives allow businesses and societies to 'feel their way forward' in the many areas where standards on acceptable management practices for business are not yet firmly established. There is some evidence that this is happening in some sectors. For example, OECD research (OECD, 2002, 2003a, pp 127–133) suggests that the published policies of OECD-based companies with outsourcing operations have tended to converge with respect to the core labour standards they ask their suppliers to observe. Nearly all companies with publicly available outsourcing policies now mention all core labour standards, whereas few covered all core standards in the late 1990s[10]. However, the research also suggests that most companies – 118 out of a sample of 147 companies operating in sectors where core labour standards are a strategic concern – do not publish their outsourcing policies. Thus, OECD research shows that sample of outsourcing companies as being divided into two sub-groups – a group of activists (within which there are clear signs of convergence – that is, of the emergence of a *de facto* standard) and a group of non-activists.

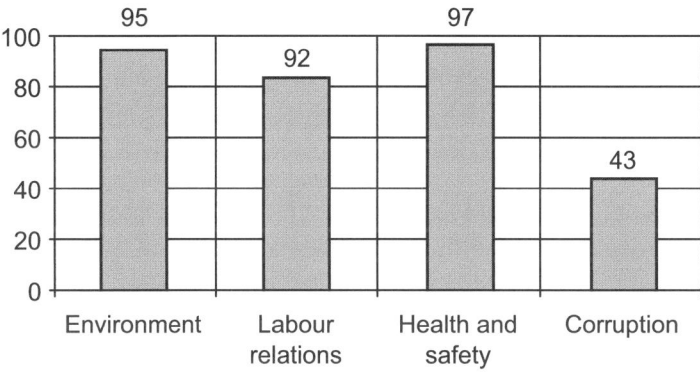

Source: 2003 Annual Report on the OECD Guidelines for Multinational Enterprises (OECD, 2003a)

Figure 6.1 Policy statements by issue area (number of companies in top 100 list making statements)

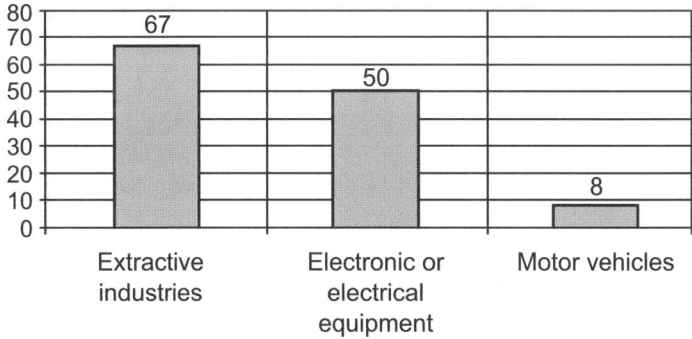

Source: 2003 Annual Report on the OECD Guidelines for Multinational Enterprises (OECD, 2003a)

Figure 6.2 Anti-corruption statements by sector of activity (per cent of companies in sector sample)

The interplay between voluntary and legal, private and public standards

There is an ongoing debate about the effectiveness of voluntary initiatives. Some parties believe that such initiatives represent the business sector's contribution to the goal of building effective standards of international business conduct. These standards clarify what is expected of managers and support social and business processes – both inside and outside the firm – that help support appropriate business conduct. This voluntary approach offers the flexibility needed to adapt to and learn from regional, sectoral and individual business circumstances. Others view these efforts as little more than public relations ploys and would favour replacing them with binding rules involving sanctions and other enforcement mechanisms. Only these, they feel, will give the standards enough 'teeth' to influence corporate behaviour in a meaningful way.

The review of human behaviour provided in the second section of this chapter suggests that it would be extremely surprising if both aspects – genuine effort and deception – were not present in private initiatives for corporate responsibility. When engaging in any group activity, the cooperative side of the human mind feels more comfortable when it can draw on group-condoned standards and norms to regulate individual behaviour. Group integration of such standards also allows other group processes to enter in play (encouragement, status, group identification and loyalty, punishment, ostracism, derision, etc). This side of the mind is also reasonably adept at detecting 'cheating', punishing it and encouraging adherence to group norms. When they are working well, private initiatives for corporate responsibility help bring these basic human capabilities to bear on the problem of observing appropriate norms for business behaviour.

On the other hand, human beings are also adept at deceit. They will try and often succeed in convincing others that they are cooperative and respectful of group norms whereas, in fact, they are acting out of self-interest. This is likely to be as present in private initiatives for corporate responsibility as it is in any other human activity.

By facilitating positive cooperative activities in the business sector in support of appropriate business conduct and by making it more difficult for people to be deceitful in this area, these initiatives help to improve the functioning of the global economy. At the same time, it would be naive to think that a meaningful system of global norms could exist without binding regulation and formal deterrence. As noted earlier, for the time being, much regulation and law enforcement is very much anchored in national economic systems. Future international regulation in some areas could emerge from gradual convergence and coordination of national practices. The OECD has taken steps to encourage this. The OECD Convention on Combating Bribery of Foreign Public Officials in International Business Transactions (OECD, 1998) – which obliges signatories to enact laws and criminal sanctions against bribery of foreign public officials – is an important example. Another example can be found in OECD work on international tax enforcement. One should take care, however, to avoid exaggerating the degree to which formal law enforcement can or should solve all the world's problems.

Moreover, many of these initiatives are not quite as 'voluntary' as they might seem. The *Merriam-Webster Dictionary* defines 'voluntary' as 'acting or done of one's own free will without valuable consideration or legal obligation'. If one accepts this definition, then many private initiatives are not really voluntary – they are private responses (built into management systems and other business practices) that are driven by powerful financial, legal or regulatory pressures created by the broader society in which businesses operate. For example, environmental regulation in the European Union provides incentives for adopting certain environmental management practices. The US Federal Sentencing Guidelines for Organizations (2004) provide another example of this deliberate coordination of public and private efforts. The sentencing guidelines provide powerful legal incentives (in the form of the possibility of more lenient sentences) for companies to adopt management systems that would allow them to show that they have made credible efforts to prevent violations of law by their employees.

Thus, the idea that there is a stark difference between binding and 'soft' initiatives is not a valid one. The challenge is to promote a workable mix of public and private initiatives and to get all actors in the broader system – both public and private – to take up their responsibilities and to assume appropriate roles in an effective manner. Private initiatives by companies are part of this broader effort, but companies cannot, by themselves, create workable norms for conduct for the global economy. Indeed, OECD dialogue on corporate responsibility indicates that the one area on which all actors – business, trade unions and NGOs – agree is that it should not be asked to take on other actors' – especially governments' – responsibilities. There should be no 'privatization' of government responsibility. If effective systems for promoting appropriate business conduct are to be built, governments and private sector actors must act in partnerships underpinned by an appropriate allocation of roles and responsibilities for each.

The OECD Guidelines for Multinational Enterprises, described below, are one of the most concrete examples in the OECD of how successful private–public partnerships can be used to help make the global economy work better.

The OECD Guidelines for Multinational Enterprises

What the guidelines are

The Guidelines are a government-backed code of conduct for international business (OECD, 2000). Thirty-eight governments – from the 30 OECD members and from eight non-members[11] – have adhered to the guidelines. Today they are exploring how the guidelines can best contribute to improving the functioning of the global economy and to promoting corporate responsibility. The guidelines are recommendations covering such areas as human rights, labour relations, environment, combating corruption and consumer protection. Observance of these recommendations is voluntary for businesses, but the adhering governments make a binding commitment to promote them among multinational enterprises operating in or from their territories. In making this commitment, governments aim 'to strengthen the basis of mutual confidence between enterprises and the societies in which they operate, to help improve the foreign investment climate and to enhance the contribution to sustainable development made by multinational enterprises' (OECD, 2000, preface).

The OECD Guidelines for Multinational Enterprises seek to encourage and reinforce the private initiatives for corporate responsibility that are described above. They express the shared views of 38 adhering governments on ethical business conduct. The guidelines provide several channels through which companies, trade unions and NGOs work with governments to promote further progress. As described below, these channels include: 1. discussions between adhering governments and other stakeholders of individual company conduct in specific business situations (including specific companies' approaches to respecting workers' rights to freedom of association or to managing the risk of employing child or forced labour); and 2. analysis and discussion of generic corporate responsibility issues.

The key features of the guidelines are as follows.

1. They contain voluntary recommendations to multinational enterprises in all major areas of business ethics.

2. Adhering governments sign a binding commitment to promote them among multinational enterprises operating in or from their territories. Thus, the guidelines represent a unique combination of voluntary and binding elements.

3. The most visible sign of adhering governments' commitment to the guidelines is their participation in the instrument's distinctive follow-up mechanisms. These include the operations of National Contact Points (NCP), which are government offices charged with promoting the guidelines and handling enquiries in the national context.

4. One of the NCPs' responsibilities is to consider 'specific instances'. Under this procedure, NCPs act as referees in multi-stakeholder discussions of specific company behaviour in specific business situations. In effect, this creates a case-based approach to the problem of building behavioural norms for appropriate international business conduct.

5. The guidelines are part of a broader and balanced instrument of rights and commitments – the OECD Declaration on International Investment and Multinational Enterprises (OECD, 1976). In addition to the guidelines, the declaration provides guidance for governments in the areas of national treatment, avoiding imposing conflicting requirements on international investors and investment incentives and disincentives[12].

The governments that adhere to the guidelines represent countries that are the source of most of the world's foreign direct investment and are home to most major multinational enterprises (97 out of UNCTAD's top 100 multinational enterprises are covered by the guidelines). Although the guidelines have been in existence since 1976, they were significantly revised in June 2000. After four years of implementation under the revised procedures, it is fair to ask what kind of impact the guidelines have had to date.

Guidelines implementation – results to date

The 2000 review of the guidelines and subsequent work by adhering governments have strengthened the instrument and raised its profile. There is growing evidence that the guidelines are becoming an important international tool for corporate responsibility. The guidelines have been translated into at least 24 languages. A recent survey asked managers of international companies to list influential international benchmarks for corporate behaviour – 22 per cent of them mentioned the guidelines without prompting. Some 60,000 web pages refer to the guidelines. Fifteen countries use the guidelines in their export credit and investment guarantee programmes. In addition to the formal adherence by 38 governments, the guidelines have received official support from business and trade union representatives at the OECD. NGOs have formed a coalition to make use of them.

The implementation procedures are being actively used, tested and refined. As of June 2004, 80 specific instances had been considered (OECD, 2003a). Some of these deal with company conduct in OECD countries, but most look at business conduct in non-OECD countries and cover issues that go to the heart of the current debate on globalization. The following cases serve as examples.

1. *Zambian copper mining.* The Canadian NCP has looked into the resettlement plans of a company operating in Zambia's copper belt. As a result of this consideration, the company agreed to postpone its resettlement plans for one year to allow time to rethink the plans – both the company and the NGO coalition (involving a Canadian and Zambian NGO) that were parties to this specific instance agreed that the procedure made a useful contribution to reducing tensions.
2. *Korean suppliers in a Guatemalan export processing zone.* The Korean NCP has looked into a Korean company's respect of freedom of association – a core labour standard – in an export processing zone in Guatemala. The Korean NCP encouraged the company to inform the Guatemalan workers of their rights and to respect these rights. The company responded by issuing a manual in comic book form illustrating workers' rights under Guatemalan law.
3. *Swedish business service provision in Ghana's gold sector.* The Swedish NCP looked at two Swedish companies' involvement (as business service providers) in Ghana's gold sector. The NCP collected information from on-site visits, from the Swedish embassy and from Ghanaian NGOs. It concluded that, while there are significant environmental and social problems in Ghana's gold sector, the two companies could not be held responsible for these problems because they were too far removed from them.

These are just a few of the many specific instances that have been considered by NCPs so far. Some of the positive developments that have been noted from these and other experiences include:

1. *Using the embassy networks as an accountability mechanism.* It is now becoming common practice for NCPs to use embassies (as well as employees from overseas development assistance programmes) as sources of information for consideration of 'specific instances', e.g. see the Swedish case given on the previous page. In 2005, nine adhering countries now feature the Guidelines as part of the training material given to embassy personnel before they take up their posts.

2. *Giving a voice to trade unions and civil society actors from the non-OECD area.* Many of the specific instances have been brought by trade unions and NGOs from the non-OECD area working in partnership with OECD-based actors. The guidelines strengthen these non-OECD actors by providing an international forum in which they can voice their concerns and by allowing them to gain experience with international institutions and procedures.

3. *A way for governments to engage with companies on issues of business ethics at a lower standard for quality of information than that required by formal legal proceedings.* A number of actors, including the UN Expert Panel on the illegal exploitation of natural resources in the Democratic Republic of Congo, have noted that the guidelines allow governments to engage with companies with greater flexibility than that permitted by legal proceedings.

4. *A tool for companies.* Trade unions and NGOs have been attracted to the specific instances procedure for some time. But companies are now starting to realize that it can be a useful tool for them as well. Business recently asked the guidelines institutions to assist them in dealing with bribe solicitation and ways of responding to this request are currently being explored. In addition, the specific instances procedures can help provide concrete guidance to companies – it can reassure them (as in the Swedish case described on the previous page) while sometimes also helping them to identify shortcomings.

Conclusions

The question addressed in this chapter is: are intergovernmental initiatives in support of appropriate standards of business conduct effective? The overall answer is 'yes' (but a qualified yes). These intergovernmental initiatives provide: 1) a framework in which the international discussions needed to build global norms can take place; and 2) a mechanism through which governments can support the functioning of basic micro-level processes that regulate how people behave in groups (including within companies) as well as the managerial, commercial and legal processes that support appropriate business conduct.

Overall, the OECD experience shows how subtle the process of building well-functioning institutions is. With the complex behaviour that typifies human beings, informal norms, formal standards and binding law all have their roles to play in creating economic systems that genuinely serve people's needs. The theme of this chapter has generally been one of progress – significant progress has been made in developing all of these on a global scale over the last half-century. Progress in anti-corruption is particularly noteworthy and illustrative. International standards-setting initiatives have turned what was once widely accepted behaviour into a criminal activity, thereby setting in motion the development of managerial policies and practices in this area that are already common in others (such as labour relations and environment). International initiatives have also supported micro-level social controls to start operating. That is, by clarifying and reinforcing the notion that corruption is an antisocial activity, the emotions and behaviours described in the second section (e.g. encouragement of pro-integrity behaviours, anger about corruption, desire for punishment, desire to be affiliated with pro-integrity groups) will start to have a pro-integrity impact, both within companies and in surrounding societies. In this area and many others, however, a great deal more work needs to be done in ongoing partnerships involving home and host governments, international organizations, business, trade unions and NGOs to create an effective system of global law, standards and norms.

Notes

1 The views expressed in this chapter are those of its author. They are not necessarily shared by the member governments or by the Secretariat of the Organisation for Economic Cooperation and Development.
2 See, for example, the emphasis on the benefits of properly functioning markets in the Monterrey Consensus (United Nations, 2002). The Consensus was endorsed by dozens of heads of state and provides using market forces in order to achieve the Millennium Development Goals (United Nations, 2005).
3 This book offers a detailed review of the role of ethical systems in human behaviour, seen from the perspectives of the biological theory of human evolution.
4 This article presents a critique of the behavioural precepts of mainstream microeconomics, an introduction to behavioral law and economics (BLE) and a consideration of how the BLE perspective might influence the design of legal systems.

5 This paper surveys results of experimental games, where the propensity toward altruism and cooperation is tested with experimental subjects. The survey points to a strong tendency toward altruism and cooperation, but also stresses the importance of the 'institutional characteristics' of the game in influencing outcomes, e.g. the game's title, the social context in which the game takes place and the approach of the person administering the game.

6 See Masters and Gruter (1992) for a series of papers on this subject. For a recent paper on the relationship between law and informal norms, see Parisi and Von Wangenheim (2004). This paper treats social norms and legal rules as mutually influencing institutions and explores what happens when they are at odds with one another.

7 This paper provides examples of how local level social capital facilitates orderly and welfare-enhancing economic transacting.

8 This paper reviews the ways that international organizations can influence one aspect of policy – the respect of human rights. Means of influence include coercion, persuasion and acculturation. The paper provides analysis that could eventually lead to a better understanding of which means of influence are most appropriate for dealing with different policy problems.

9 Friedman states that business has 'one and only one' responsibility (profit maximization), though he goes on to note that business should obey the law (Friedman, 1962).

10 The core labour standards are set forth in the International Labour Organization's Declaration on Fundamental Principles and Rights at Work (International Labour Organization, 1998). They include freedom of association, elimination of all forms of forced or compulsory labour, effective abolition of child labour and the elimination of discrimination with respect of employment and occupation.

11 The eight countries are Argentina, Brazil, Chile, Estonia, Israel, Latvia, Lithuania and Slovenia.

12 For fuller information on the OECD Declaration, see OECD (1976).

References

Alexander, Richard (1987) *The Biology of Moral Systems* New York: Aldyne de Gruyter

Bowles, Samuel and Gintis, Herbert (2000) Social Capital and Community Governance. Santa Fe Institute Working Paper 01–01–003, Dec.

FATF (1990) The Forty Recommendations of the Financial Action Task Force on Money Laundering. Available at: http://www.fatf-gafi.org/dataoecd/25/61/33635879.pdf

Friedman, Milton (1962) *Capitalism and Freedom*. Chicago: University of Chicago Press

Fukuyama, Francis (1999) *The Great Disruption: Human Nature and the Reconstitution of Social Order*. London: Profile Books

Goodman, Ryan and Jinks, Derek (2004) How to influence states: socialisation and international human rights law. *Duke University Law Journal* 54:3 621–704. Available at: http://www.ssrn.com/abstract=519565

Henderson, David (2001) *Misguided Virtue*. Auckland: New Zealand Business Roundtable

International Labour Organization (1998). *Declaration on Fundamental Principles and Rights at Work*. Available at: http://www.ilo.org/dyn/declaris/DECLARATIONWEB.INDEXPAGE

Jones, Owen (2001) Time-shifted rationality and the law of law's leverage: behavioral economics meets behavioral biology. *Northwestern University Law Review* 95. Available at: http://ssrn.com/abstract=249419

Masters, Rober and Gruter, Margaret (eds) (1992) *The Sense of Justice: The Biolological Foundations of Law*. Newbury Park, CA: Sage Publications

Merriam-Webster Online Dictionary. Available at: http://www.m-w.com/

OECD (1976) *Declaration on International Investment and Multinational Enterprises*. Paris: OECD. Available at: http://www.oecd.org/daf/investment/instruments/

OECD (1998) Convention on Combating Bribery of Foreign Public Officials in International Business Transactions. Paris: OECD. Available at: http://www.oecd.org

OECD (2000) *OECD Guidelines for Multinational Enterprises*. Paris: OECD. Available at: http://www.oecd.org/daf/investment/guidelines

OECD (2001) *Corporate Responsibility: Private Initiatives and Public Goals*. Paris: OECD

OECD (2002) Managing working conditions in the supply chain – a fact finding study of corporate practices *2002 Annual Report on the OECD Guidelines for Multinational Enterprises*. Paris: OECD, pp 111–124

OECD (2003a) *2003 Annual Report on the OECD Guidelines for Multinational Enterprises*. Paris: OECD

OECD (2003b) *Guidelines on Managing Conflict of Interest in the Public Sector*. Available at: http://www.oecd.org/dataoecd/17/23/33967052.pdf

OECD (2004) *Principles of Corporate Governance*. OECD: Paris. Available at: http://www.oecd.org/dataoecd/32/18/31557724.pdf

Parisi, Francesco and Von Wangenheim, Georg (2004) legislation and countervailing effects from social norms. George Mason Law & Economics Research Paper No. 04–31 (July). Available at: http://ssrn.com/abstract=569383

Stout, Lynn (2001) Other-regarding preferences and social norms. Georgetown University Law Center Working Paper Series in Business, Economics and Regulatory Policy, Working Paper No. 265902

United Nations (2002) *Report of the International Conference on Financing for Development, Monterrey, Mexico, 18–22 March (Monterrey Consensus)*. Available at: http://www.un.org/esa/ffd/aconf198–11.pdf

United Nations (2005) *Millenium Development Goals*. Available at: http://www.un.org/millenniumgoals/

US Federal Sentencing Guidelines for Organizations (2004) 18 U.S.C. §3553(a). Available at: http://www.ussc.gov/orgguide.HTM

7

The Role of Ethical Business Practice in Latin America – The Case of Mexico

Patricia Greaves

The globalization of economic activity, together with the predominance of market forces, has clearly encroached upon the importance of the state and its traditional role. The privatization of state-owned companies, the liberalization of trade and the increasing integration of markets have facilitated this decline and weakened the state's regulating function. This process has created a vacuum, and has also yielded terrain to the self-regulation (whether real or fictitious) of corporate activity.

This chapter offers a general overview on codes of conduct and ethics in Mexico, in terms of the magnitude and factors that inhibit or foster the development and drafting of such codes, as well as the institutions responsible for promoting them. This overview is situated in a context of the existing relations between the government and the private sector, both nationally and internationally, and this is what is addressed in the first part of this chapter. The codes of four Mexican transnational companies from different industries are then analysed, according to their content and the functions they fulfil. These companies were chosen because they are four of the most prestigious nationwide, according to a survey conducted by the *Financial Times* (*Financial Times* and PricewaterhouseCoopers, 2004).

International context

Even though companies are the principal defenders of self-regulation, their involvement in accounting scandals, the violation of human rights and environmental deterioration have brought their reputation into question and affected their image.

This situation has spurred greater demands and complaints in relation to two aspects of the ethical behaviour of businesses (principally multinational corporations): on the one hand, the defence of human dignity (human and labour rights) and the environment, and on the other, the defence of the global market and free competition through a battle against corruption and bribery, in order to protect the interests of investors and companies.

In the field of human and labour rights, the Organisation for Economic Co-operation and Development (OECD), the United Nations (UN) through the Global Pact, and the International Labour Organization (ILO), as well as civil society organizations, unions and consumer organizations from developed countries, have all exerted pressure on corporate conduct.

Some international entities and governments have come to the defence of the global market, carrying out efforts to combat corruption and end poor ethical corporate behaviour, since the latter distort free competition, affect corporate performance, increase the risk to investors and trigger additional costs. Two of these primary instruments are the Principles of Corporate Governance developed by the OECD (OECD, 2004) and the Extortion and Bribery in International Business Transactions Rules and Recommendations launched by the International Chamber of Commerce (ICC) (ICC, 1999). These initiatives seek to consolidate a fairer and more honest global market in an increasingly interdependent world (OECD, 2000).

Companies aim to self-regulate through the use of conduct codes, guidelines and company principles or, to be more precise, social responsibility practices. Such codes are tools or mechanisms that tend to play a complementary role in relation to existing legal frameworks derived from values previously established in the company's mission. On the one hand, these instruments articulate a company's values, responsibilities and obligations; on the other, they serve to guide employee behaviour in given situations. These initiatives, which are voluntary in nature, vary in terms of their content, level of specificity, scope and rigorousness, as well as their mechanisms for communication and implementation.

In this sense, there is no universal model or code. Variations arise depending on business goals, industry sector, company size and context, among other factors.

The Mexican context

Mexico is the largest Spanish-speaking country in the world with a population of a little over 100 million people. It is the second largest economy in Latin America behind Brazil and is classified globally as a middle income economy. There is also a persisting problem of poverty and marked regional disparities in economic structures and income levels.

It is important to highlight that, beginning in 1982, a 'modernizing' project took root in Mexico and was continued during the following administrations and strengthened in the 1990s. From that time on, as in many other countries, the Mexican government began to focus more on attracting foreign investment, than on regulating transnational corporations (Jenkins, 2004). The goal was to make Mexico an appealing and reliable country for attracting flows of direct foreign investment. In the interest of facilitating such investment (to generate employment), the government began to implement reforms favourable to investors.

On the one hand, this led to a decrease in state intervention and its regulating function, and, on the other, it led to an opening and the possibility granted to foreign capital to access strategic sectors previously exclusive to the state's domain (energy and banking, to name just two examples) and considered to be essential components of national sovereignty.

These new policies and the globalization of the economy took shape through a series of initiatives. For example, in 1994, the North American Free Trade Agreement (NAFTA) went into effect. This treaty reflected the trade opening process based on deregulation, privatization, the dismantling of the structure for protecting businesses and a move towards unrestricted mobility of capital. The treaty offered treatment normally afforded only to foreign investors, in addition to guarantees of filing for compensation in the case of any harm to their interests (REMALC, 1997). Moreover, agreements for the promotion and reciprocal protection of investments were signed with several different countries. These bilateral agreements contain measures and clauses for protecting investments through international law. In the case of the Free Trade Area of the Americas (FTAA), this treaty also favours the interests of multinational corporations, mainly from the United States, by permitting the exploitation of the region's natural resources.

Furthermore, not only foreign companies, but Mexicans as well, have benefited from governmental prerogatives. For example, the recently proposed modifications to current federal labour law –

Ley federal del Trabajo – reduce the demands placed on employers and deprives workers of certain guarantees. Among other aspects, the new legislation does not force employers to hire workers during the six month training period, allows employers to determine the working day and increases the requirements for creating a union (De Buen, 2003 p 17). This implies the preservation of the state's discretionary intervention in strikes and unions, to the detriment of collective bargaining practices.

In this same fashion, the national bailout package for Mexican banks in response to the crisis of 1995 was a singularly important event that favoured private sector interests. This package led the federal government to channel resources to banks (initially Mexican-owned enterprises, and later mostly those in the hands of foreign investors), which then contributed to an enormous increase in public debt. The total amount paid to banks is estimated at five times the amount of public spending on the fight against poverty.

Codes of ethics in Mexico: a general overview

Among Mexican companies, having a code of ethics or conduct is a recent phenomenon that began in the mid-1990s as a result of the globalization process and the growing demands of the international market.

Nevertheless, there is very little information available regarding the number of companies that have a code of ethics, making them difficult to quantify. The President of Administración por Valores (AVAL) affirms that approximately 300 companies (including foreign companies) have a code or programme of this nature, and that progress in this field has been modest and slow (De la Torre, 2004). If we consider that there are a total of 500,121 companies, this figure is quite insignificant[1].

Furthermore, the level of the development of these codes is unknown, nor whether or not their specifications are implemented. Available information, besides being scarce, can also be contradictory. Some companies may have written codes that are actually implemented, while others may only have formal written documents and lack enforcement. Additionally, some companies may not have written rules (as in the case of many family-owned businesses) but only implicit conventions or agreements to which the employees abide.

Only 66 Mexican companies have been found to comply with a code of ethics that is actually respected. These are the companies that have received recognition as 'socially responsible businesses' named annually by the Centro Mexicano para la Filantropía – CEMEFI (The Mexican Center for Philantropy). Approximately half of these 66 companies are of Mexican ownership, almost all of them are large businesses and in two cases they belong to the state.

A 1999 study by the Instituto Panamericano de Alta Dirección de Empresas – IPADE (The Pan American Institute of Top Mexican Executives and Officials) and the *Mundo Ejecutivo* magazine, in which 300 companies were surveyed, found that although 81 per cent of the companies had developed a code of ethics, 57 per cent lacked the necessary mechanisms for putting it into effect and 36 per cent transmitted company values and norms to their employees in a verbal and poorly institutionalized manner (quoted in Ibarra, 2002).

Likewise, another study conducted in 2000 on codes of ethics in companies in the food industry found that, despite the fact that not a single company had a code of ethics *per se* in a written document, they did have internal policies and company values in their mission or vision statements that were transmitted to employees through formal channels such as orientations, workshops or seminars (Miceli, 2000).

Specifically, for larger Mexican companies (particularly those linked to international trade), having a code of conduct becomes both a demand and a convenience. The enactment of the Sarbanes-Oxley Act of 2002 in the United States aims to create confidence in investors, establish more rigorous measures and controls for corporate self-regulation in regards to their responsibilities and sanctions for accounting and auditing practices (Sarbanes-Oxley Act, 2002). This became obligatory for all US public companies and thus for Mexican companies on the New York Stock Exchange.

Furthermore, having a code of ethics or conduct becomes a factor for greater competitiveness and added value: 'The new corporate environment characterized by globalization calls for companies to pay more attention to their ethical performance in order to achieve the levels of service, quality and prestige required by global competition.' (SECODAM, p 28). Similarly, intangible assets – the company's image and the perception of consumers and investors – acquire special relevance.

Among small and mid-size companies (those which contribute the most to the national economy and to creating new jobs), codes are not very common, either because they are considered to be unnecessary or due to the lack of the financial and human resources they require. Companies that do have these types of internal policies and procedures are usually those that are part of a chain of suppliers in a larger company, which extends certain requirements in regard to ethics, transparency and social responsibility and makes them obligatory to all.

A number of specialists believe there are three factors that obstruct corporative ethical practice and the fight against corruption within Mexican companies.

The first factor is the fear of losing ground to one's competition, which could benefit from special treatment or favouritism in commercial transactions, and the second is fear of reprisal from certain authorities accustomed to bribery and pay-offs. According to a survey conducted by the Instituto Tecnológico de Estudios Superiores de Monterrey – ITESM (Technological Institute for Higher Studies of Monterrey), 62 per cent of enterprises recognized that they make extra-official payments or bribe public authorities (especially mid-level officials) and that such expenses represent 5.1 per cent of their incomes (ITESM, 2002). In addition, the third factor is the fear of consequences from publicly announcing company commitments and values, and then being exposed to public scrutiny.

Organizations that promote ethics

Although a recent phenomenon that is not widespread in Mexico, organizations of both a public and private nature do exist to promote business ethics.

At the governmental level, the Secretaría de la Función Pública (SFP)[2] is responsible for fostering a culture of transparency and legality, and has developed and promoted two proposals for ethical business practice. One of these proposals is the 'Integrity Program' focused on fighting corruption in any and all kinds of organizations (including businesses), and which proposes the development of codes of conduct to guide their members' behaviour (Secretaría de la Función Pública, 2003). The other is the 'Business Ethics' proposal that promotes corporate social responsibility, understood as commitments and responsibilities that companies should adopt towards their key audiences.

Another organization, Administración por Valores – AVAL, was established in 1999 as the Latin American secretariat for the international organization called Caux Round Table and as a member of ALIARSE, a body that brings together several business groups interested in promoting and disseminating information regarding corporate social responsibility (ALIARSE, 2000). AVAL is specifically dedicated to promoting the use of ethical business principles through training programmes, consultation and dissemination. Furthermore, although the Caux Round Table promotes a culture of legality as part of its principles (especially the fight against unlawful operations and respect for the law), it also stresses corporate social responsibility and declares itself to be a defender of international trade (Caux Round Table, 1994).

The influence of the Unión Social de Empresarios Mexicanos – USEM (The Social Union of Mexican Businessmen), founded by Catholic businessmen in the 1970s – is also noteworthy. USEM developed a model of the ideal company (entitled 'highly productive and completely human') founded on the values of the Catholic Church's social doctrine. This model, which USEM promotes among its members, proposes the need for a code of ethics and for socially responsible actions (USEM, 1993).

At the same time, there are two other bodies that promote positive corporate conduct by institutionalizing awards and special recognitions. For example, CEMEFI annually grants an award to the company with the best corporate social practices for its ethical performance, its policies towards employees and the environment, and its ties to the community. As previously mentioned, the 'Socially Responsible Company' award requires, among other criteria, the adoption of a code of ethics and its effective implementation.

In addition, the Confederation of Industrial Chambers (CON CAMIN) grants an award to companies, chambers and business associations that carry out ethical business practices and have values-based administrations. Nevertheless, not only are ethical criteria considered for conferring the award, but also 'productive, exemplary and successful' performance and the implementation of actions to benefit the community (CONCAMIN, 2002).

Case studies

In Mexico, corporate codes, usually called 'codes of ethics', are documents that generally contain the company's mission statement and company values, in addition to norms of conduct that company members should follow. On occasion, these documents also include business principles, principles for behaviour, principles of social responsibility or company core beliefs.

Generally speaking, the contents of these codes mainly vary according to the importance given to the codes of labour conduct (that is to say, the ones that must be heeded by company personnel), to the company's commitments and responsibilities for conserving the environment, and to different internal and external stakeholders: clients, shareholders, employees, suppliers, the government and the community. In general, such codes also specify which entities are responsible for supervising compliance.

The norms of conduct established by companies are very similar, and usually refer mainly to the use of the organization's resources and protection of its assets, the management of confidential information, conflicts of interest, participation in political activities and relations among employees.

The commitments and responsibilities that companies establish with different audiences are, in turn, more unequal. They differ in questions of labour policy, human rights and community relations. However, these commitments in regards to company relations with shareholders, clients and suppliers tend to be very similar. These commitments make an explicit pledge to providing quality goods or services, offering reliable and timely information, pursuing the company's profitability, and maintaining fair and equitable treatment without showing favouritism.

However, we should mention that not all commitments and responsibilities assumed by companies are included in these codes. Sometimes companies have adopted practices of social responsibility that are only mentioned in specific written reports.

As previously mentioned, this section analyses the contents of the codes of ethics of four Mexican companies, placing a special emphasis on labour issues and community relations, which we believe to be the most important questions regarding corporate self-regulation. We will also refer to the function that these codes fulfil.

The companies in question are Teléfonos de México (TELMEX), Cementos Mexicanos (CEMEX), BIMBO and GALVAK. All of these are very strong, competitive corporations with high profitability and presence on the national and international market, and are seeking to consolidate their leadership.

CEMEX

CEMEX is a leading company in the production and commercialization of cement and pre-mixed concrete, and it exports its products to 15 countries in Latin America, the United States, Asia, Africa and Europe (CEMEX, 1906). CEMEX aspires to consolidate itself as the most efficient and profitable multinational cement organization in the world.

Some five years ago, CEMEX developed a code of ethics that refers to norms of conduct or key principles that should serve as a guide to CEMEX personnel. This code also includes the company's commitments to all of its key audiences (clients, suppliers, the government, the community, the environment and personnel) in the terms of a model for corporate social responsibility (CEMEX, 2000).

The commitments specified by CEMEX regard the following: compliance with labour law and regulations; respect for other people's differences and opinions with the consistent prohibition of all types of harassment and discrimination; industrial safety and occupational health for personnel; and protection of the environment.

The commitments that CEMEX establishes to its employees refer basically to protecting the employees' health and maintaining safety conditions. Other commitments that the company adopts refer to a series of economic benefits (incentives, compensations), modernization and professional development, as well as recognition on the job, merit-based promotions and open communication with personnel.

CEMEX does look at its own role with the community in regards to social responsibility and sustainable development, referring to its own commitment to address the needs of its context: the environment and communities around it. Since it is a company that depends on natural resources and energy, it values the importance of taking pertinent measures to protect its employees, neighbours and the environment. CEMEX also operates several community development programmes that, although not specified in their code, are included in their social responsibility reports.

For CEMEX, the code is a relevant document that provides the basis for a 'guide to consolidate its development at a global level'. The code affirms that a culture based on CEMEX values of collaboration, integrity and leadership fosters its virtues and capacities at the same time that it contributes to increasing and prolonging the company's value for all stakeholders.

The value of 'integrity' is considered to offer them comparative advantages, since acting with honesty, responsibility and respect builds lasting ties of trust and mutual benefit in each of CEMEX's interactions.

In summary, it can be said that the company's values, the function of the code itself and the CEMEX concept of social responsibility called 'responsible competitiveness', interconnect the company's ethical and social performance to its competitiveness.

TELMEX

TELMEX is a leading company in the field of telecommunications that seeks to consolidate its leadership in the national market and further its penetration of services in other countries (TELMEX, 1990).

Besides its mission and vision statements, the TELMEX code of ethics includes the company's values, its business principles and its principles and norms of conduct (TELMEX, 2005). The norms of conduct predominate in the document. These norms, as well as the principles of conduct, and the enunciated values (work, growth, social responsibility and austerity), refer to the behaviour and responsibilities of members of the company and the treatment that interested parties (mainly clients, suppliers and other employees) should receive.

The TELMEX business principles (quality, client service and being at the technological forefront) refer to the business goals and the specific activity at hand: telecommunications. The behaviour principles are general principles more of an ethical nature that should be applied in all kinds of circumstances and are established to guide employee behaviour. They do not refer to the commitments adopted by the company. They are as follows: respect for the established norms; no discrimination in terms of respect and recognition of the same rights for all people; and integrity. The integrity principle is understood to be respect for established norms and respectful and professional treatment of others.

In sum, we can affirm that the TELMEX code does not distinguish between the obligations or commitments assumed by the company. The exception is a reference to the company's obligation to its stockholders to seek profitability and a clause about relations with competitors which exclusively refers to respect for these norms. However, we should mention that TELMEX has principally been questioned for its monopolistic practices and the high number of complaints filed by its clients to the Procuraduría Federal del Consumidor (Federal Attorney General for Consumers).

The code contains no information whatsoever regarding labour issues or community relations, despite the fact that the company, through its foundation, carries out important actions in the fields of education, culture, justice and emergency relief for natural disasters.

Like CEMEX, TELMEX finds having a code of ethics to be of added value and a comparative advantage: 'The code of ethics promotes ethical conduct as an advantage over our competitors. With our current access to technology, capital and human labor, honest conduct and behaviors of integrity become an added value to the goods and services that companies offer.' (TELMEX, 2005).

Ethical behaviour is also important to the company's image: 'Based on our conduct and our values, we want to be an example to our country. We wish to show how work can be carried out efficiently. We aspire to be recognized as a company that respects the law and people, as being honest in our negotiations and a promoter of social well-being ... ' (TELMEX, 2005)

GALVAK

GALVAK, a Grupo ALFA company, is part of HYLSAMEX and is dedicated to producing, transforming and commercializing steel products in the United States and several Latin American countries. GALVAK aims to improve its competitive position and to become a world-class company with great profitability.

GALVAK has a code of ethics that establishes its mission statement, vision, values, company core beliefs and norms of conduct for its employees (GALVAK, 2003).

Since this is an industry with very significant environmental impact, in its mission statement, GALVAK highlights the importance of contributing to improving its surrounding ecological and social environment. In addition, the company expresses its concern for satisfying the expectations of its shareholders, clients, suppliers and employees.

GALVAK sets forth both organizational and personal values. The latter refer to values such as responsibility, collaboration, integrity and dignity that should orient employee behaviour during daily interactions.

The organizational values point to the responsibilities that the company adopts in regards to ecology, the workplace, safety and human resources. Above all, these values emphasize the protection of each person's physical integrity and the integrity of the surroundings.

The labour issues (addressed from a human resources perspective) found in the code mainly refer to promoting opportunities for worker training and personal development, placing the family in a prominent place within the company's organizational context. On the one hand, the code addresses aspects referring to employee treatment (recognition of merit and participation in decision-making) and some worker rights: training, promotion of holistic development and freedom of expression. Within the training section, scholarships, courses and even the Galvacer university are mentioned.

The GALVAK code does not make any mention of the company's involvement in the surrounding community. GALVAK's relationship with its surroundings is reduced, on the one hand, to the employees' obligation to look after the company's image to the outside world and, on the other, to an indirect relationship through the workers' families. GALVAK considers that employee self-improvement and development implicitly constitute a contribution to the community.

The GALVAK code is conceived of as a philosophy, as a collection of ideas that unifies all the members of the organization. It turns out to be an important component that creates institutional identity and simultaneously permits the company's favourable economic performance and fulfillment of its mission.

> 'By having capable and committed people on board who embrace our values, we ensure the mission of our organization.' (GALVAK, 2003, p 2)

> 'These ideas, together with our technological development . . . are what help us to better involve ourselves in GALVAK goals and strategies, and consequently give a sense of identity and transcendence to the daily tasks of our organization.' (GALVAK, 2003, p 2)

Overall, it can be said that the code of ethics is seen as a factor that creates identity and is also directly tied to greater levels of company productivity.

BIMBO

BIMBO is a leading company in the food industry not only in Mexico, but throughout Latin America.

The BIMBO code of ethics is basically a document that lays out the company's commitments and responsibilities to different interested parties: consumers, clients, stakeholders, partners, employees, suppliers, competitors and society at large (Grupo BIMBO, 2001a). Like CEMEX, BIMBO also announces its commitment to respect legislation in countries where it does business.

Unlike the other cases mentioned thus far, the code has very few references to the conduct of its members, mainly referring to conflicts of interest, the efficient use of resources and the protection of company assets.

The BIMBO code does not mention the organization's mission or vision statements, nor its general values. It only refers to values or principles to be applied in concrete situations.

BIMBO specifies the company's commitments to its employees in regards to employee treatment. These commitments refer to respect for their individuality (dignity, diversity), their personal development, and the promotion of moral value and ethical norms. It also includes a section on the company's relationship to labour organizations. It is noteworthy that BIMBO is the only company that mentions this point and pronounces its commitment to respect the independence of labour organizations that represent the workers' legitimate interests, always seeking relations based on cooperation and mutual benefit. Since true unionism has many times become distorted in Mexico, BIMBO stresses that union representation should always protect collective interests and the common good above personal interests.

Unlike others, BIMBO identifies its commitments to its surroundings and the terms of these commitments in a much broader and explicit fashion. It broadly points to three areas: the environment, publicity and community development.

In regards to the environment, BIMBO mentions environmental conservation and restoration projects that it promotes outside of the company.

It also specifies its commitment to employ publicity that promotes values that do not harm individuals, the family or society. These values include family unity, personal physical and emotional integrity, respect for the universal rights of children, people with disabilities, the elderly, ethnical groups and all people, regardless of their social condition.

In regards to community development, it is interesting to note BIMBO's commitment to promote the social and economic growth of the communities where its employees live, through the creation and preservation of sources of productive employment.

BIMBO, as a company influenced by USEM's values and principles, aspires to be a productive and yet human company that shapes human beings, 'because we do our business in several parts of the world, in a diversity of languages and cultures, because we want to be a company with high principles and values, that shapes human beings and respects society to which we owe so much, our code of ethics is a universal guide for our business practice.' (Grupo BIMBO, 2001b)

The code is conceived in terms of the principles, values and philosophy of the company, as a reflection of the company's personality. For BIMBO, ethical behaviour is a company's most distinctive character trait.

'We share a common goal of wanting to distinguish ourselves by a certain way of thinking and acting, being open and clear about what we, as a group of human beings, believe to be essential.' (Grupo BIMBO, 2001a, p 1)

Final comments

Mexican companies that develop a code in which they set forth their values, principles and norms of conduct are uncommon, although this is becoming more widespread. However, the absence of a code of this nature does not necessarily signify inadequate, reprehensible or unethical behaviour. Nor does it imply that the company is behaving adequately. This is the case in the central region of the country where labour abuses seem to be permanent occurrences in the maquila garment industry that supplies big name brand companies (Juárez, 2005).

In Mexico, corporate codes are generally called 'codes of ethics' which set forth the norms that should guide employee conduct. The obligations and commitments adopted by the company tend to be less important or are not completely included in these declarations.

In the case of Mexican companies, the adoption of these codes responds to both internal and external factors. Among the internal factors, the need to align the behaviour of the company's members to favour company performance and avoid illicit or unethical conduct or behaviours that simply do not keep with the established values is of particular importance. The external factors that favour this kind of document undoubtedly include globalization, greater demands of the international market and the emergence of a new business culture. In addition, the importance of intangible assets such as image and reputation also add to the convenience of setting forth the organization's values in such an explicit fashion. Unlike other countries, in Mexico, civil society organizations, unions or consumers do not provide sufficient counterbalances for pressuring companies.

Generally speaking, we can say that, in Mexico, the development of these codes has been promoted to fight corruption at every level, that is to say, incorrect practices of employees and company relations with public officials or other authorities, and in response to the demand for socially responsible companies.

Most of the time the commitments and obligations that companies adopt voluntarily are part of their social responsibility or corporate philanthropy practices, more so than from their codes of conduct.

It is important to note that, in Mexico, corporations seek to forge a good image more concerned about their presence in the community and their participation in social programmes to benefit the community, than for example, for their internal policies towards employees, suppliers or contractors. Abuses committed in regard to the latter are rarely made known to the public.

In terms of labour issues, the contents are few or solely refer to questions of training, personal and professional development, and matters of occupational health, safety and hygiene. Not a single mention was found in reference to wages and collective bargaining agreements. With the exception of BIMBO, the companies also fail to mention the right to freedom of association and collective bargaining. This could also be due to the fact that many times labour rights are understood to be protected when the companies state that they will abide by and respect existing legislation.

Moreover, although companies establish commitments with the community such as social or sustainable development programmes and their broader surroundings in general, such commitments are often not specified in the codes and are rather found in other kinds of documents or reports.

Given the information presented thus far, we can affirm that the role of self-regulation fulfilled by the codes of Mexican companies is less important when compared to codes adopted by other transnational companies. This is because the emphasis of the codes studied here is placed more on regulating the employees' internal conduct than on the company's behaviour in regards to more relevant and more controversial labour and social issues.

The adoption of codes in Mexico has emerged in the context of professionalism in the face of global competitiveness and brings common benefits for all companies. But each code also fulfils a specific role within each company, according to its particular characteristics, needs and interests, and serves to help explain its values.

Notes

1 Besides, more than 90 per cent are small enterprises.
2 This ministry was previously the Secretaría de Contraloría y Desarrollo Administrativo (SECODAM).

References

ALIARSE (2000) Alianza para la Responsabilidad Social Empresarial. Available at: http://www.cce.org.mx/CCE/ALIARSE/

Caux Round Table (1994) *Principles for Business*. Available at: http://www.cauxroundtable.org/principles.html

CEMEX (1906) Available at: http://www.cemex.com

CEMEX (2000) *Code of Business Conduct and Ethics*. Available at: http://www.cemex.com/ic/pdf/codigo_de_Etica_Ingles.pdf

Confederation of Industrial Chambers (CONCAMIN) (2002) Available at: http://mx.groups.yahoo.com/group/Responsabilidad_Social_Empresarial_AliaRSE/message/839

De Buen, N (2003) *La Jornada* 21 April p 17

De la Torre, G (2004) Presidente de AVAL, entrevista realizada el 22 de Diciembre

Financial Times and PricewaterhouseCoopers (2004) 7a. Encuesta sobre las Empresas más respetadas del Mundo. *Reforma* 23 Nov.

GALVAK (2003) *Código de Ética, haciendo vida los valores* Mexico City: GALVAK

Grupo BIMBO (2001a) *Código de Ética*. Mexico City: Grupo BIMBO. Available at: http://www.grupobimbo.com.mx/admin/content/uploaded/codigoetica.pdf

Grupo BIMBO (2001b) Available at: http://www.grupobimbo.com/display.php?section=1&subsection=1&topic=8

Ibarra, R (2002) *Códigos de Ética, cómo implantarlo en la empresa*. Mexico City: Trillas

ICC (1999) *ICC Extortion and Bribery in International Business Transactions*. Available at: http://www.iccwbo.org/home/statements_rules/1999/briberydoc99.asp

Instituto Tecnológico de Estudios Superiores de Monterrey (ITESM) Centro de Estudios Estratégicos (2002) *La investigación versa sobre la percepción que el sector empresarial tiene sobre la corrupción existente en sus relaciones y trámites con el gobierno federal, estatal y municipal*. Available at: http://www.funcionpublica.gob.mx/indices/doctos/indicetec.pdf

Jenkins, R (2004) Códigos de conducta empresariales:autorregulación en una economía global. *Comercio Exterior* 54:9 764–778

Juárez, H (2005) Allá . . . donde viven los más pobres: cadenas globales-regionas productoras. La industria maquiladora del vestido. Mexico: Universidad Autónoma de Puebla (UAP)

Miceli, E (2000) *Estudio Exploratorio de Códigos de Ética en la industria alimentaria Mexicana*. Tesis de Maestría en Ciencias. Mexico City: Instituto Tecnológico de Estudios Superiores

OECD (2000) *No Longer Business as Usual: Fighting Bribery and Corruption*. Paris: OECD

OECD (2004) *Principles of Corporate Governance*. Available at: http://www.oecd.org/dataoecd/32/18/31557724.pdf

Red Mexicana Frente al Libre Comercio (REMALC) (1997) *Espejismo y Realidad: el TLCAN tres años después. Análisis y Propuestas desde la Sociedad Civil*. Mexico City: REMALC

Sarbanes-Oxley Act (2002) Available at: http://www.sec.gov/about/laws/soa2002. pdf. See also: http://www.sec.gov/spotlight/sarbanes-oxley.htm

Secretaría de la Controlaría y Desarrollo Administrativo (SECODAM) *La Ética es un Buen Negocio*. SECODAM: Mexico City. Available at: http://www. funcionpublica.gob.mx/publicaciones/folletos/doctos/ebn.pdf

Secretaría de la Función Pública (SFP) (2003) *Construyendo un Programa de Integridad: el papel de los códigos de conducta*. Mexico City: SFP

TELMEX (1990). Available at: http://www.telmex.com

TELMEX (2005) *Code of Ethics*, 3rd edn. Available at: http://www.telmex.com/ explorer/esto/pt_seccion.jsp?p=esto_infcorp_codigo.html

Unión Social de Empresarios Mexicanos (USEM) – The Social Union of Mexican Businessmen) (1993) *La empresa altamente productiva y plenamente humana: manual de transformación*. Mexico: Edamex

8

The Development of Business Ethics and Corporate Governance in Latin America

Albrecht Mueller

Latin America may not perhaps seem the obvious place to search for a reference when it comes to business ethics; yet the continent is moving to align itself with the global trend by developing standards similar to the laws and practices found in OECD countries.

Similarly, although democratic political structures may only have flourished in the last two decades or so, this is equally the case in parts of Europe such as Spain and Portugal.

The purpose of this chapter is to explain the socio-economic landscape in Latin America and its influence over the current state of business ethics and corporate governance in general.

Historical background

The status and potential of business ethics and corporate governance in Latin American companies is best understood by placing the current state of affairs in historical context.

With the exception of Brazil, which was under the influence of the Portuguese, all Latin American countries were colonies of the Spanish crown, which about 500 years ago established their economic and political control system.

De facto control was either assigned or simply claimed by *caudillos* (Portuguese: *coroneis*), who were often adventurers acting either openly or tacitly in the name of the crown. Their aim was to establish a patriarchic hierarchy to exploit the countries they controlled. Typically, they established a proprietary army and interpreted the law and its enforcement to their benefit, or simply created and enforced their own laws and rules.

These self-styled rulers secured their power base through nepotism and the granting of rights and benefits to cronies. Links based on mutual benefit were maintained with the current political class.

The key result of this process was a complete failure to instil a set of ethics suitable to community life; instead a recipe for success based on egoism, power-brokerage and patronage was created.

Traces of this mindset can still be found today, helping for example to shape the social landscape formed by dominant parties in countries like Argentina or Mexico. They also remain vivid in the North Eastern part of Brazil, whose states retain a dominant representation in the Brazilian federation.

Although the identity of the ruling clans or families may have changed over time, as the political system mutated from colony to dictatorship to military rulers to democratic systems, they have always remained dependent on their relationship with the prevailing political elite.

Perhaps predictably, these dominant clans, families or individuals are generally not at all interested in seeing the values of transparency, internationalism and professionalism being promoted. In contrast, they continue to foster local isolation and political dependencies.

Social and economic realities

As the previous section illustrated, Latin American societies were, and to some extent still are, under the significant influence of relatively few ruling clans or families.

Some of those families and clans promote their continuity via power-broking and influence peddling, thereby undermining any assimilation of the concept of meritocracy based on expertise and competency.

Income distribution is still very unequal and the middle classes remain particularly exposed to the effects of the recurring economic crises that remain a feature of many Latin American countries. Members of the middle class are the first to lose a job or see their hard-earned savings and pensions evaporate due to imprudent politics.

Given this scenario, it might be expected that the middle class would be the social group most interested in seeing transparency and accountability permeating their societies and through that the good practices that are a feature of sound corporate governance. Later it will be shown why this has not yet been accomplished.

As mentioned earlier, ruling families and clans resorted, and in some cases still resort to, collusion with politicians and government officials. Furthermore, a significant number of politicians continue to base their political weight and fortune on the extent to which they can support or promote vested interests. One outcome is that business processes and practices remains opaque, suiting the involved parties' interests and, in extreme cases, facilitating unethical behaviour.

The Nobel Laureate Dr Douglas North referred to the heritage of Latin American economies as being based on personal exchange whereas developed countries have already migrated to impersonal exchange (North, 2003).

The personal exchange model means that the institutions within an economy function solely through the network of personal contacts. By contrast, a society based on impersonal exchange creates a framework of legal and regulatory structures backed by enforcement that guarantees economic activity can take place without personal friendships being required.

Under this system, business transactions are predictable and their related costs are lower than in a society based on personal exchange. This is an important prerequisite for an economy to grow. Ethical behaviour and good corporate governance can also be implemented more easily in an economy based on impersonal exchange.

How does this translate to current economic circumstances within Latin America?

All Latin American economies consist of an official market and an unofficial or parallel market. The individual Latin American countries differ only by the size of their respective parallel market, although it is difficult to estimate their size due to their obscure nature. The size or importance of the parallel market within a specific country depends also on the state of economic stability. For example, during the Argentinean crisis of 2001/2002 the parallel market jumped significantly to comprise roughly 40 per cent of the total economy.

The unofficial market is characterized by small scale enterprises which circumvent labour, environmental or safety regulations, often in combination with tax evasion. The owners or the controlling parties entertain good relations with lenient government officials and police. Large party or election contributions to some local politicians secure benign treatment and a convenient political or juridical protection.

Drug production and trafficking represents another important share of the parallel markets in Latin America.

It is obvious that the parallel market distorts the competitiveness of the official market. Companies in the parallel market can out-manoeuvre the companies who play honest, since not paying taxes or not respecting safety or labour regulations creates a pecuniary advantage which is greater than the disadvantage of having a lesser skilled workforce or a less efficient company.

Also the official market consists of mostly small to medium size enterprises; they are the backbone of the official economy. Larger companies were, in the not too distant past, either state-controlled companies or large family-controlled companies and conglomerates.

Ownership statistics for listed companies located in the six largest economies in Latin America – Argentina, Brazil, Chile, Colombia, Mexico and Peru – show that on average the three largest shareholders of each corporation constitute 73 per cent of the total ownership (Lefort, 2003).

Furthermore, with the exception of Argentina, the majority of those largest shareholders are either domestic owners or the state itself. The remaining shareholders are basically domestic institutional investors like pension funds (Lefort, 2003). Foreign shareholders are most frequently multinationals, followed in second place by external institutional investors.

A lot of companies also issue different classes of shares, allowing the controlling entities to wield a much wider influence through the holding of voting shares, while the free floating shares are often of the non voting variety. Not surprisingly, the resulting free floating activity is very minuscule, share turnover is low and stock exchanges are managed in a clubby atmosphere.

One other important consequence of this situation is that the middle class tends not participate as an individual shareholder; being involved instead via privately held investment funds or indirectly via an employer pension fund.

This in turn leads to a relatively low degree of engagement in the implementation and oversight of business ethics and good corporate governance. In cases where major fraud has been uncovered, such as the Parmalat Brazil incident, public reaction is generally muted. This is because incidents such as these serve to confirm the middle class perception that illegal business practice is both still widespread and ultimately an insoluble problem.

Illegal business practice and corruption

Recent scandals at companies such as MCI Worldcom, Enron, Tyco, Parmalat and Vivendi notwithstanding, corporate governance in OECD countries has been driven primarily by the need to regulate the protection of minority shareholder rights. Crime prevention had been only a secondary goal.

Minority shareholder rights are even less protected in Latin America. It is common practice for dominant shareholders and shareholder groups to control a larger share of the cash flow than their nominal shareholding suggests.

This is achieved either through the issuance of voting and non-voting share classes referred to earlier or even by pyramid shareholding

Often this dominance over a corporation is misused by the controlling shareholders to let the corporation enter into commercial relations that are not priced at market values but at much less favourable conditions, which for example favour a related company in which the controlling shareholder has a higher stake. This problem is known as expropriation or asset stripping. The consequence in macroeconomic terms is the destruction of value and a severe impediment to the competitiveness of domestic businesses (Oman *et al.*, 2003).

The risk of ignoring statute laws and regulations to gain an advantage for personal or corporate enrichment is higher in an environment where the aforementioned shareholder structure prevails in conjunction with a system based on the concept of personal exchange.

By contrast, share price manipulation tactics are a much less common practice in Latin America than in the developed countries. If share price manipulation is conducted at Latin American exchanges then often it involves the lead owners of a company colluding with brokers in order to sell out at a higher price. Share price manipulation is not an attractive option in the face of high ownership concentration together with the long-term holding of stakes in a company. Manipulation of the share price via the creation of a phantom business, through the suppression of unfavourable company data or via insider trading are all relatively uncommon in Latin America compared to European and other markets.

The most important reason to promote ethical business behaviour and good corporate governance in Latin America is because of its potential impact in reducing the incidence of corruption, which is still endemic.

A survey undertaken amongst businesses by Transparência Brasil and Kroll International in 2003 found that, after the prevailing high tax structure, the next biggest problem in Brazil was corruption (Abramo, 2004).

The survey also found that corruption is most likely to be suggested by government officials and then in second place by individuals who represent a company.

Clearly, corruption is a major impediment to practising good corporate governance in Latin America (Abramo, 2004; Apoyo Opinion y Mercado, 2004). But it also requires a parallel system of good political governance.

Transparency International, the NGO watchdog of worldwide corruption, conducts a yearly survey. Results for 2003 show that Chile or Uruguay are placed at the lower end of the first quartile, on a level comparable with OECD countries. Brazil, Colombia, Peru and Mexico can be found around the average level and Argentina, Bolivia and Venezuela manage to be among the last third, amongst the poor performers (Transparency International, 2003).

Corruption perpetrated by public officials will always flourish in an environment where extensive discretionary power is delegated to government officials without the establishment of adequate accountability and control, as is still quite characteristic of Latin America.

Resisting corrupt approaches carries the risk of an adverse economic effect to the corporation, of course.

Multinationals can clearly cope with any negative economic impact without endangering their existence. So to, although to a lesser extent, can the so-called 'regionals'. Regionals are a group of either formerly state controlled or already private companies now controlled by either a major private individual, local investor or the state acting as controlling shareholder which started as a national player but later gained a regional footprint.

It is the smaller national company where the greatest risk exists of being seriously weakened by refusing to participate in corrupt practices.

Fortunately, some Latin American central, federal and local governments realize that poor political governance encourages corruption, with its sub-optimal allocation of resources and the proliferation of government ineffectiveness. Collateral destructive moral effects show a long-term impact. Some are already using technology to promote transparency in economic dealings and reduce the potential for corruption.

In Brazil, for example, all imports and exports are registered in an online databank, called Siscomex. Tax declarations are filed electronically, thereby giving the tax authorities a superb tool to analyse data chronologically and conduct consistency cross-checks. Public offices in various countries use the e-procurement concept as a means of increasing transparency.

Some Brazilian regional governors are also taking drastic measures, spurred on by the poor state of national public finances. In the state of Minas Gerais, the governor recently introduced a performance measuring system for the administration that offers incentives once targets are met or surpassed (Governor Aécio Neves, 2004). This is already common practice in the private sector but novel to the public sector.

In two years, the governor managed to turn around the near defunct state finances to zero deficits, an impressive result that has led other governors to consider copying this policy. While these measures were primarily directed towards cost-cutting with simultaneous augmentation of tax collection, they certainly had a collateral effect by reducing the level of corruption.

As mentioned earlier, corruption and illegal acts perpetrated by employees are a major problem in Latin America and corporations are making a considerable effort to reduce it.

To combat this, multinational subsidiaries and regionals long ago introduced robust control systems such as internal and external auditing, the 'four eye' and double signature principles and clear segregation of corporate duties. These are reinforced in many cases by a code of ethical conduct.

Transparency is further enhanced through management tools such as ERP (enterprise resource planning) that allow for standardized work processes that can be monitored remotely to be implemented throughout the world, and also allow processes such as open tendering and benchmarking of outcomes.

Recent moves towards corporate governance

After managing the debt crisis of the 1980s with its restructuring through Brady bonds, the larger Latin American capital markets reshaped in the 1990s and at the start of the 21st century. This was in large part due to a wave of privatization, principally in the energy, financial and telecommunication sectors. Multinational companies poured in foreign direct investment (FDI) to capture a share in the privatized companies and in some cases supported the formation of so-called 'regionals'.

Interestingly, after some initial shakeout, the Spanish returned to be one of the largest foreign investors within Latin America.

Some of those privatized companies that are now controlled by foreign multinationals maintain a local listing, but not necessarily so. Even where these companies are taken private, they adopt the management policy of the controlling multinational investor, due to the global reach of the business practices of investor companies.

In recent years, borrowing in the local credit market has also turned out to be too costly, even for well-rated commercial borrowers, with interest rates often being in the double digit range for a lot of Latin American markets.

To help finance their expansion, these companies resorted to the only option left, namely to tap the equity/capital markets, either by issuance of new shares or corporate bonds. Here, good business practices can make a significant difference. McKinsey in collaboration with the Korean Institute of Directors demonstrated through a joint survey in 2003 that foreign institutional investors are willing to pay a premium in the *P/E* ratio for good corporate governance to the tune of 20–23 per cent (McKinsey/Korean Institute of Directors, 2003).

In the 1980s all Latin American countries were ruled by military governments or through a dictatorship whose intention was to secure its mandate through isolation from the rest of the world. High tariffs isolated national products from international competition.

When democracy returned, governments opened the domestic markets and soon it became evident that national products stood next to no chance of competing with their more advanced international equivalents. This created a strong need for finance to upgrade and update local production. Since a lot of local production was still state controlled, the only realistic way to finance the future was through privatization. Globalization provided an important part in the supply of fresh capital.

This wave of privatization and the related FDI caused local regulators and governments to confront the need to update their respective laws and by-laws which regulate the capital and equity markets, thereby managing the surging challenges and raising the attraction of further foreign investment.

Based on an OECD initiative in 2000, Latin American regulators, policy makers, business leaders and private sector experts launched a round table discussion with the support of the World Bank and Inter-American Development Bank[1]. The outcome was a White Paper with recommendations on how to implement good corporate governance in Latin America. The study was presented in 2003 (OECD, 2003).

The recommendations basically follow those already published by the OECD and are very comprehensive. They express the expected actions to be taken by each stakeholder, whether it is the company management, the institutional investor or the policy maker in either the legislative or the government official in the administration.

The level of progress achieved over the last few years is generally very encouraging, with Brazil, Chile and Mexico in particular reforming their laws and regulations in order to attract more capital.

However, in other countries, notably Argentina, Bolivia and Venezuela the trend is to ignore, if not to obstruct, the basic foundation of any investors' confidence, namely the unconditional protection of property rights and impartial enforcement of rules.

Venezuela is currently challenging ownership rights in its land reform laws, while Argentina appears willing to break any conventional rule in order to recover from its recent economic crisis.

First the country froze all bank deposits, and then it continued with the asymmetric devaluation of commercial bank assets and liabilities, thereby asking the banks to foot the devaluation bill. Utility tariffs for energy, water and gasoline were frozen while at the same time continuous investment was required to ensure that licences are not revoked.

Furthermore, administrative guidance issued by Argentina provided overprotection to debtors in default, depriving creditors of their due rights. The same attitude is applied in its negotiation to settle its international debt. Political governance that favours populism is counterproductive to investment and ultimately to growth in the economy, as it obstructs good corporate governance, lowers investor confidence, depresses the return on investment and raises property risks.

The latest OECD White Paper report summarizes the progress already achieved in fostering corporate governance in Latin American countries (OECD, 2003).

Brazil suffered from a similar economic crisis in 1999 and 2000 but, in contrast to Argentina, is taking a much more sober stance.

It has, for example, introduced a range of measures that can only help to inspire investor confidence. First the Brazilian regulator, CVM, was granted more financial support together with more independence in 2001.

In the same year the Sao Paulo stock exchange, BOVESPA, created three new separate listings: Special Corporate Governance Level 1, Level 2 and the *Novo Mercado*. The first one requires improved disclosure only, the second also includes strengthened shareholder rights while the *Novo Mercado* requests further an arbitration system and prohibits the issuance of non-voting shares.

The *Novo Mercado* got off to a slow start but passed its first major acceptance test in 2004, when in that year the local market showed a strong IPO activity with five out of seven new listings placed at the *Novo Mercado*.

We will also soon see the benefits of changed lending practices instituted by the Brazilian National Development bank, BNDES, which launched a new regulation in 2003 that discriminates positively in favour of those borrowers who apply good corporate governance (BNDES, 2003).

Elsewhere, the Chilean regulator SVS was granted more influence as the result of a law passed in 2000 to improve the regulatory framework of share transactions in areas such as minority shareholder protection and the setting of a stricter corporate governance framework (see OECD, 2000).

Similar initiatives began during 2001 in Argentina, Mexico and Colombia while the Peruvian regulator CONASEV issued its own Principles for Good Governance of Peruvian Corporations in 2002 (CONASEV, 2002).

The influence of multinationals and regionals

Multinationals, whether or not they are locally listed, import and implement global corporate policies that are based on OECD conventions and reporting standards as defined by Financial Accounting Standards Board (FASB) or International Accounting Standards Board (IASB).

Regionals often follow suit, not least because they are keen to attract foreign finance via commercial bonds or share offers. The American Depository Receipt (ADR) is a popular means to issue shares outside the region, for example. FASB disclosure compliance is a prerequisite for ADR issuance.

For much the same reasons, it is also common to see the adoption of standards required from legislation such as Sarbanes-Oxley (Sarbanes-Oxley Act, 2002) and compliance with international guidelines with regard to child labour, sweatshops, environmental standards and the like.

The global influence is also found in the relationships formed by these companies with their customers or their suppliers. Some companies who have committed to follow international standards ask their commercial partners to apply certain minimum standards on pain of losing their contract.

This can include audits conducted by the procuring multinational at the subcontractor to ascertain whether this partner applies the required safety or labour standards. Another example concerns the legislation on outsourcing that is common in most Latin American countries. This legislation includes the concept of substitution, i.e. when a subcontractor fails to pay social security for its staff, then the temporary employee can claim compensation from the company who contracted the subcontractor. Consequently, smart companies ask their subcontractors at the time of contract negotiation and during the contract period to provide a negative certification that no social security contributions were pending.

With the onset of the global corporate governance forum and the regional policy dialogue roundtable, a joint initiative of the OECD and the World Bank, as decreed in June 1999 by both institutions, discussions over corporate governance have proliferated in Latin America, resulting in the conclusions laid down in the White Paper on corporate governance referred to earlier (Nestor, 2001). Today, major Latin American markets have established institutes for directors in order to train and coach directors in their roles and responsibilities, particularly in terms of protecting the interests of their stakeholders.

Good corporate governance is also becoming a sales tool to retain employees and attract recruits. Multinationals and regionals require well-trained and highly skilled personnel and these companies look to the alumni of the best universities, who in a lot of cases have received some exposure to foreign countries either via education or employment.

Young professionals are becoming increasingly keen to work in an environment comparable to the best international standards. They also wish to avoid any company that has a tarnished image, making them keen supporters of good corporate governance. Once hired, they frequently assume the role of the guardian of good standards, particularly as any wrongdoing at the company might reduce their individual market value or dent their future career.

Ways government can help

That there is a positive correlation between good corporate and political governance is quite clear, as an aid to both greater transparency and accountability. Actions by government in this area can help to optimize the resources available for the underlying objective of sustainable growth.

Individual governments have a positive role to play through reining in the influence of vested interest groups by, for example, simplifying the tax structure or passing laws which clearly lay out shareholder and ownership protection.

However, Latin American societies are still in the phase of personal exchange. In other words, the institutions that represent enforcement, i.e. legislation, jurisdiction and police, require a serious overhaul in order to warrant an impartial and equal treatment of every individual through clearly-defined rules and responsibilities with stringent supervision.

Good political governance is also given important expression in a just and effective taxation system.

Brazil and Argentina have both introduced a cheque tax, levied on movements between bank accounts or cash transfers. Simplification of the taxation structure could be achieved quite easily if Governments standardized their VAT and otherwise relied solely on the cheque tax.

As it is a fixed percentage of the underlying value, the cheque tax is very simple to calculate. Levies are directly correlated with the amounts transferred and it is therefore also socially fair. The banks act as the tax collector; hence it does not need many tax inspectors to control the collection.

All other taxes, with the exception of VAT, would be redundant. The ratio of collection would be dramatically improved while at the same time the collection and administration work would be reduced significantly. Vested interest groups would also have far fewer opportunities to impose unfair advantages and create distortions in general competitiveness.

The role of the private sector

As demonstrated earlier, companies in Latin America reveal a high shareholder concentration, exercised by either families or clans or by the states via partial privatization.

Pyramid, cross-shareholding and different share class structures, or in the case of state controlled companies the golden share, allow the controlling entity to yield much higher influence than actual investment suggests.

These structures invite sub-optimal use of resources and impede transparency and accountability.

The capital and equity markets can contribute via tighter regulations with regard to the minimum requirements to list stock. Action could be required in a range of areas, including tag along rights, the 'one share one vote' concept, minimum free floating share percentages, minimum numbers of independent directors and the setting up of appropriate board committees.

Business associations, chambers of commerce, merchant guilds and consultancies are the right organizations to jointly promote the benefits of corporate governance as a means to prevent an organization becoming entangled in corruption and to enhance the efficiency of the use of resources within corporations.

Financial institutions would also be very well advised to include the existence of corporate governance policies and standards as a credit rating aspect when evaluating their new and existing clients.

Outlook

Good corporate governance principles help foster a better allocation of resources under a transparent structure of clearly expressed rules, whether it relates to the utilization of capital or a better equipped and motivated workforce. This improved allocation of resources leads to economic growth for the corporation itself and benefits its shareholders and employees. When corporate governance acts in synchrony with good political governance then society is the prime beneficiary.

Both an individual government as well as any entrepreneur acting in Latin America has to understand that corporate governance is a competitive issue in a global world under which any outside investor or trading partner is benchmarking countries or companies.

So, we should not view the demands of international lenders for improvements in areas such as the judiciary, legal framework or police as an interference in the internal affairs of another sovereignty but as a responsible act designed to help achieve a more prosperous society.

The articulation of such requirements is of vital importance to most Latin American countries because internal forces are still too entrenched in the personal exchange concept to be able to instigate and execute the needed reorganization towards an impersonal exchange concept.

Diplomacy, patience but also perseverance are all vital in order to keep the government of a developing country and the outside trading partner, sponsor or donor focused on the ultimate goal of realizing the impersonal exchange concept and the benefits it brings to the majority of human beings. This strategy is a marathon task.

At the same time we should also recognize that improving education provision is a precursor to raising the standard of living on a broader scale, although the full impact will show only in the long term. Education is the most important contributor to the enlargement of the middle classes. The middle classes in any society are the driver behind the calls for changes to improve either political or corporate governance. Therefore, fostering mass education should be the second point to focus on.

In conclusion it can be said that institutions in Latin America have already embarked on a road to better corporate governance. However, more is required by governments to aid the development of the impersonal exchange concept and more can also be done by outside trading partners, governmental and non governmental organizations. Only then will parity be achieved with OECD countries.

Notes

1   This was founded in 1959 and today the IDB is owned by 47 member states, of which 26 are borrowing members in Latin America and the Caribbean. Each member country's voting power is based on its subscription to the institution's Ordinary Capital (OC) resources.

References

Abramo, Claudio Weber (2004) *Corruption in Brazil, Perspective from the Private Sector. 2003 Survey by Transparência Brasil in Association with Kroll International.* Available at: http:// www.transparencia.org.br

Apoyo Opinion y Mercado (2004) *Segunda encuesta sobre corrupción.* Lima: Proetica. Available at: http://www.proetica.org.pe/Descargas/SegundaEncuesta_20040210.pdf

BNDES (2003) BNDES program to encourage adoption of corporate governance practices, announced 2002, translated by International Finance Corporation

CONASEV (2002) Principios de Buen Gobierno Para Las Sociedades Peruanas. Available at: http://www.conasev.gob.pe/Acercade/BuenGobierno/principios%20buen%20gobierno.pdf

Governor Aécio Neves (2004) *Cidades do Brasil.* Interview, 56 (Nov.) Available at: http://cidadesdobrasil.com.br/cgi-cn/news.cgi?cl=09910510009710010 1098114&arecod=25&newcod=828

Lefort, Fernando (2003) *Ownership Structure and Corporate Governance in Latin American Countries – An Empirical Overview.* Available at: http://www.sumaq.org/sumaq_summit_2004/documentos/documentos2/Corporate Governance_FernandoLefort.pdf

McKinsey/Korean Institute of Directors (2003) *Survey on Corporate Governance.* Washington, DC: McKinsey and Co.

Nestor, Stilpon (2001) *International Efforts to Improve Corporate Governance.* Paris: OECD. Available at: http://www.oecd.org/dataoecd/61/1/1932028.pdf

North, D (2003) *Promoting Institutional Reforms in Latin America. Conference organized by the center for International Private Enterprise (CIPE) and the Ronald Coarse Institute.* Presentation, 12 Dec.

OECD (2000) *Tender Offer and Corporate Governance Law: Chilean New Set of Rules to Integrate the Global Marketplace,* Alvaro Clarke de la Cerda, Superintendente de Valores y Seguros de Chile. Available at: http://www. oecd.org/dataoecd/56/58/1922398.ppt

OECD (2003) *White Paper on Corporate Governance in Latin America.* Paris: OECD

Oman, Charles, Fries, Steven and Buiter, Willem (2003) *Corporate Governance in Developing, Transition and Emerging-Market Economies.* OECD Development Centre Policy Brief no. 23

Sarbanes-Oxley Act (2002) Available at: http://www.sec.gov/about/laws/soa2002. pdf. See also: http://www.sec.gov/spotlight/sarbanes-oxley.htm

Transparency International (2003) Available at: http://www.transparency.org/ pressreleases_archive/2003/2003.10.07.cpi.en.html

9

Ethics in Financial Markets

Andreas Prindl

Ethical scandals in financial markets continue unabated. As WorldCom and Enron become old news, we hear of corrupt practices in the US mutual fund and insurance industries including late trading breaches, mis-selling of financial products and deliberately misleading analysts' reports.

Such ugly events happen across the whole spectrum of finance: retail and investment banking, securities operations, pension sales, insurance broking and investment funds, and they happen worldwide. While it is not easy to estimate whether the incidence of malfeasance is greater than in, say, manufacturing, certainly financial frauds and crimes are bigger and more visible as a rule.

This chapter looks first at ethical problems in the financial markets more generally, then analyses what is specific to those markets that may give rise to ethical breaches. Finally, it outlines internal and regulatory actions that are needed, many already underway, to diminish them.

It argues that the nature of financial markets, especially the opportunity and temptations for wrongdoing, gives rise to many real or possible breaches of ethical behaviour. The complexity and size of transactions increase steadily. Conflicts of interest abound.

It also points out that financial misbehaviour in the corporate sector – which often takes place in the accounting/disclosure lapses of non-financial corporations – seems in the public eye to be related to financial markets, compounding the perception of widespread iniquity there. To the extent that some financial institutions have helped to disguise and misrepresent accounting results, or to hide profits, the financial services sector is indeed again directly involved. Yet that perception is generally unfounded; all business dealings eventually involve finance.

The situation is made worse by inadequate or fragmented regulatory supervision, although this is improving in the European and US markets. Internal controls and audit functions are being strengthened as well.

Recent scandals

The common perception that the financial markets are full of scandals is fuelled by constant media headlines. Transgressions reported, indictments issued and penalties imposed involve staggering amounts.

Many breaches of proper behaviour take place in the accounting statements of corporations, but these seem to be part and parcel of the same problem, and abetted by the system. In 2003–4 we have seen the following.

*   A total of $1.4 billion in fines and other punishment for 10 Wall Street firms to settle charges that their research reports were deliberately misleading about customers whose business they sought.
*   Over $3 billion in monetary penalties imposed on US mutual fund complexes for market timing and late trading violations.
*   The indictment of Marsh McLennan and other firms in the US for bid-rigging and contingent commissions in insurance brokerage business; in the case of Marsh it is claimed that it gained over $1 billion in incorrect commissions.

All of these were based on investigations and suits instigated by the New York State Attorney General Eliot Spitzer. We have also seen the following.

* $550 million in losses from irregular trading of derivatives in Singapore by China Aviation Oil.
*   Accounting lapses in two American government sponsored enterprises (GSEs) Freddie Mac and Fannie Mae, in the latter amounting to a reported $9 billion.
*   False accounting in Parmalat, an Italian food company, where up to $12 billion of assets have turned out to be non-existent.
* $2.7 billion of assets allegedly fraudulently accounted for by HealthSouth Corporation.

The latter two examples are not directly related to the financial sector *per se*. As Elaine Sternberg points out:

'Major business scandals tend to be associated with finance, because they are associated with financial losses. But it would be wrong to conclude that financial wrongdoing is the cause of these losses, or that finance is especially unethical. . . . Unethical conduct in finance may be as much a response to financial losses as a source of them; it is when businesses are weak that the temptation to falsify may be the greatest.' (Sternberg, 1994)

Causes of ethical problems

The nature of the financial markets, which exist to safeguard and transfer claims on financial assets, creates a breeding ground for ethical problems. The sheer size of financial firms and the complexity of the marketplace in which they compete are difficult to understand and control. Transactions are so large, and nowadays so complex, that unethical practice can be very rewarding if undetected.

Financial firms have themselves become very large, and spread across the world. Aggressive new entrants have come in. Consolidation of firms has resulted in ever growing financial organizations with multiple product lines and presences in widespread geographic markets. For example, the world's largest financial organization has more than $1 trillion in assets and operates truly worldwide.

Assets held or traded in financial markets are immense. External assets of EU banks are over £1.8 trillion. Outstanding traded bond issues in the US are some $11 trillion. The cash flow of US corporations in 2004 amounted to $1.3 trillion; their outstanding cash holdings at year end alone were about $600 billion. It is estimated that funds equal to half the world's GDP move through the SWIFT interbank payment system every day. The value of shares traded in New York can be over $1 trillion per month. Individual deals are also often enormous; it may be tempting to some financial employees to try to skim off a tiny, perhaps unnoticeable, part of a deal, for possible large gains.

Market complexity is also a significant factor. The banking and financial world today is far more complex than that of a generation ago. There are more voracious players, many new and much more complicated products, more emphasis on the distribution of risk and more uncertainty about the rewards of risk. Transactions are much larger and have bigger stakes, requiring more intricate negotiation.

New information and communication technology has led to the rapid extension of markets worldwide. The Internet connects the world seamlessly and immediately. Any market can be instantly accessed; most continue trading around the clock. For example, we in London trade with the Far East in our morning and with America in our afternoon. As the American West Coast begins to finish its day, the Far East markets open up.

New technology has also heightened competition, with many opportunities for new entrants to come into the market, e.g. banks in the securities business, securities firms in the banking business, banks and securities firms in the insurance business. This intensified in the US after the passage of the Gramm-Leach-Bliley Act in 1999, allowing financial holding companies and effectively scrapping the divisions in the banking industry imposed by the Glass-Steagall Act of 1932.

Competition in the marketplace has been fuelled by the ability to offer innovative new products and the race for increased market share. Many complex financial products require a high degree of mathematical modelling and/or involve off-balance sheet operations. These include derivatives, swaps and exotic new financial instruments; hedge funds are a structural representation of the same process. The world of derivatives has opened up new ways for transactions to be hidden or transferred off-shore beyond the reach of the tax inspector.

But these products and the resultant position taking can be harder to understand and can result in more rapid losses and profits. In the case of the hedge fund Long-Term Capital Management, two Nobel Prize winners and a former Federal Reserve Board Vice Chairman were involved, yet the company nearly went bankrupt in 1998 as a result of its trading positions. It had to be rescued by a \$3.65 re-capitalization package under the auspices of the New York Federal Reserve Bank.

The language and practices of finance are arcane and little known outside its markets. Huge sums can be dealt between two, often junior, people using public communications media. Secret information lies at the heart of these markets: not yet released information on sales and profitability, corporate strategy, planned mergers and acquisitions.

Corporate cultures in financial houses also seem to have radically changed. The old structure in Anglo-Saxon countries of traditional merchant and investment banks and retail banks included limits on the products offered and interest rates earned or paid. Thousands of country banks in the USA, and thousands of bank branches in the UK, knew their customers intimately and offered them similar, mostly on-balance sheet services.

Self-regulation was possible in wholesale banks, whose homogeneous and closely-knit staff knew each other and their competition well.

Remuneration was typically based on general contribution to the firm, not specific profits gained. Their ethical cultures were set by the example of management and long-established in-house procedures. Self-regulation was also important in the securities and insurance industries, where longstanding procedures influenced how employees approached ethical rules and provided guidance in difficult cases.

But this type of company culture appears to have disappeared in many financial institutions. An emphasis on short-term profits, after traditional intermediary functions became less profitable, seems instead to be all-pervasive. Salaries, commissions and bonuses are based in many instances on deals brought in or trading profits earned by individuals, not how well the employee assisted customers in their problem solving and the resultant lending or hedging transactions. Total remuneration can be astonishingly high: the Credit Suisse First Boston investment banker Frank Quattrone once made $120 million in a single year. He is now a convicted felon awaiting 18 months in prison for failing to cooperate with a federal investigation into kickback allegations.

An obvious question would be: given the high incidence of reported wrongdoing, do the financial markets attract personnel of less morality? I wouldn't like to think so. Are bankers less ethical than lawyers, insurance executives less ethical than manufacturers of pharmaceuticals, securities dealers less ethical than tobacco company managers? All of these groups contain bad apples. Many industries have had egregious cases of insider dealing, tax fraud, false accounting, overcharging on defence contracts and so on. It is, however, possible that the reputed high compensation levels in financial services attract people whose primary motivation is making money. To such people, the perceived financial rewards of malfeasance may be more difficult to resist.

Other ethical problems exist at the employee level as well. Despite the strictest of controls, collusion between two individuals is still possible. Indeed, a single trader can – for a while – commit fraud or theft, or place their firm at risk to crippling losses, all by themselves: witness Nick Leeson of Baring, Toshihide Ibuchi of Daiwa Bank in America or Yasuo Hamanaka of Sumitomo Shoji.

The opportunities – one could also say temptations – to act unethically in financial markets are greater than in most other business areas, because of the relatively easy access to funds or deals involving large sums. Access to non-public information, which can be used to take profitable trading positions, is often present. A further conflict is to try to bring in more business by voracious, sometimes false, marketing, for the resultant commissions or bonuses. One could be an unethical supplier of, say, shoes, but it would be much harder to reap huge financial rewards thereby.

The client–bank relationship – in both directions – seems to be weaker than it was. Whereas before, large corporates might rely on a few 'house banks' for most of its advice and financing, now they deal with many firms. They can pick and choose those which give the best advice in different areas, or offer the most imaginative financing schemes. Banks have been seen to drop longstanding customers for dealings with newer, more promising ones, including in hostile takeovers. This trend may lead to short-term relationships, less than complete understanding of the firm's operations on the part of the advisor and reduced personal knowledge of each other's management.

Furthermore, disintermediation plays a role here. Businesses can side-step banks by issuing their own commercial notes or by securitizing assets. Bank loans in the US are often a source of back-up liquidity rather than to provide funding. Increased institutionalization of savings in the form of pension and retirement plans, and the management of these funds by professional non-bank money managers, diverts away from banks' vast pools of funds that otherwise would have been placed on deposit (Fein, 2005).

These changes have brought new conflicts of interest, especially for investment and universal banks. Such banks can now play a variety of roles, often simultaneously; they can be at one time underwriter, financial advisor, trader, principal and fair value opinion provider. Universal banks in many places can own shares directly as well. For example, in the securities area, a bank might underwrite bonds for a client, purchase bonds for its own account, advise investors on bond purchases and manage bond portfolios.

Potential conflicts of interest are inherent in the multiple roles a financial institution can play. A bank's concern about its underwriting risk could influence its recommendations to investors. Its own holdings of bonds might influence the way it manages customer portfolios. Its goal of winning investment fund business might influence the terms of its bond underwriting, or it might give special treatment in the form of allotments of sought-after issues (typically new shares in initial public offerings) to top executives of big existing or potential clients. Its security analysts might come under pressure to write overly positive or inaccurate reports on clients whose future business it hopes to obtain. Investment banks can represent both sides in a merger of equals, which can create a conflict of interest in negotiating the terms of a transaction. In a leveraged buyout a bank can represent a buyout group as advisor and also be a member of that self-same group (Regan, 2004).

Banks can play multiple roles without always very clear perimeters because they are not in all cases regarded as fiduciaries. Generally, relations between banks and customers are governed by rules that apply to parties engaged in arms-length relationships.

Ethical conflicts arise as well in relationships with stakeholders, with holders of information and with society. They may originate in the area of shareholder and creditor arrangements, especially in bankruptcy or reorganization, in egregious management incentives, or again in the overwhelmingly short-term focus of analysts and investors. Conflicts between holders of information are well known, insider trading being the most pronounced. While some commentators judge that insider dealing promotes market efficiency, others conclude that it seriously endangers the fiduciary relationships which are essential.

Conflicts with the society in which financial firms operate may appear. While these arise in all business sectors – think of pollution or other types of endangering the environment, or dangerous products – financial houses can act against societal interests by helping tax evasion or promoting unfair or misleading services, especially in areas such as pensions or other types of long term saving.

Marketing practices in the financial services sector are not always transparent or in the best interests of customers, especially in the retail area where individual clients are less knowledgeable. The term 'confusion marketing' is often heard in the United Kingdom; it refers to the unethical practice of banks and insurance companies offering a confusing array of retail products in which the risks are understated or obfuscated, or the indicated returns overstated. The Financial Services Authority (FSA) in the UK has investigated over 145,000 alleged cases of deceitful mortgage endowment policies.

The absolute size of financial transactions can even negatively impact governmental finances or reserves. For example, the daily average volume of foreign exchange transactions worldwide is at least $2 trillion. The total reserves of all central banks amounted in late 2004 to $2.4 trillion. If a group of speculators, consisting of financial houses or their largest customers, wishes to speculate against a currency, many countries with modest reserves will not be able to withstand market pressure, and be forced to devalue. Even the UK fell victim to this action in 1992, when the pound was forced to devalue. The same happened in the Asian currency crisis in 1997. It is hard to consider these attacks ethical, even if they are legal.

Personal experiences

Many persons with responsibility in financial markets are confronted with conflicts of interest or temptations to act in a less than ethical way. I have been faced with this myself.

As examples, I have been offered bribes (in the form of potential large and profitable transactions for my firm) from a discredited business tycoon, now dead. He wanted the cachet of being seen as a major customer of a reputable house; he may have also planned to hide some of the pension funds he was stealing from his pensioners through us.

I have been offered 'hot' stock market tips by the head of the investment department of a major financial house if I would occasionally tell him in return which mergers and acquisitions we were working on before they became public. I have been offered inappropriate, lavish entertainment in possible exchange for favourable treatment on future loan applications. I could have acted – by myself – on information my company knew but which wasn't generally yet public or reflected in market prices. And I have been tempted, as a brash young account officer, to show off to my friends by telling them details of confidential, often very impressive, transactions.

I didn't succumb to any of these, but they are typical of the ethical conflicts that can arise in a financial manager's career. Some did not offer immediate prospects of any financial gain. What I didn't face, but is not completely infrequent, was any request by a superior to act in an unethical way.

A typical further individual conflict of interest is to enhance one's reputation, promotion or bonus by acting in a way that is not in all stakeholders' interests. This can come up for managers too. Again a personal example: I once employed a brilliant young bond trader, who consistently made profits in good markets and bad, indeed was usually the biggest contributor to our bottom line in a time when traditional lending brought poor returns. He never respected trading limits and often was outside them; once or twice he even breached the guidelines of the central bank. The dilemma for me was how to discipline him, by sharp reprimands or reducing his bonus perhaps, without driving him away. Doing nothing would show the rest of the treasury department that controls and discipline were not serious matters. Here I dithered and didn't come down hard enough on him, falling prey to my own conflict of interest of trying to keep the bank's profitability high.

What best to do?

What then can be done about unethical behaviour in financial markets? If the nature, size and structure of these markets continue to allow fraudulent or criminal activities, what measures can its participants and their regulators adopt?

Eliminating conflicts of interest in finance completely is not realistic. Competitive and profit pressures creating them will likely only increase. The Nobel Laureate Joseph Stiglitz says:

> 'Conflicts of interest will never be fully eliminated, either in the public or private sector. But by sensitizing ourselves to their presence, by increasing required disclosures – as the old saying goes, sunshine is the strongest antiseptic – by becoming aware of the incentives that are in place that can exacerbate these conflicts of interest, and by imposing regulations that limit their scope, we can do much to mitigate their consequences, both in the public and the private sector.' (Stiglitz, 2004)

The management of financial institutions and their regulators have both manifestly worked for decades to reduce ethical problems. Regulation of financial markets in many jurisdictions, however, may have been inadequate. It can be difficult for regulatory officials to keep abreast of rapidly changing markets and products. Market players can sense which regulators can be persuaded – or duped – to condone transactions more competent regulators would identify and forbid. This could happen in Western counties, but more frequently appears in off-shore centres where regulation is *de minimis* or non-existent.

Furthermore, regulatory fragmentation is a related issue. For example, there are 50 state insurance commissioners in America and it is unlikely that the smaller states can easily understand all the activities of a multinational insurance company under their scrutiny.

A review of the financial scandals of the last decade will show how many involved off-shore vehicles. Banking secrecy is claimed to be one of the virtues of these centres, but it can also cover up deals that are illegal. The proceeds of organized crime mostly wind up in banks; as tougher disclosure and money laundering laws are applied in the USA and Europe, these funds gravitate to unregulated markets (or Switzerland and Austria still). A kind of regulatory arbitrage is possible for unethical players. Some indication of the attractiveness of these off-shore markets to its users, many of whom have something to hide, is the estimated total of $5 trillion in financial assets held in off-shore accounts, spread among banks, mutual funds and other institutions which are all but unregulated.

Even governments themselves may act questionably in financial markets. Certain large central banks are known to speculate in currency markets, not as a diversification of reserves, but for profit. This may negatively affect other governments and central banks and is ethically unacceptable.

A striking case of apparent government malfeasance in markets is that of Credit Lyonnais, until recently owned directly by the French Government. It pled guilty to charges that it hid for years from the US regulators its illegal ownership of a California insurance company and the secret agreements in France made to disguise this. The French Government made attempts at the highest level to induce the US Government not to prosecute the bank or its culpable top officials for their criminal actions; the US authorities didn't give in to pressure and criminally indicted the bank and some executives. Credit Lyonnais made a $600 million settlement to the California Department of Insurance and paid a $100 million fine as a result.

When Daiwa Bank in New York was indicted for conspiracy, mail fraud and other crimes (and later shut down), it was reported that the Bank of Japan knew what that branch had been doing, but had not passed this on to the US authorities.

Stronger internal processes are required, however. A number of measures can minimize the potential for ethical breaches in the financial industry.

The starting point for companies themselves is *unambiguous rules of behaviour*. This applies equally to financial and non-financial firms and is based on written operating procedures taught to and understood by all staff. *Codes of conduct* are typically part of this process. These are discussed elsewhere; I will only comment that such codes not only have to be correctly imparted, but also openly exemplified by top management. Although it is now a requirement of the New York Stock Exchange that any listed company have a code of conduct, this is by itself only the first step. Even Enron had a code of conduct for a time.

Management example – demonstrating the values of a company – is one of the most critical factors in supporting correct behaviour. As Sir Adrian Cadbury points out: 'The glue which holds a company together is its beliefs and values, rather than its structures and systems.' (Cadbury, 1990). Visible ethical behaviour by management permeates throughout the firm; conversely, less than ethical behaviour will eventually be obvious to the dimmest employee and shape their behaviour. Proper procedures, policies and examples lead to an *ethical infrastructure*, which promotes ethical behaviour in the face of competitive and other pressures.

Morgan Guaranty, when I worked there from 1964 to 1984, was an outstanding example of this; in my opinion, no other bank can be considered more ethical than it then was. Honest open behaviour was the norm. If Morgan couldn't do something for a client, it openly acknowledged it. If persons in one profit centre acted in their own interests and not the bank's, they were faced with dismissal. Ethical expectations were self-fulfilling. One would no more walk into Walter Page's or Lew Preston's office (one could always walk right into the President's office) with a suspect deal – helping to falsify a client's accounting with transactions in an offshore vehicle, for example – than one would have sold his children into slavery. It of course helped that Morgan Guaranty was a relatively small company, with a limited number of wholesale clients and a homogeneous, well-educated and well-off officer corps.

The only ethical lapse I know of at Morgan Guaranty in this period was a private one. A Morgan officer, once married to the president of Brazil's daughter and well known in South America, dealt with the US investments of rich Latin American clients. He routinely shaved off a small portion for himself, stealing several million dollars over a period of time. The clients didn't scrutinize, or question, the returns they achieved and his rich lifestyle didn't attract attention. Of course he was eventually caught and sent to prison. Ironically, the impeccable reputation of Morgan Guaranty probably helped him defraud, since almost no one at that time would have questioned a transaction or a rate quotation from it.

The old Morgan Guaranty is now gone, and with it apparently some of its ethic. The merged J P Morgan Chase, now a huge company with manifold activities around the world, consented in 2003 to pay $135 million in disgorgement, penalty and interest after being charged with helping Enron mislead its investors by characterizing what were essentially loan proceeds as cash from operating procedures. Citicorp consented to pay $100 million for the same alleged offence.

Stronger and more independent boards and audit committees are essential. This will be reviewed later in the discussion of the Sarbanes-Oxley Act (2002), but it is a universal *sine qua non*. It is obvious that some of the fraudulent behaviour in financial markets has been condoned by, misunderstood by or not imparted to the relevant board.

Some board members in some companies may have been too complacent, too much in the pocket of management or too unwilling to lose their fees and perks to properly do their job, but it is their primary responsibility to see that ethical behaviour is maintained. Tough, questioning and impartial directors are needed.

The audit committee, not always historically as independent or powerful in many companies as it should have been, is a critical ingredient here. So is the internal audit department, which has to be completely independent in its reporting and responsible only to outside directors.

A strong internal audit team, in my experience, is one of the best tools management can have to deal with ethical conflicts, and not just those which breach regulatory guidelines or laws. It can be the first point of guidance and advice to employees with ethical concerns, indeed to management itself. I have seen cases where management of banks wished to keep their audit department quiescent and tame; this is a serious mistake.

Strict separation of activities – the so-called *Chinese walls* – reduces the chances of insider trading, or of analysts being pressured to give inaccurate or over-generous opinions on public shares so other departments can win more business, as was seen in Wall Street recently. Chinese walls still can be much better enforced.

The role of self-regulation and government

Other measures can be taken outside of individual firms. General *market awareness* of its participants – through informal and quite proper sharing of information – can be used to judge individual firms or their employees. In the case of BCCI in London, the market sensed that something was fishy about this Asian-controlled and inadequately regulated bank, which turned out to have had at least three sets of books and massive criminal activities, long before the responsible central banks in Luxembourg or England did anything. Many banks pulled their lines to BCCI without clear evidence, based on market perception.

The great trading room of Lloyd's fulfils a similar unofficial function. The underwriters all sit in their boxes and deal with the brokers openly; transactions pass from box to box as various syndicates sign up for risk participations. Deals, companies or individuals with unsavory reputations are widely known. The probable move to electronic trading which Lloyd's will eventually adopt could affect somewhat the outstanding market intelligence which is one of Lloyd's key success factors, and some of that market's ability to identify and curb questionable activity.

On the other hand, the discipline of electronic data exchange will help ensure that risk and other data is shared with all underwriters in an equitable way. Transparency can fail in a face-to-face subscription market based on pairwise conversations. An electronic audit trail would be facilitated.

Good market intelligence helps *self-regulation*, still an active force in policing markets. Lloyd's still acts somewhat in this capacity, although its main emphasis is to control unjustified risk-taking or inaccurate pricing. As another example, the National Association of Securities Dealers, which acts for the US securities industry, banned or suspended 830 individuals from the securities industry during 2004 and collected more than $102 million in disciplinary fines.

Government also has a major part to play. A complex set of laws and regulations exists in all advanced financial markets. These are augmented by administrative guidance, close contact between the regulatory authorities and those they regulate, and inspections.

Accounting standards, however, are not uniform internationally or always respected. This makes the task of the regulators that much harder.

The Financial Services Authority (FSA) in the UK, responsible for regulating the financial markets, their firms and employees, has an interesting and imaginative approach to ethics. It attempts to differentiate the institutions it regulates as to their perceived approach to ethical behaviour and the values they display. Firms that demonstrate their commitment to ethical practice experience a much lighter regulatory regime, while those where doubt arises face tough, intrusive and constant scrutiny, as shown in the FSA's published framework (Financial Services Authority, 2002):

Values and cultures of firms	Regulatory relationship
Minimum standards	Policing
Compliance culture	Supervising/educating
Beyond compliance	Educating/ consulting
Values-led business	Mature relationship/benchmarking

More rigorous and focused analysis by the FSA should help ethical standards of financial firms in the United Kingdom, although it will not eliminate crimes of rogue individuals as in the Baring case. In the US, the new Sentencing Guidelines adopted in 2004 (US Sentencing Commission, 2004) may allow mitigation of fines if companies can prove they have ethical guidelines in place and seek to train their employees about ethical behaviour.

Tougher legislation has inevitably followed. A striking example is the Sarbanes-Oxley Act of 2002. It puts the onus firmly on boards and top management to eliminate illicit financial behaviour, specifically in reporting and disclosure. Following widely published financial and reporting scandals, the Act sets much higher standards for corporate governance, promotes transparency of financial statements and establishes a tougher set of sanctions and penalties for violations of securities law.

For example, it is now unlawful to fraudulently influence, coerce, manipulate or mislead auditors. The audit committee of company boards must now approve in advance any non-audit services contracted with their outside auditor (this reduces the auditor's own conflict of interest to perhaps be less demanding about the accounts if it can win significant other business). The lesson learned from the demise of the leading accounting firm Arthur Andersen, found to be in collusion with its customer Enron, was certainly a contributing factor to this rule.

The Act requires independent auditors to report to audit committees all alternative accounting treatments of company data discussed with management, the implications of those treatments and the actual methodology they recommended. Audit committees are empowered (although this was already commonly possible) to retain their own outside advisors, including lawyers. The Public Accounting Oversight Board was created to review industry adherence to the new rules.

Sarbanes-Oxley also requires issuing companies to impose and disseminate a code of ethics specifically for financial reporting personnel and gives audit committees the duty to establish confidential procedures for employers wishing to point out illegal or questionable accounting practices. It creates a private right of action for such 'whistleblowers', who have often faced retaliation for their commendable behaviour.

Crucially, the Act requires each quarterly and annual report of an issuing firm to include certification signed by the CEO and CFO, stating that they have reviewed the report, it contains no material misstatement and any significant deficiencies have been disclosed to the firm's independent auditor and audit committee. No longer can top managers in the USA claim they didn't know what was going on, or were misled by subordinates.

The Sarbanes-Oxley Act is not a reform of the financial services sector *per se*, but more specifically of the accounting and disclosure structures that underlie its activities. It should reduce the incidence of financial fraud, at least by US companies, by more clearly spelling out who is responsible for overseeing financial reporting and disclosure, empowering them to do so and making transgression here more severely punished.

Alongside this, nine-figure fines and disgorgement penalties have become more frequent. But even these are not so large in the context of mega-companies. Furthermore, little reputational loss is apparent, possibly because so many financial industry leaders have been fined or have settled suits out of court. Few customers of such firms seem to have gone away.

Even stronger sanctions could be envisioned, for example suspending a market participant from trading for a period if it is found guilty of malfeasance or assisting crime. This happened in the case of Nomura Securities and Daiichi Kangyo Bank, which suffered suspensions of own-account trading and loans to new clients respectively in Japan in 1997 after revelations about their dealings with underworld gangs. Daiwa Bank was ordered to close its US operations for good in 1996 after the extent of its hiding of documents from and lying to American authorities was revealed.

But there is a moral hazard here. A large firm such as J P Morgan Chase or Citibank, or their equivalents in other markets, cannot realistically be suspended or closed down. They are too large and too important in the economic system. Long Term Capital Management was kept afloat for this reason. Furthermore, although such banks have been involved in quite serious offenses, the actual miscreants were individuals or departments; there was no concerted firm-wide attempt to deceive or defraud.

Culpable management could face stiffer penalties, and more executives could be dismissed by their board or by the authorities for malfeasance by the firm. Those unambiguously involved in crime should be sent to prison *pour encourager les autres*, which so far has rarely happened. Maybe every jurisdiction should have an Eliot Spitzer.

Conclusion

Apparent opportunities to gain wealth and myriad conflicts of interest will continue to arise in today's vast and complex financial markets.

These will lead to crimes, especially fraud and hiding of profits, misuse of information and of the intermediary function of financial firms.

A stronger regulatory structure is appearing in many countries and more progress can be expected. Yet it is up to the financial market participants themselves to ensure more appropriate behaviour. Many of the internal measures suggested in the previous pages have been adopted by the leading industry firms. The optimal solution will be when the preponderance of financial houses in a position to affect market behaviour can be characterized as ethical organizations, or value-led companies.

The nature of value-led companies has been well described in the recent literature of ethics. They have an open organizational hierarchy and structure of responsibilities, especially regarding compliance in all its senses. Ethical organizations understand their role in the society they operate in, and their obligations to all stakeholders. Such firms think long-term and are not swayed by short-termism. Organizational goals are realistic and do not put undue pressure on staff for performance or profit levels. The internal and external audit functions are clear, independent and powerful. Employees are educated about ethical behaviour and adhere to an ethical code promulgated by the firm and continually exemplified by its management. Remuneration is not solely based on profits gained for the company.

Pace Milton Friedman, it can be argued that all companies are part of the social system and have a responsibility to it beyond simply making profit. The Bank of England Governor, Mervyn King, has said that in this respect profits are a by-product of the successful company; its ethical role is one it should stress and be proud of.

Only a few financial companies now can undoubtedly be designated as value-led, despite protestations to the contrary. Some are more obviously in this category, among which are those financial firms that concentrate solely on investing in or lending to what they see as ethical businesses. Successful ethical funds have been set up, although these are still rather small.

The combination of sanctions by government and the move of customers to financial companies that are perceived to be ethical will eventually weed out questionable players and increase the scope and success of the more ethical ones.

Ultimately, I believe that we in the financial services sector will act more ethically, because to act ethically 'pays off' in the long run. Some researchers have found that investments in firms that engage in unethical behaviour earn abnormally negative returns for prolonged periods

(Long and Rao, 1995). Others find that firms that have better corporate governance also have higher stock market valuations, higher profitability and faster sales (Gompers *et al.*, 2003).

While such evidence is not yet totally convincing, it is certain that a reputation for ethical behaviour, above all in an industry which holds, protects, transfers and helps to invest the financial assets of a country, will ultimately bring more client business and longer lasting relationships. A better class of personnel will be attracted to work in ethical firms, and they will remain longer. Suppliers and the community will be better long-term partners. Government relations will be smoother and regulation more benign.

All those benefits should indeed be reflected in profitability over time and higher share prices. Those firms that can see such long-term advantages do not need much government pressure to do what is best in any event for them, and for their customers.

References

Cadbury, Sir Adrian (1990) *The Company Chairman*. London: Institute of Directors

Fein, Melanie L. (2005) *Banking and Financial Services: A Regulatory Guide to the Convergence of Banking, Securities and Insurance in the United States*. Boston: Goodwin Procter

Financial Services Authority (2002) *An Ethical Framework for Financial Services*. London: Financial Services Authority

Glass-Steagall Act (1932)

Gompers, Paul, Ishii, Joy and Metrick, Andrew (2003) Corporate governance and equity prices. *The Quarterly Journal of Economics* **118**:1

Gramm-Leach-Bliley Act (1999). Available at: http://www.ftc.gov/privacy/privacyinitiatives/glbact.html

Long, D Michael and Rao, Spuma (1995) The wealth effects of unethical business behaviour. *Journal of Economics and Finance*. **19**:2

National Association of Securities Dealers (NASD) (2004) News Release – NASD: 2004 in Review. Available at: http://www.nasd.com

Regan, Milton C Jr (2004) *Eat What You Kill: Ethics, Law Firms and the Downfall of a Wall Street Lawyer*. Ann Arbor, MI: University of Michigan Press

Sarbanes-Oxley Act (2002). Available at: http://www.sec.gov/about/laws/soa2002.pdf. See also: http://www.sec.gov/spotlight/sarbanes-oxley.htm

Sternberg, Elaine (1994) *Just Business*. London: Little, Brown

Stiglitz, Joseph (2004) *The Guardian*. 4 July

US Sentencing Commission (2004) *Amended Organizational Guidelines* 13 (Apr. 30). Available at: http://www.lrn.com/library/whitepapers/ussc_guide_print.pdf

10

Ethics and Entrepreneurship – A Comparative Perspective

Philip A. Dover

'If you gain financial success at the expense of your integrity, you are not a success at all.' John Cullinane, founder of Cullinet Software Inc (Rollag, 2003).

This is a very pertinent time to talk about ethical business behaviour when major US corporations such as Enron, Tyco and Arthur Anderson have managed to set such appallingly low standards. Much has been written about ethical management and the strategies required to implement it. We will start with a fairly simple dichotomy – that managers use one of two strategies when dealing with ethical situations. The first is referred to as compliance strategy (Paine, 1994) and involves conformity with externally imposed standards. It tends to be lawyer driven and relies heavily on auditing, controls and penalties. The Sarbanes-Oxley Act (2002), requiring specific financial and accounting disclosures, is a recent example of such compliance standards and systems. The other approach – and the one we will concentrate on in this chapter – is known as integrity strategy (Paine, 1994) and focuses much more on the ethos of self-governance and self-imposed standards. Its focal points are management leadership, the determination of company values and effective training and communication. This viewpoint can be summarized as follows:

'From the perspective of integrity, the task of ethics management is to define and give life to an organization's guiding values, to create an environment that supports ethically sound behaviour, and to instil a sense of shared accountability among employees.' (Paine, 1994)

This leads us to two interesting and related questions. Do entrepreneurs exhibit more or less ethical behaviour than their management counterparts operating in the ranks of the larger corporations? Similarly, do ethical attitudes and behaviour vary by entrepreneurs in different countries? At this point, it may be useful to relate a personal story. Having lived and worked in the United States for the past 25 years I had become comfortable with the concept of the entrepreneur as hero. From teaching on the faculty of Babson College, ranked as the number one business school in the world for the study of entrepreneurship, the adoption of an entrepreneurial mindset had become part of my professional DNA. Indeed, my colleagues at Babson define this mindset as:

> 'a way of thinking and acting, that is opportunity obsessed, holistic in nature, and leadership balanced for the purpose of value creation'.

In their excellent book, *The Entrepreneurial Mindset*, McGrath and MacMillan (2000) identify the following characteristics of the habitual entrepreneur.

- They passionately seek new opportunities.
- They pursue opportunities with enormous discipline.
- They pursue only the very best opportunities.
- They focus on execution – specifically, adaptive execution.
- They engage the energies of everyone in their domain.

As is intimated by the above classifications, the concept of entrepreneurship provokes a strong, positive affective reaction among the American population. And official statistics bear out the importance of entrepreneurial activity to the US economy. The *2002 Global Entrepreneurship Monitor* (2003) revealed that 10.5 per cent of the adult working population in the United States was involved in the start-up process or in a business less than 24 months old. The United States outranks the rest of the world on key entrepreneurial framework conditions such as financial support, education and training, and culture. On the issue of cultural and social norms, the United States scored significantly higher than the remaining 36 GEM countries (developed or rapidly developing countries). The items that comprised the cultural and social norms measure were the following.

1. National culture is highly supportive of individual success achieved through own personal efforts.

2. The national culture emphasizes sufficiency, autonomy, and personal initiative.
3. The national culture encourages entrepreneurial risk taking.
4. The national culture encourages creativity and innovativeness.
5. The national culture emphasizes the responsibility that the individual (rather than the collective) has in managing their life.

These observations were vividly underlined by a recent experience. On returning to the UK to take up the position of Dean at the University of Buckingham Business School, I decided to give my inaugural address to the academic community and the citizens of Buckingham on the topic of corporate entrepreneurship. After an uneventful lecture, I was somewhat taken aback by the nature and passion of some of the questions. There was a vocal subset of the audience who clearly saw entrepreneurs as a rather untrustworthy and seedy bunch. Terms such as 'fly-by-night', 'price shavers' and 'smoke and mirrors' were bandied about and the analogy of the second-hand car salesman was implicit. Clearly, I should be cautious not to over-interpret such idiosyncratic observations, but it did bring to mind my recent experiences of teaching and consulting in Germany. Retained by DAX level companies, we have worked on a number of assignments designed to inculcate an entrepreneurial mindset in currently bureaucratic and slow-moving organizations. The work has been well received although we have been cautioned to use the term 'entrepreneurship' somewhat sparingly and instead to use such euphemisms as 'innovation management' and 'business development'. From these semantic niceties it can be inferred that, at least in some sectors, the concept of the entrepreneur carries some negative baggage. Certainly, levels of total entrepreneurial activity were considerably lower in the UK and Germany than in the United States, with about 5 per cent of the adult working population in the UK and Germany active in 2002 in nascent or new businesses (*Global Entrepreneurship Monitor*, 2003). Recent research (van Houdt, 2005) suggests that ambivalent attitudes towards entrepreneurship come, in part, from EU citizens preferring to be an employee with a regular fixed income, a stable job and less risk. The level of employment protection is also a contributing factor.

Understanding entrepreneurship

Given these disparate transatlantic views of entrepreneurship, let us return to the question of ethics and the entrepreneur. What evidence do we have that the entrepreneur is more or less ethical than their corporate counterpart? Let's start by establishing, in a broad sense, what entrepreneurship means. In French, the word 'entreprendre' means to undertake[1]. Coined by French economist J B Say in 1800, the term 'entrepreneur' referred to a person who 'shifts economic resources out of an area of lower and into an area of higher productivity and greater yield' (Drucker, 1985). Contemporary theorists, however, have amended this definition to focus primarily on the entrepreneur's role as an innovator. Drucker, for example, considers entrepreneurship to be spotting opportunities and marshalling resources to produce innovation.

Entrepreneurs have much in common with other managers. They are risk takers, but they are not the only businesspersons who take risks, as all economic activity involves uncertainty. They innovate, but all managers have the potential to produce innovations. What distinguishes entrepreneurs – whether in the private or public sector – is that innovation is much more central to their role and they exhibit a greater-than-average willingness to take risks in pursuit of their projects. In Drucker's formulation, they 'search for change, respond to it, and exploit it as an opportunity' (Drucker, 1985).

As important as what entrepreneurial innovation does entail, however, is an understanding of what it does not. For example, it is not simply a new business. Some new businesses merely undertake, in a new location, an enterprise that already exists in hundreds of other places, as when partners open a fast-food franchise. Such small businesspersons are owner–managers, but they have not done much that is new. Nor is entrepreneurship just the process of bringing a new invention to market, as the inventor must employ managerial skills to translate ideas into market opportunities.

Entrepreneurs often seem larger than life. The brilliant loner, the outsider who 'pulls a fast one' on the entrenched powers, the maverick who lives by their wits on the edges of civil society, all tend to stimulate mixed reactions. Some perceive enduring appeal in these traits (mainly American?) while others treat the phenomena with doubt and suspicion (mainly Europeans?). Critics of entrepreneurship complain, 'individualism, profit, selfishness and shrewd calculation become the norm' (Stever, 1988). Among the aspects of the entrepreneurial character that elicit concern are the moral traits of egotism, selfishness, waywardness, domination and opportunism (deLeon, 1996). But are these necessarily undesirable characteristics for the entrepreneurial role?

The role of the entrepreneur

We will examine these entrepreneurial traits shortly but it might be useful to first consider the nature of the entrepreneurial role. While bureaucracy, as manifested in most organizations, is well designed to solve routine problems (where goals are unambiguous and the means to achieve them involve familiar technologies), relatively few problems are now thought to be so simple. In particular, entrepreneurship plays an essential role in addressing a specific type of problem – those where goals are ambiguous or conflicting and where the means to achieve them are unknown or uncertain. Cohen and March (1986) have portrayed the task of the entrepreneur as managing 'organized anarchies'. Again, to quote from deLeon (1996):

> 'In the absence of group consensus on goals, personal vision finds room for expression; in the absence of knowledge about means, the entrepreneur must experiment; in the absence of sufficient budget allocations, s/he must scrounge for resources. To go one step further, in an anarchic problem situation, the entrepreneur's personal vision is a *necessary* precondition for action.'

In this kind of situation the entrepreneur identifies the problem (although they would classify it as an opportunity), then pours energy and resourcefulness into finding a resolution. Such 'inspirational' action coincides with Schumpeter's (1934) view of entrepreneurship as a sort of creative destruction. In his view, the entrepreneur not only exploits change, they create it, generating dynamic disequilibrium by the pursuit of innovation.

For many scholars of management (e.g. Drucker, 1985) it is clear that entrepreneurship is fundamentally a moral enterprise. The entrepreneur is the catalyst who brings together problems and solutions that would otherwise remain unresolved. Moreover, many of the attributes that provoke criticism – their egotism, selfishness, waywardness, opportunism and domineering style – are the extremes of qualities that are functional for their role as innovators. We should, therefore, examine these attributes in a little more depth.

Entrepreneurial traits

Individualism and single-mindedness is often cited as a core trait of entrepreneurs. This has often been portrayed as a selfish pursuit of their own ends rather than an exercise in corporate good behaviour. However, it has been pointed out that 'the effective entrepreneur works on the fringes and not the mainstream of societal ventures,' as opportunities for innovation generally lie on the margins (Fisher, 1983). This means that the entrepreneur has the benefit of constantly observing the operation of the industry and company value chains from the outskirts of the system with the commensurate ability to quickly exploit weaknesses.

Can we then level the charge that the entrepreneur is motivated by self-interest? The answer is almost certainly 'yes'. But this is a specious argument as *everyone* acts in their own self-interest. There is evidence to suggest that, although the entrepreneur's motives are self-centered, social good is often a moderating influence or by-product of their efforts (deLeon, 1996). Market success requires a deep understanding of employee and customer needs that are often underestimated or ignored by the bureaucrat or politician.

The fact that entrepreneurs are often stereotyped as loners or mavericks seems to justify regarding them with the suspicion commonly accorded 'outsiders'. This leads to the view that wayward entrepreneurs are willing to use any means necessary to achieve their own self-interested goals. Lewis (1980) comments on this quality:

> 'This is not to suggest that (they) were criminals in any conventional sense. Rather, they were "rule benders." They were crafty, and they pushed the limits of what was legal and permissible time after time ... '.

And yet entrepreneurs are wayward because they require some freedom to innovate or experiment outside the boundaries of the usual rules and procedures. While innovations, especially significant ones, need space in which to flourish it is important that limits on entrepreneurial autonomy be self-imposed rather than legally mandated.

Stever (1988) considers opportunism to be one of the defining characteristics of an entrepreneur and suggests that the opportunist is fickle, a careless risk-taker and heedless of the welfare of their clients and associates. On the other side, Drucker views an opportunist as someone who takes advantage of an opportunity, a valuable trait in the entrepreneur. The contrast between the two perspectives suggests that there are two types of entrepreneurs, whose different characteristics account for the different moral judgements of those who value entrepreneurship and those who fear it. On the one hand, there are opportunistic entrepreneurs who seize upon trends, hoping to profit from them. They move restlessly from one venue to another, often less concerned about ethical niceties and looking for the 'quick hit'. Drucker (1985) has criticized these entrepreneurs for their deficiencies in organization and discipline and has accused them of being 'still inventors rather than innovators, still speculators rather than entrepreneurs'. On the other hand, we have what deLeon (1996) has called the tenacious entrepreneurs. In contrast, they rely upon purposeful, systematic management and steadfastly pursue their goals despite many obstacles. For tenacious entrepreneurs, who intend to stay in a line of endeavour for the long term and who therefore prefer to develop lasting alliances with suppliers and customers, a reputation for ethical conduct is important. At Babson College we talk a great deal about the paradox of entrepreneurial activity. Part of the time we expect the entrepreneur to be innovative, imaginative and inspirational, as he/she identifies and exploits market opportunities. For the rest of the time, however, we expect the entrepreneur to use the left side of their brain to conduct deliberate market and financial due diligence to reduce the risk of opportunity failure. It is the tenacious entrepreneur that we have in mind when we introduce this operational model.

These arguments would suggest that affective interpretation of the entrepreneur's key traits (e.g. self-interest, opportunism) lies in the eye of the beholder – an interpretation, moreover, that may contain some cultural bias. Further, the concept of entrepreneurship has a range of possible hues from the exploitative opportunist to the person who balances self-interest with longer term social concern. It would be interesting now to turn to a few specific research studies that examine the ethical context of entrepreneurship. It is significant that the literature available on this topic comes predominantly from US sources.

Entrepreneurship/ethics research

In a recent study of 165 entrepreneurs and 128 large-company managers, the entrepreneurs proved more likely to regard certain actions as unethical (Love, 1998, commenting on Hisrich, 1998). Here are some actions described to the survey participants, with the percentage of entrepreneurs who said such action is unethical, followed by the percentage of business managers who made the same judgement:

• using company services for personal purposes: 82 per cent of the entrepreneurs, 72 per cent of the business managers;

- using company time for personal benefit: 81 per cent and 70 per cent;
- taking longer than necessary to do a job: 91 per cent and 78 per cent.

Some care should be taken with these findings as they reflect attitudinal statements rather than actual behaviour although they do suggest an intriguing trend.

A later interpretation of this research study (Bucar and Hisrich, 2001) consistently confirmed that entrepreneurs were more prone to hold ethical attitudes than their managerial counterparts. These findings are in line with the theory of property where we would expect someone to be more ethical in dealing with their own property. This suggests that, through increased ownership, managers in larger companies might be given incentives to have more ethical dealings with their company's assets. Profit-sharing companies can perhaps reduce the possibilities of moral hazard and opportunistic behaviour within the company through some form of managerial ownership. Further research is needed to determine other factors that may influence the ethical conduct of managers and entrepreneurs. Perhaps core values implanted by family members, teachers and mentors early in life determine ethical decision-making. Possibly ethical values and behaviour are influenced by school curricula, including those found in business schools (a recent GEM study showed that, despite increasing awareness of the importance of entrepreneurship education, teaching entrepreneurial values and skills is still not widespread within the EU). It may be that external conditions, such as public versus private ownership, have an overarching role.

In addition to delineating accountability and responsibility in the decision-making process, future research should do more to include entrepreneurial and managerial samples from outside the United States, reflecting differing socio-economic and cultural backgrounds. Much of the research exploring business ethics to date reflects the Judeo-Christian heritage and individualistic orientation of the United States, and misses the normative context where collective dependency is primary. There is, however, one recent study (Bucar *et al.*, 2003) that offers some insight into cross-cultural differences in ethical attitudes of entrepreneurs and managers. Here a comparative analysis was done between entrepreneurs and managers in Slovenia, Russia and the United States.

Cross-cultural findings

The research used social contract theory and stakeholder theory as the framework. Social contract theory posits that countries with institutions of higher quality will have more efficient economic integration. The comparison of some key societal institutions (law, educational system and government) and of the quality of economic interactions led to the hypothesis that the US would rank the highest in ethical standards, followed by Slovenia and then Russia. The hypothesis was confirmed, with Slovenian businesspeople exhibiting a surprisingly high level of business ethics (sometimes higher than American standards) and, in some cases, Russian entrepreneurs revealing a rather discouragingly low level of ethical attitudes. This was particularly true regarding gifts/bribes, insider trading, ignorance of violations of company policy and the law. This may reflect the lack of tradition of market economics and the harsh reality of the country's economic situation where survival might become a priority over ethics.

A comparison between entrepreneurs and managers in Slovenia and the US was based on the assumptions of stakeholder theory. Due to a different type and degree of financial risk assumed by entrepreneurs compared to managers, it was hypothesized that entrepreneurs would be more sensitive to the ethical aspects of decision-making. The hypothesis was not confirmed in Slovenia, where a large proportion of entrepreneurs originated from previous managerial positions. These findings are revealing and should act as a harbinger for further research. It emphasizes the need to identify authentic behavioural norms for different international communities by exposing the relevant existing cultural and social underpinnings. The key to national policy relating to entrepreneurship must then concentrate on the development of formal and informal structures that are conducive to high ethical standards and that facilitate the creation of wealth and the efficient allocation of resources.

Although the development of official structures (e.g. an ethics better business bureau for entrepreneurs and corporate managers that fields complaints but does not act as a judicial body) can discourage or prevent entrepreneurial talent from devoting itself to unproductive courses, at the end of the day the solution must principally lie in formal and informal ethical structures that emerge, over time, within the entrepreneurial firms themselves. This final section extracts some useful findings from a recent study (Morris *et al.*, 2002) that sought to understand the evolution of the ethical climate within entrepreneurial firms as they grew and developed.

Entrepreneurial taxonomy

The *Economist* (2000) notes that small firms pay far less attention than bigger rivals to normalizing ethical issues, while Robinson *et al.* (1991) found that monitoring and enforcement of ethics policies are not very effective in small firms. She also found that more than 60 per cent of larger companies had a written code of ethics and 38 per cent had an ethics training programme, while the numbers for small firms were 33 per cent and 7 per cent, respectively. This lack of formal ethical structures, of course, does not imply a weak ethical climate within the entrepreneurial venture. Informal systems dominate in the looser, less hierarchical environment found in the start-up or small firm. Such informal activities would include genuine top manager concerns about ethics, ethics as a topic of conversation among employees, and stories of ethical behaviour communicated within the firm. Indeed, it was found that four distinct clusters of firms emerged based on their formal and informal ethical structures. Morris *et al.* (2002) referred to them as superlatives, core proponents, pain and gain, and deficients.

At one end of the ethical spectrum are the superlatives. These firms clearly place a priority on ethics, their efforts encompassing both formal and informal mechanisms. The fact that one in five firms falls into this category appears reassuring. At the other end of the continuum one finds the deficients: firms that lag behind others in almost every area of formal and informal ethical structures. While these firms are not inherently unethical in their behaviour, motivating the ethical climate is apparently not viewed as a high managerial imperative. The fact that such firms represent almost half the firms sampled gives some pause to the earlier postulate that small firms have higher ethical standards. Between these two endpoints are the core proponents and the pain and gain firms. Core proponents pursue the basic and more formal ethical elements. It appears they do the more symbolic things, such as mentioning ethics in their mission statement and having a code of conduct. However, activities that are more interventionist and hands-on are not pursued. The pain and gain is rather a small group who do not do the symbolic things such as value statements. Yet they are reinforcers, employing the more activist types of behaviour. For example, they tend to talk to employees about ethical issues on an ongoing basis.

The authors explored a number of possible variables that might explain these differences in the ethical behaviour of entrepreneurs. Need for achievement was negatively associated with the tendency to ignore the ethical factors, suggesting that accomplishments such as innovation and growth need not come at the expense of ethics. There were also some interesting links between the life cycle development of the firm and ethical practices. It appears that superlatives will support lots of ethical initiatives from the early days of the firm onwards, while deficients resist doing so, regardless of their stage of development. With regard to the characteristics of the business itself, 'lifestyle' types of ventures[2] are not as focused on ethical structures. Consequently, the tendency to be more labour intensive, sell services and to have a strategic focus less centred on growth was all associated with being in the deficients cluster. The ethical nature of an entrepreneurial way of life was further reinforced by the finding that entrepreneurs holding more equity in their own firms were more likely to engage in multiple initiatives to encourage ethical behaviour.

These findings imply that we may be oversimplifying when we generalize about entrepreneurial firms being more or less ethical. There appear to be identifiable categories of firms with significant differences in their approach to the management of ethics. We would do well to learn more about the characteristics that stimulate such variance. Examples that may warrant future attention include demographics (e.g. age, sex, religion), additional characteristics of the firm (e.g. cost and margin structures) and the external environment in which the firm operates (e.g. pace of technological change, level of competitive intensity). And, of course, further comparative analysis by country and culture holds much potential.

Summary

This brief review of the literature (supported by some unscientific personal observations) has failed to categorically answer the two initial questions: Do entrepreneurs exhibit more or less ethical behaviour than their management counterparts operating in the ranks of the larger corporations? Do ethical attitudes vary by entrepreneurs in different countries? As is so often the case with this type of research, the answer emerges as 'it depends'. Not surprisingly, there is no 'one-size-fits-all' designation for entrepreneurs, leading to considerable difference in ethical attitudes and behaviour across the category. There are, however, some important indicators that correlate strongly with ethical actions, such as need for achievement and level of equity involvement. Note that these factors are often absent in the corporate or public sector employee, providing little stimulus for the creation of an ethical environment.

Insufficient evidence is available to draw strong conclusions on any possible variance in ethical approaches by entrepreneurs from different countries. It can be speculated, however, that the public view of entrepreneurial ethics is greatly coloured by general attitudes towards the role of the entrepreneur in society. Considerable ambivalence remains in Europe towards the entrepreneur, where adversity to risk and the stigma of failure remain major deterrents to entrepreneurial activity. At the very least, entrepreneurship education should be greatly extended in Europe to provide wider teaching of entrepreneurial values and skills, including guidance on ethical issues.

Notes

1   Ideas for this section have been adapted from an excellent article by Linda deLeon (1996).
2   Entrepreneurs are often categorized as either 'lifestyle' or 'growth'. The 'lifestyle' entrepreneur is often looking to exit the corporate rat race, pursue a long-held personal initiative but not to grow much beyond a one or two person business.

References

Bucar, B, Glas, M and Hisrich, R D (2003) Ethics and entrepreneurs: an international comparative study. *Journal of Business Venturing* **18** 261–281
Bucar, B and Hisrich, R D (2001) Ethics of business managers vs entrepreneurs. *Journal of Developmental Entrepreneurship* **6**:1 59–82
Cohen, M D and March, J G (1986) *Leadership and Ambiguity* 2nd edn. Boston, MA: Harvard Business School Press
DeLeon, L (1996) Ethics and entrepreneurship. *Policy Studies Journal* **24**:3 495–510
Drucker, P (1985) *Innovation and Entrepreneurship*. New York: Harper & Row The *Economist* (2000) Doing well by doing good. 22 Apr.
Fisher, F (1983). The new entrepreneurs. In: Moore, B H (ed) *The Entrepreneur in Local Government*. Washington, DC: International City Management Association, pp 9–14
Global Entrepreneurship Monitor, 2002 Executive Report (2003) Office of Publications, Babson College
Hisrich, R D (1998) *Ethics of Business Managers vs. Entrepreneurs*. Washington, DC: Research Institute of Small and Emerging Business (RISEbusiness)
Hisrich, R D and Peters, M P (1998) *Entrepreneurship*. Boston, MA: McGraw-Hill
van Houdt, F (2005) Entrepreneurial challenges and policy responses in the EU, presentation at the launch of Global Entrepreneurship Monitor, London,

20 January 2005. Brussels: European Commission. Available at: http://www. gemconsortium.org/document.asp?id=374

Lewis, E (1980) *Public Entrepreneurship*. Bloomington, IN: Indiana University Press

Love, T (1998) Taking the ethical temperature of entrepreneurs and managers. *Nation's Business* 86:9 12

McGrath, R G and MacMillan, I (2000) *The Entrepreneurial Mindset*. Boston, MA: Harvard Business School Press

Morris, M H, Schindehutte, M, Walton, J and Allen, J (2002) The ethical context of entrepreneurship: proposing and testing a developmental framework. *Journal of Business Ethics* 40: 331–361

Paine, L S (1994) Managing for organizational integrity. *Harvard Business Review* Mar.–Apr.

Robinson, P B, Stimpson, D V, Huefner, J C and Hunt, H K (1991) An attitude approach to the prediction of entrepreneurship. *Entrepreneurship Theory and Practice* 15:3 13–31

Rollag, K (2003) Fast organizational growth: ten insights from successful managers. *Babson Insight* (an e-journal published for selected clients)

Sarbanes-Oxley Act (2002). Available at: http://www.sec.gov/about/laws/soa2002. pdf. See also: http://www.sec.gov/spotlight/sarbanes-oxley.htm

Schumpeter, J. (1934) *The Theory of Economic Development*. Cambridge, MA: Harvard University Press

Stever, J A (1988) *The End of Public Administration*. Dobbs Ferry, NY: Transnational Publishers

11

Ethics and Management Challenges

Philippa Foster Back

Introduction

The 21st century organization faces wider scrutiny than its 20th century counterpart. Scrutiny is from not only the shareholders as to whether or not the company is making a profit and paying a dividend, but from others who are interested in how the company's profits are being made. They question whether the company is acting responsibly and behaving ethically in providing the goods and services that it does.

The purpose of this chapter is to:

- identify the management challenges;
- suggest mechanisms and processes to meet the challenges;
- identify the issues underlying the challenges;
- comment on whether the challenges are being met.

The management challenges

There are three main challenges facing management today:

- long-term growth versus competitive pressures;
- producing products and services responsibly;
- building and keeping a good reputation.

Competitive pressures

This challenge is that of a company's management seeking to grow and maintain long-term growth against the backdrop of competitive global markets. The challenge becomes acute when management seek to do their business ethically knowing they may lose business to others who, in the company's view, are prepared to cut corners or behave unethically. Such instances highlight the problem, as interpreted by some people, that doing business ethically can 'cost' a company in terms of lost revenues, contracts and work.

Two companies that walked away (*Ethical Performance*, 2003)

Kuoni – Europe's sixth-largest travel company – has announced it will stop offering holidays in Burma at the end of 2003.

The company has been on a 'dirty list' of firms in the country published by the Burma Campaign UK.

Kuoni managing director Sue Biggs said: 'We look forward to returning to Burma once the British public demands it back, which we expect to happen as soon as democracy is restored.'

US retail group Saks and French clothing retailer Bonmarché also recently said they will not source from Burma.

Competitive pressures abound in all markets, though there is a perception in the business community and public arena that there are certain countries where such pressures are greater. This is primarily due to the expectation that bribery and corruption are rife. Bribery and corruption is a difficult issue for companies to face up to.

Transparency International publishes annually a Corruption Perceptions Index which in 2003 ranked 133 countries in terms of the degree to which corruption is perceived to exist among public officials and politicians (Transparency International, 2003). It is a composite index, drawing on 17 different polls and surveys from 13 independent institutions carried out among business people and country analysts, including surveys of residents, both local and expatriate. The top and bottom countries perceived to be the least and most corrupt, respectively, in 2003, are as shown in Table 11.1.

Many companies will try to take a stand against corruption knowing it to be illegal let alone unethical but it can be difficult to walk away from a contract knowing the knock-on effect on the rest of the business by not winning that particular contract. This is especially difficult for medium-sized companies new to bidding for overseas contracts. Large companies may be able to 'afford' their refusal to be involved

Table 11.1 Least and most corrupt countries (from Transparency International, 2003)

Top	Bottom
Finland	Myanmar (Burma)
Iceland	Paraguay
Denmark	Haiti
New Zealand	Nigeria
Singapore	Bangladesh

in corruption and certainly in some countries companies in the same sector are clubbing together and refusing to pay bribes. There is also an initiative called 'publish what you pay' whereby companies are openly disclosing amounts paid to foreign governments for licences.

The *Publish What You Pay* campaign (PWYP) and EITI, the UK Government's Extractive Industries Transparency Initiative

PWYP is a campaign backed by more than 70 NGOs, including Transparency International (Publish What You Pay, 2002). It calls for the mandatory disclosure by natural resource extraction businesses of all payments they make to national governments in the countries where they operate. EITI is a UK government initiative aiming to bring governments together to address this transparency issue, along with companies and civil society (Extractive Industries Transparency Initiative, 2002). It recognizes the seriousness of the problem but without, at this stage, recommending a solution and allowing for, if not actually favouring, a voluntary process.

An example of this was BP in Angola in 2002 where the company published how much it paid for an operating licence in that country (BP, 2002, p 24).

Competitive pressures can lead companies to skimp on quality, perhaps using sub-standard materials or employing cheap labour through gang masters to do the work at less than the statutory minimum wage, or to use child labour. Such business practices may help the company to reach its short-term financial goals but in the main such practices are not sustainable in the long-term. This has been highlighted in recent years as the wider public have become interested in how goods and services are supplied. Companies have had to review their supply chains and sometimes had to drop, or change, suppliers as the potential loss of reputation would be severe to the company if malpractice was to be found in its supply chain. Any such malpractice could be exploited by pressure groups and/or the media. This adds to the management challenge as the world is now a 'global village' in this respect.

Producing products and services responsibly

Companies are under pressure in today's business environment to be responsible in how they conduct their business. These pressures come from many quarters, some of which are listed in the following diagram.

Each 'pressure', each grouping or special interest group, as shown in Figure 11.1, will have valid concerns as to how the company is undertaking its business. The management challenge is to manage them

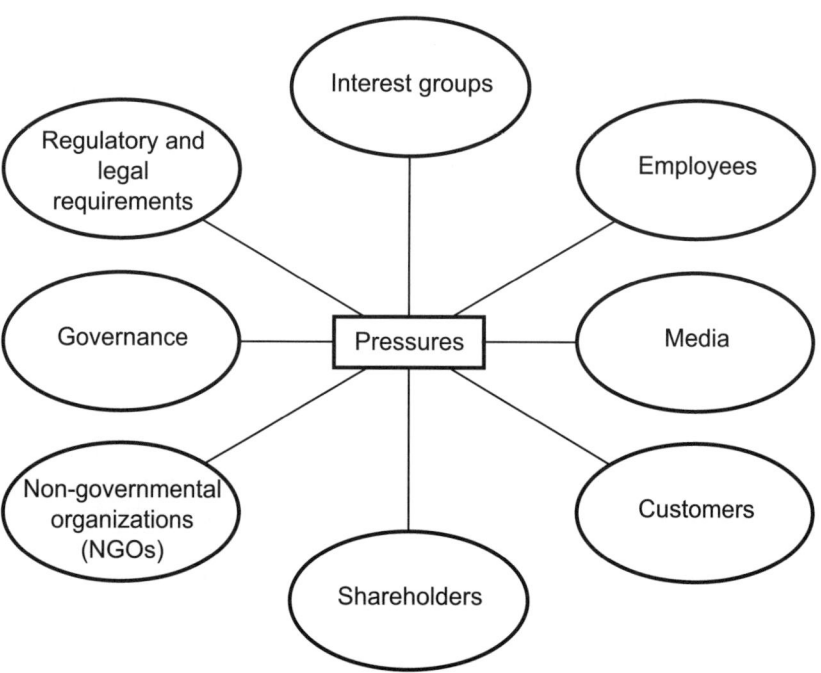

Figure 11.1 Pressures on companies

in a coherent way and still create profits in the business in order to pay dividends to the shareholders. In this respect it falls chiefly to the large institutional investors, who manage insurance and pension funds, to view critically how companies create their wealth, how they produce their goods and services and how they behave. At present it is still a minority of institutional investors who are in this category referred to as 'socially responsible investors', or the SRI community. The number is growing as there is a recognition that companies who do undertake their business responsibly do tend to be more financially successful over the longer term.

In 2003 the Institute of Business Ethics published *Does Business Ethics Pay?* (Webley and Moore, 2003). In the study, having demonstrated that having a code of business ethics could be used as a proxy for company behaviour, companies with codes outperformed those without codes clearly in three financial performance measures (economic value added, market value added and *P/E* ratios) over a five year period. In the fourth financial measure (return on capital employed) there was a positive change during the study period (see Figures 11.2–11.5). The Institute concluded that having a code was an indicator of a better managed company.

Active fulfilment of corporate responsibility is the subject of current research by the IBE. Hearsay evidence from a number of companies implies that better-managed businesses, including those which actively pursue a corporate responsibility agenda, are more able to recruit talented staff and to retain existing staff and that they have a lower cost of capital and insurance. Preliminary evidence supports this view.

In 2004 Deutsche Bank analysts (Cornelius, 2004) undertook research based on a system of quantifying risk associated with different company attitudes to corporate governance. They took 50 attributes of corporate governance, most of which were factual and objective, and scored the companies accordingly. The results were matched against the companies' share performance. They found that shares in companies with high corporate governance scores outperformed by 25 per cent those companies with low scores.

Building and keeping a good reputation

Benjamin Franklin once said 'Glass, china and reputations are easily cracked and never well mended' (Franklin, 1750). It is a constant challenge to management to maintain a company's good reputation. Without it, the company will lose customers, its ability to raise finance

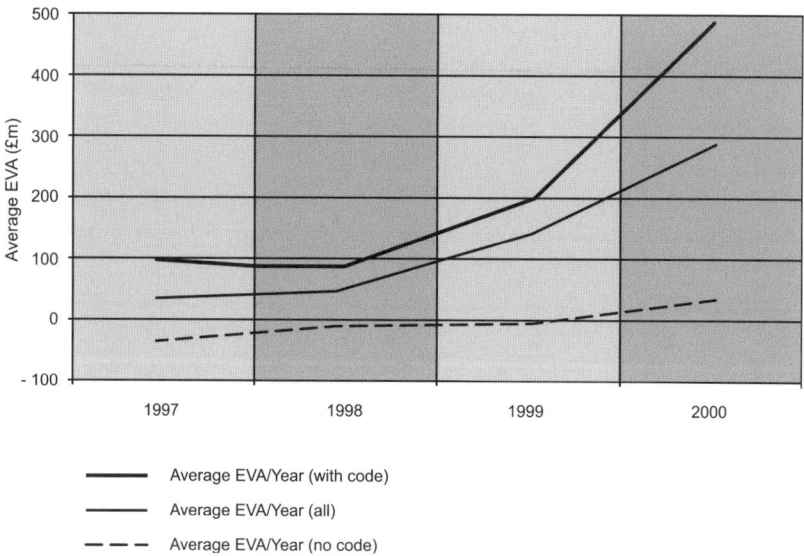

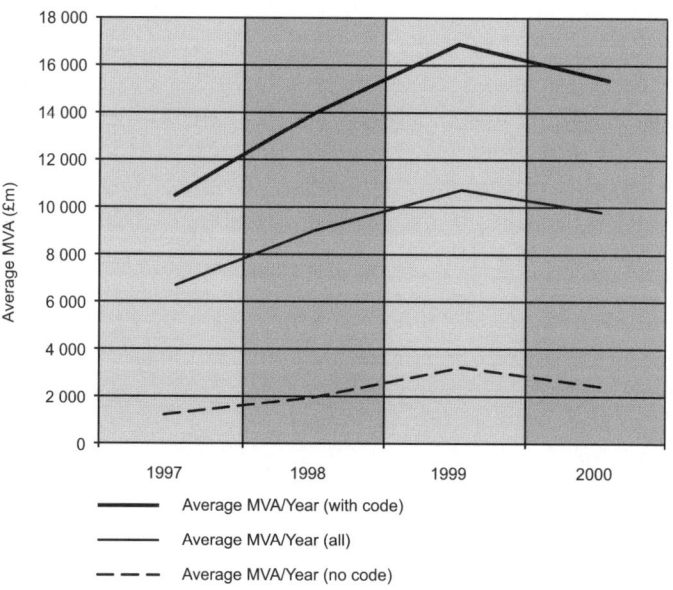

(from Webley and Moore, 2003)

Figure 11.2 Financial performance of companies with and without a code of business ethics

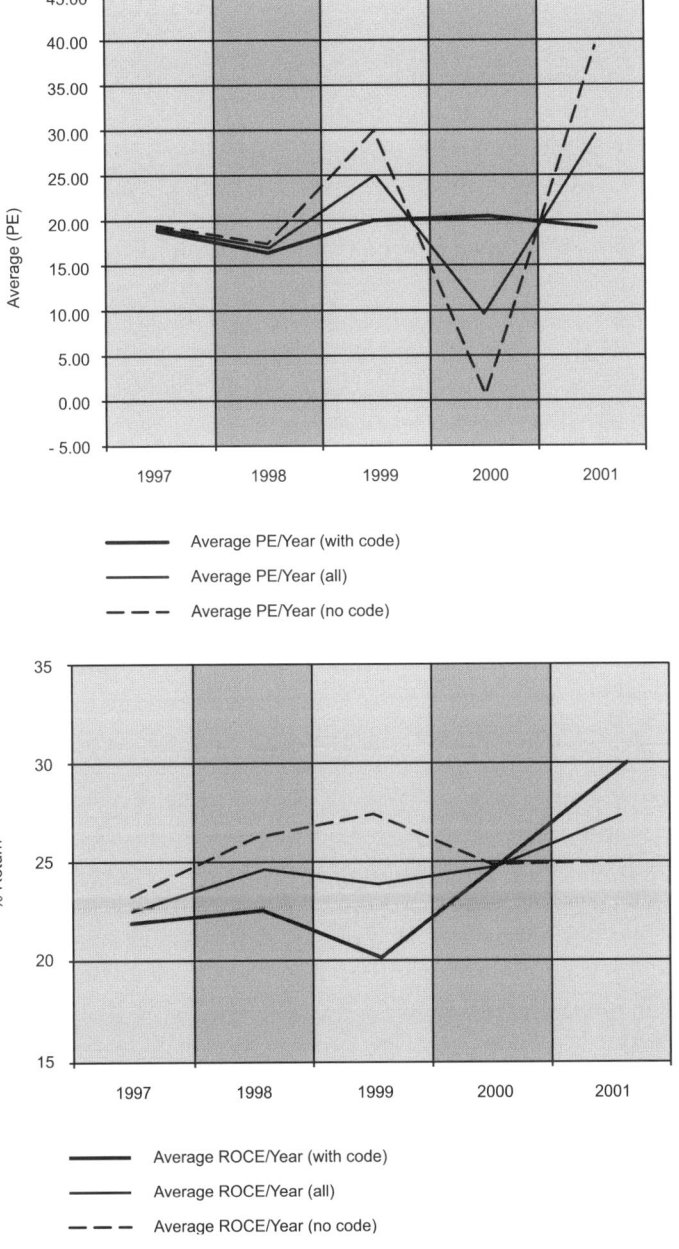

(from Webley and Moore, 2003)

Figure 11.2 Financial performance of companies with and without a code of business ethics (continued)

and perhaps its 'licence to operate' from society. The result might be bankruptcy at one extreme or to be taken over by another company at the other extreme.

Much has been written in recent years about how companies should protect their reputations and how to manage or mitigate the risk of losing their reputation. This has been the result of the frequently cited examples of corporate misbehaviour in recent years. In the UK there was Maxwell, Polly Peck, Barings, BA; in the US there was Enron, WorldCom and Tyco; in Europe there was Ahold, Parmalat, and in the Far East there was Daewoo and Mitsubishi Motors. There have been many reported cases too of companies or individuals within companies behaving with double standards, notably the investment bankers in New York who talked up their own book in order to make money for their firms and bonuses for themselves. In nearly all occasions of corporate misbehaviour, the misapplication or ignoring of ethical values has been at the root. There have been many instances of unfair behaviour, such as the misuse of privileged information or the exercise of influence over vulnerable customers and clients, and instances of blatant dishonesty and lack of due care or responsibility to others. The most obvious abuse of ethical values has been greed, both at the corporate level, to be 'number one' and, at the personal level, to further personal wealth and status.

These examples and their consequent 'hits' to the reputation of the companies and individuals concerned have caused many businesses to reflect on their practices and how they may be perceived. However, there are still many instances when outsiders, usually through the media, will question the wisdom of certain behaviours such as a seemingly over-generous remuneration package to a chief executive or a misguided sales campaign. It is likely that greater awareness of the fragility of reputation today will curb some of the excesses of the recent past as directors look to their own reputations as well. But it is hoped that obvious excesses may be curbed by the greater transparency demanded of corporate governance by the expectations of the market. Sadly a determined fraudster or bully is often difficult to deal with, but this does not mean that an effort to deter them should not be made.

Much of reputation risk management has to do with how the company, the industry sector, business or commerce *per se* is viewed or perceived to behave by the public. MORI regularly undertakes opinion polls on behalf of individual companies and corporate sectors to gauge public opinion in this area. One annual poll is that done by MORI for the British Medical Association which looks at the question 'who would you trust to tell you the truth?', asking the general public to rank a number of professions and job roles (MORI, 2004). Consistently over the 21 years that this poll has run, business leaders have polled about a 30 per cent trust rating, against doctors at 90 per cent and politicians and journalists at 20 per cent (see Figure 11.3).

To build a strong reputation a company needs to engender trust in its products and services, for quality, price and reliability. It is this that managers seek to achieve in managing this challenge.

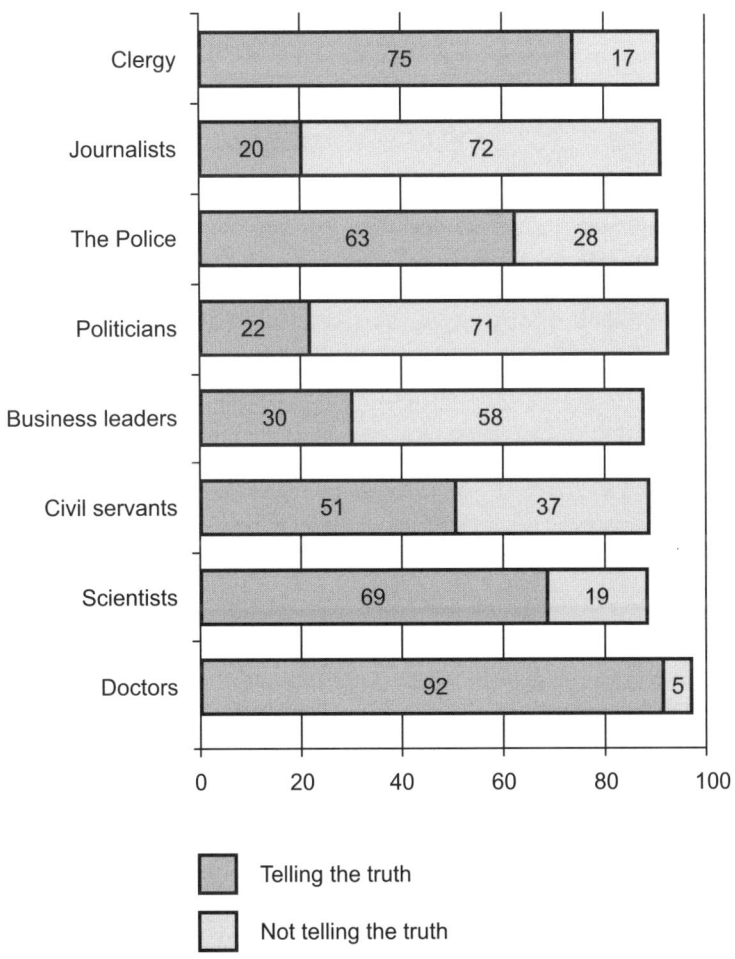

Figure 11.3 Trust ratings, 2004. Question: Who would you generally trust . . . to tell the truth, or not? Base: c. 2,000 adults across Britain, March 2004 by MORI

Who are the players in meeting these challenges?

There are many players in the running of a company who are responsible for meeting the management challenges. At the top there are those in the boardroom, the directors, who collectively are accountable to the company's shareholders for running the company. The board sets the strategic direction and policies by which the company will be run. Below the board in the company hierarchy are senior managers, with managers and teams reporting to them. They are primarily responsible for implementing the strategy laid down by the board, and adhering to company policies. Finally at the 'coal face' are the employees who interact with suppliers and customers and usually have to face difficult business decisions in carrying out instructions given to them by their managers.

Taking each group in turn, how do they cope, react or deal with the three challenges identified?

The board usually comprises the chairman, chief executive officer (or managing director), chief financial officer (or finance director), executive and non-executive directors. Collectively they set the tone for the organization as to how it will react to challenges, such as competitive pressures, doing business responsibly and managing the reputation of the company.

In reality their responsibilities often tend to be split between the chairman who guards the reputation of the company, the chief executive who manages competitive pressures and the non-executives who look at whether the business is being conducted responsibly through their oversight of the audit and control processes within the company. This is an arbitrary distinction to make the point, as in law they are collectively responsible.

From time to time a board may face a dilemma. An example could be one of setting a company policy about the marketing and selling of its products in Libya.

Widget Autos is seeking to expand its market presence in Libya. It is bidding for a contract to sell 100 vehicles to a state enterprise. It is potentially a big order for the company but the board is concerned about the potential pitfalls of doing business in Libya. The country was ranked 118 on Transparency International's *Corruption Perception Index* in 2003, and they will need to appoint a local agent. The board concludes they should bid but will refuse to pay any form of bribe to win the contract, though they recognize this could put them at a competitive disadvantage.

In this instance the board has recognized the potential issue of bribery, and decided they will not pay a bribe, knowing it to be illegal and fearing a loss of reputation.

At the next level, of senior managers and their teams, they are charged with implementing the strategy and policies. Continuing the dilemma faced by the board, at this level it is often interpreted slightly differently:

John, country sales manager for Libya, is told the board has given the go-ahead to bid, using an agent, for the vehicle contract. He is really pleased. It is a big deal and could help him to raise his profile in the company, and earn a big bonus too. He knows just the agent to use. He notes the board's decision not to pay a bribe to get the contract but John is realistic about the competition. He reckons it will be alright in the end.

Often at senior management level the drivers to undertake business are different. They may be personal ones, such as achieving targets and so meeting bonus criteria, or gaining status within the company. Such drivers can cause individuals to interpret policies differently from what was intended.

At the lower level are the individual employees in the field who have to transfer the policy or instruction into actual reality. They too may be driven by personal ambitions.

Frank, local salesman in Libya, has lived there for five years and cultivated many contacts in the country. These are in the ministry, local government, police force and with many potential agents. He feels by spreading his contact base he will be best placed in bidding for the vehicle contract. He talks to Ali, an agent he has worked with before. Ali explains the contract is big so he will be asked whether the bidder will make a welfare contribution as well to help road accident victims. Frank is unsure whether to say yes or no – is it a bribe? If he says no he knows the competitor will say yes and he'll lose the deal.

This is an example of the ultimate challenge as the three 21st century challenges come together: competitive pressure, doing business responsibly and maintaining the company's reputation.

How do companies meet such challenges?

The best way to meet challenges and to ensure that they are dealt with appropriately is through setting the tone and creating a culture in the company where people naturally do the right thing when faced with dilemmas. Companies need to be open and transparent in meeting business challenges. Primarily though, it is about the tone set from the top and the leadership example of the senior team.

If the leadership of a company is clear in how it wishes business in the company to be transacted, and it leads by example, it is more likely to achieve that objective.

There is a process, which is introducing a code of business ethics, that leaders can follow to engender a culture of 'doing the right thing because it is the right thing to do'. This process can begin as a top-down exercise but to have the greatest support it will need to combine with a bottom-up approach too. This will get employees to buy-in to the concepts the leader is trying to instil. The process is therefore as follows.

1. Identify core values
    Ensure that your company has established core values such as openness, integrity, fairness and respect by which business will be undertaken. If they do not exist, identifying them must be the first step.
2. Get endorsement from the chairman and the board
    Corporate values and ethics set the tone for effective governance. The board must be enthusiastic not only about having such a policy but also about receiving regular reports on its operation.
3. Find out what bothers people
    Merely endorsing a standard code or copying that of another company will not suffice. It is important to find out the topics on which the company's own employees require guidance.
4. Pick a well-tested model
    Use a framework which addresses issues as they affect different constituents or stakeholders of the company.
5. Try it out first
    The code needs piloting, perhaps with a sample of employees drawn from all levels and different locations.
6. Produce a company code of business ethics
    The code will be individual to the company and may incorporate some existing policies, for example on giving and receiving gifts or the private use of company assets. Include guidance on how to use the code and its implementation in the company.

7. Issue the code and make it known

   The code should be distributed in booklet form or included in a staff manual or on company websites. Send the code to all suppliers and others as well. State publicly that the company has a code and an implementation programme that covers the whole company. Put the code on your website and send it to joint-venture and other business partners.

8. Make it work

   The policy needs to be endorsed and launched by the CEO and cascaded down to all levels and locations. Practical examples of the code in action should then be introduced into all company internal (and external) training programmes as well as induction courses. Managers should sign off on the code regularly and a review mechanism should be established.

Setting up a code is just a first step in giving guidance to staff about how they should behave when facing ethical dilemmas. Employees need to understand that the company is serious about the purpose of the code. It is a matter of leadership to ensure that this is made clear. Leadership can make this clear through two mechanisms primarily. The first is to ensure that employees can raise concerns about issues they may come across with confidence that they will be taken seriously. Also they need to have confidence that there will not be any retaliation or retribution against them for having done so. This is very important.

People raising concerns are often called 'whistleblowers', which is not a helpful term as in the UK it has connotations of telling on someone in open forum, when really the company wants to encourage individuals to 'speak up', anonymously if they wish, about concerns they may have. Such concerns may be about what they have seen others do or say, or about how they should deal with a business dilemma. In an open culture people will come forward, particularly if they are given feedback and can see their concerns are taken seriously.

A second mechanism is through the company's remuneration policies. Companies should have regard to how people do their jobs, not just that they achieve goals or targets set them. This should come through in the individual's appraisals and reviews.

There is a series of further actions that a leader can instigate in order to support the ethics programme and embed the message:

1. training;
2. introduce speak-up/help lines;

3. performance appraisal;
4. remuneration policies;
5. disciplinary policies;
6. monitoring;
7. auditing and assurance;
8. reporting.

These actions will help to bring the ethics programme alive and make it meaningful for all employees. They begin with internal processes and end with the external one of reporting to those interested outside the company, notably shareholders, about how the company is undertaking its business. This information is often contained in a company's social or corporate responsibility report. However, from 2005 companies will reflect on such issues in their operating and financial review (OFR) sections in their annual report and accounts. The OFR regulations were published in November 2004 (Operating and Financial Review, 2004). They require a company to review its performance in a wider context and to look forward by assessing trends and issues that may affect its future performance. These, of course, need to be grounded in the company's 'statement of business, objectives and strategies. These should be driven by the underlying purpose and values of the business, including its ethical stance.' There is a new requirement as of 1 April 2005 to report on matters relating to a company's social and environmental performance. As the OFR will be the directors' view of the relevant and significant issues that may be of interest to shareholders, in theory they can decide that social and environmental factors are not material to the company. In such a case, they would need to be explicit about this.

The regulations also make clear that other information should be included in the OFR 'to the extent necessary', meaning that it is for the directors to decide but that the information should include details on employees, environmental matters, social and community issues and key stakeholders 'which are essential to the business'. It is likely that the directors will take a risk-based approach as to what to include in or exclude, focussing perhaps on reputation risk as being a key driver – backed by the corporate values of trust and integrity.

What are the issues underlying the three management challenges?

The issue of bribery and corruption has already been mentioned but it is a key one for businesses. There are many other ethical issues facing companies today. These include the issues of harassment, bullying and discrimination in the workplace; issues of appropriateness of gifts and entertainment with clients and customers; issues of conflicts of interest; issues of outsourcing or offshoring operations; issues of labour practices in the supply chain; issues of antitrust or tax avoidance; and issues of excessive remuneration and corporate greed. Each of these issues can raise dilemmas for employees as they have to deal with them. This is why explicit guidance in the form of a code of business ethics is important to a company in helping their employees deal with these matters. If there is no guidance each employee could potentially choose a different option or way to deal with the dilemma. That inconsistency could easily lead to a loss of the company's reputation or trust and ultimately a loss of revenue if the problem were severe.

The market reaction to companies facing trust issues, particularly those based around remuneration or corporate failure due to greed and ambition in the boardroom, has been to introduce corporate governance procedures. During 2002–4, 28 countries published new governance codes of best practice. In the US this has taken the form of the Sarbanes-Oxley Act (2002). In the UK during 2003 there were two governance reports: the *Review of the Role and Effectiveness of Non-Executive Directors* by Derek Higgs (Higgs, 2003) and the *Guidance on Audit Committees* by Sir Robert Smith (Smith *et al.*, 2003); their findings were collated into a revised version of the combined code, which was published in July 2003 (Financial Reporting Council, 2003).

The company reaction to the ethical issues they face is to try to be more open and to monitor, report and audit their activities more closely. This has led to increasing levels of internal training and attempts to embed the corporate message of 'this is how we do business round here'.

Are the management challenges being met?

It is always a valid question to ask whether or not companies are meeting their management challenges. Most often the public, through institutional investors, will only look at the financial consequences of how companies are doing their business in assessing whether or not the challenges are being met. Nowadays a review of company performance has to be wider than just the company's financial results alone. Companies do have a role to play in society. They have to behave responsibly in order to maintain their 'licence to operate' and to play their role in the communities in which they operate. This is because a company is made up of the individuals that work for it and they, in the main, want to work in a pleasant, happy environment and for an entity that cares, not only for individual employees, but for the wider community too. Creating trust is extremely difficult in an environment of short-term demands from the financial markets which expect companies to grow and develop continuously. A balance has to be sought, with investors recognizing the long-term gain for those companies which do undertake their business ethically. Short-term gain can lead to long-term pain if corners are cut constantly and unethical behaviour comes to light, leading to a hit to a company's reputation and consequent financial loss. A company that ignores these issues is taking a short term view and is unlikely to survive into the 22nd century.

References

BP (2002) *BP Environment and Social Report 2002.* London: BP

Cornelius, P (2004) *Corporate Practices and National Governance Systems: What do Country Rankings Tell Us?* Deutsche Bank Research, Research Notes Working Paper Series no. 16. Frankfurt am Main: Deutsche Bank Research

Ethical Performance (2003) Volume 5, issue 2, June, p 5

Extractive Industries Transparency Initiative (2002) Available at: http://www2.dfid. gov.uk/news/files/extractiveindustries.asp

Financial Reporting Council (2003) *The Combined Code on Corporate Governance.* Available at: http://www.asb.org.uk/documents/pagemanager/frc/ combinedcodefinal.pdf

Franklin, Benjamin (1750) *Poor Richard's Almanack*

Higgs, D (2003) *Review of the Role and Effectiveness of Non-Executive Directors.* DTI, London: The Stationery Office. Available at: http://www.dti.gov.uk/cld/ non_exec_review

MORI (2004) Available at: http://www.mori.com/polls/trends/trust.shtml

The Operating and Financial Review Practical Guidance for Directors (2004) London: DTI. Available at: http:// www.dti.gov.uk/cld/financialreview.htm

Publish What You Pay (2002) Available at: http://www.publishwhatyoupay.org/ english/

Sarbanes-Oxley Act (2002). Available at: http://www.sec.gov/about/laws/soa2002. pdf. See also: http://www.sec.gov/spotlight/sarbanes-oxley.htm

Smith, R *et al.* (2003) *Audit Committees – Combined Code Guidance* London: Financial Reporting Council. Available at: http://www.icaew.co.uk

Transparency International (2003) *Corruption Perceptions Index.* Available at: http://www.transparency.org.uk/pb-003.pdf

Webley, Simon and Moore, Elise (2003) *Does Business Ethics Pay?* London: Institute of Business Ethics

12

Shaping Tomorrow's Managers – How can Business Schools Tackle the Teaching of Responsible Business Behaviour?

Patricia Hind

A plethora of headline corporate scandals in recent years, such as Enron, WorldCom, ImClone, Parmalat and others, have put the spotlight on the question of managerial ethics. The business response to such events has been to assume that we must immediately 'fix' the problem. The 'fixes' have tended to be high level responses from companies, such as adopting codes of ethics, developing corporate social responsibility (CSR) strategies and policies, and/or offering 'transparent' reporting and have been seen as being delivered as an answer to the reaction by civil society against perceived unethical behaviour by organizations.

These responses have, of course, been taking place against a backdrop of social developments which have also been fuelling the smouldering CSR fire, such as the increasing power of the environmental and human rights movements, along with the growth of the concept of 'sustainable development' – which is an effort to integrate environmental and economic development values.

Companies are facing increasing pressures from government and customers to account for the impact of their operations, and they are recognizing that doing so is more than simply risk management. Operating responsibly offers opportunities for building competitive advantage, creating shareholder value, business development, innovative product development and best practice management.

As a result, what was once an interesting theoretical debate, worthy of passing executive interest, is fast becoming a compelling business concern and therefore an issue that must be addressed by business schools whose objective is to shape and inform the thinking of future business leaders.

Current attitudes in business schools

Examination of the curriculum of many business schools often reveals gaps in an understanding of the ethical dimensions of business and management despite having been acknowledged as an academic discipline in 1974 when the first national conference on business ethics was held at the University of Kansas. The USA is considerably ahead of Europe in a widespread acceptance of business ethics as a taught discipline in business schools and indeed the AACSB, the accrediting body of American business schools, insists that business ethics in some form must form part of all curricula. Further support comes from federal government legislation which encourages companies to actively engage in ethics training. However, the European picture is somewhat different. In 1999 a survey of British management schools conducted by the Institute of British Ethics indicated that, whilst the teaching of business ethics was increasing in many institutions, this was largely, if not solely, as a result of the personal interest of a minority of faculty and was not perceived as having institutional support. The report concluded that only a few professional institutions included ethics teaching in management development programmes, and even those who had did not include it in all programmes:

> 'Most have yet to consider it seriously and many do not regard it as an issue which needs addressing in a professional course syllabi'. (Cummins, 1999)

Another reason for this poor integration of ethical issues into business teaching has been the assumption that there is a moralistic stance to the teaching of 'ethics' as a discipline that involves absolute criteria of right and wrong. It has been taken for granted that such a framework does not allow for the contingencies of real managerial life, and has therefore been dismissed as irrelevant to the business of running organizations effectively. Schools and institutions that place emphasis on the practical application of knowledge in the real world of business, as opposed to the 'ivory tower' academic pursuit of knowledge, have argued that business ethicists have not provided the practical help and assistance with the practice of management which warrants inclusion into their programmes. The emphasis in many business schools on managing for corporate survival and growth takes the stance that the managerial requirements of delivering shareholder value whilst providing motivating and satisfying work for employees and meeting the needs of customers are all simply the *means* of managerial work, the purpose of which is to take the organization forward, rather than the *ends*. This position avoids the question of the moral rightness or wrongness of management and assumes that the work of a manager or leader is morally neutral.

An opposing reason for omitting ethical issues from syllabi is offered by the other end of the management education spectrum, and concerns the lack of a coherent body of knowledge, based firmly in empirical research, which would make the teaching of the discipline comparable with, for example, marketing, strategic management or organizational behaviour. It has been argued (Robertson, 1993; Cowton, 1998) that much research in the field is based on subjective self-report surveys designed to measure individual attitudes on ethical issues rather than actual managerial behaviours. As well as expressing concern about the validity and reliability of the instruments used, authors are worried that the resulting body of knowledge shows a fundamental 'lack of theory development' which prevents the more august academic institutions from giving the subject prominence in their courses. Indeed, it is fair to say that within the business and management academic community, an interest in issues of social responsibility and sustainability has often been regarded as 'career limiting' in that the research output from the area rarely finds its way into the most respected of peer reviewed journals and therefore is of no help in the vital research assessment exercise, which contributes a great deal to determining the level of public funding received by British universities.

It can be concluded that the needs of business have not yet been addressed by offerings under the 'business ethics' umbrella and even, perhaps, that this gap in business schools syllabi is felt to be perfectly acceptable, the current interest in ethical and socially responsible issues being simply a fad that business schools can comfortably ignore. However, the alternative view is more compelling on two fronts. The first is the role of business schools in the personal development of individuals and the second is their contribution to developing skilled and responsible managers capable of running businesses effectively.

There has undoubtedly been a slow, but inexorable, focusing of corporate and academic thinking around the issue of CSR which is helping to clarify the relevant concepts. As noted earlier, the notion of 'business ethics' has not proved sufficiently relevant to engage either businesses or regulators. 'Ethics' is a term that typically is invoked when considering the behaviours and attitudes displayed in situations that involve implicit prejudice, conflict of interests, favouring one's own group or a tendency to over-claim credit (Banaji *et al.*, 2003). It is therefore easy to see how the term is tangential when applied to organizations. For example, organizational success is often defined by favouring one's own group and ensuring that it outperforms the competition. Organizational survival depends on exactly that, and yet a successful company is not 'unethical' simply because it outperforms its competitors.

Part of the historic confusion in this area has been the proliferation of phrases that have been coined to reflect the linkage between moral and ethical values and business performance. They include terms such as 'business sustainability', 'pro-social behaviour' (from the psychological literature) and 'corporate citizenship'. There is considerable overlap between these concepts, but all share a broad notion of socially desirable behaviour and include cultural beliefs that people and organizations *should* behave pro-socially – for the benefit of others. Thus the notions go beyond the assumption that individuals and organizations should avoid damaging others, or the environment, to add the implication that they should add positive social value to their operations.

The term 'corporate social responsibility' (CSR) is broader and potentially much more relevant than these others. In the past the term has been used to mean, rather simply, philanthropic donations, or participating in community events, or other ways of spending the money the company has already made on 'doing good things'. However, the term is now taken to include all the ways that a business, its products and services interact with society and the environment. CSR is about all the organization's stakeholders – employees, customers, owners, investors, suppliers and pressure groups. Thus it is more about how organizations make their money than on how they spend it. Ultimately, CSR is an attitude of mind which informs behaviour and decision-making throughout the company.

> '... how we work together to translate the widespread social concern that exists among employers and employees alike into

effective action for the common good'. The Rt. Hon. Gordon Brown MP, Chancellor of the Exchequer (2004)

The questions that must now be asked are, first of all, how can managers better understand their role in this complex subject and either play a part in what their wider organizations are trying to achieve, or indeed influence their aims? The second, and equally important, question is how can business schools help them in this task?

Effective CSR teaching in MBA programmes

A first issue to be addressed is one of 'embeddedness' and responsibility. Whose responsibility is it to ensure that CSR is at the forefront of organizational consciousness? It is often difficult to answer this question. When managers are asked directly, they often respond that the responsibility lies with the PR department, or with the chief executive. It appears that one of the problems may be that organizational strategies and policies, such as ethics initiatives, can be felt to be 'disconnected' from the rest of the organization. CSR strategies exist technically, but in practice have little impact on everyday work. There are many possible explanations for this – it may be intentional, where the CSR strategy may indeed be simply cynical PR 'window dressing'. It may be the case that the fault lies simply within the term *corporate* social responsibility – individuals feel that it is 'done' somewhere else, by the 'corporation'. It is equally possible that such policies do not have the engagement or commitment of the work force, particularly the managers, for reasons such as resource shortages, lack of communication, an inappropriate skill base or a mismatching of core values between the stated strategy and operational management. This last possibility is critical as companies increasingly need to operate globally, in countries with differing core values, and yet CSR strategies need to be operated on the world stage. These may be some of the reasons why CSR development is not always high on the list of skills that companies want business schools to develop in their managers.

Business schools and management development professionals can and should be playing a crucial role here. CSR within management development is at an early stage. Issues such as corporate governance have been integrated into many MBA and management development programmes, as have environmentally responsible issues, but, on the whole, CSR has been largely ignored. This is in part because the theoretical 'managerial ethics' courses mentioned earlier have been seen as seen as giving sufficient attention (lip service?) to the issues. Most significantly, it has been viewed as a 'nice to have' or an optional extra, so therefore has not been in demand by MBA students as much as subjects such as strategy or finance – these are more clearly seen to aid graduates on the corporate ladder. It is true that this is changing, A recent survey of student attitudes in the United States (Aspen Institute, 2003) indicated that it suggested that the greatest change the students wanted in their MBA programmes was the integration of social responsibility issues into their core coursework of finance, marketing, organizational behaviour and accounting. So students are beginning to realize the importance of the links between business and society and that long term sustainable business success can be achieved only through socially responsible behaviour.

Where does this leave business schools? For almost 40 years, the MBA qualification has offered specialized knowledge in all the areas of business. This has resulted in many courses simply presenting functional silos supposedly representing the world of business. This wasn't wrong – business needs knowledge, and the 'professionalization' of management needed a Kitemark – but it has been increasingly recognized that this is not sufficient.

Developments in the design and delivery of MBA programmes have been, in large part, a response to what has been termed 'the new psychological contract' – or the implicit, unwritten set of rights, obligations and expectations that determine the nature of the employee/employer relationship. In the past this relationship included security, predictability of career progression and probabilities concerning reward and remunerations. The current realities of the world of work are such that employees can no longer count on such stability, even if they do their jobs well and are loyal to their organization. It seems that the traditional contractual focus on employment is no longer appropriate and that the focus of the psychological contract should now be on employability or the development of competitive skills for individuals to be able to find work when and where they need it. Thus, the 'new' contract offers individuals the tools for assessing and developing their own skills and in return employees accept responsibility for offering organizations an adaptable and responsive skill base and for managing the relationships which will affect their careers.

MBA programmes have responded to these new expectations in the world of work by acknowledging that people now expect and need to be managed differently. The shared responsibility for careers, and indeed the general social 'zeitgeist' which has moved away from an acceptance of authoritarian management styles, has resulted in an effort to graft 'people skills' and attributes onto the knowledge base. Emphasis has been placed on developing the personal skills of leadership, emotional intelligence, effective team working and managing ambiguity. Many MBA courses now have a pronounced emphasis on the 'people' skills needed to operate globally, to think imaginatively and strategically and personal and career development figure prominently in many brochures. Emphasis on 'effective business leadership', therefore, is no longer innovative and has become required programme content.

This relatively recent emphasis on personal leadership in MBA programmes is interesting. It has been pointed out that many of the prominent business leaders whose misbehaviours have received such sensational publicity of late are graduates of MBA programmes! So it would seem that something is clearly lacking in the leadership skills of many managers – perhaps the issue of integrity, trust and social responsibility!

That there is a 'felt need' for increasing management education in general is indisputable. In October 1999, *Business Week Online* reported a rise in corporate training and development for managers of 17 per cent on the previous year, up to $16.5 billion. The Aspen Institute's Business and Society Programme (Aspen BSP) conducts regular research into what corporate leaders need from business development and what is the current provision. The mission of Aspen BSP is:

> 'To increase the supply of business leaders who understand – and seek to balance – the complex relationship between business success and social and environmental progress'. (Aspen Institute, 2003)

The most recent findings from this programme find that there is agreement that current and future leaders in a complex and global environment need greater skills at understanding changing stakeholders (consumers, employees, suppliers, governments, communities, etc.) They need to see where business needs fit into a larger picture of societal needs and understand the interdependence of these overlapping aims. In other words, the business leaders interviewed expressed a 'felt need' for programmes that address the challenges of social impact management.

However, this felt need has not necessarily translated into an expressed demand from business customers to the providers of management education. The Aspen work confirms the demand from their corporate customers for immediate and directly applicable learning in the functional business areas – the need for simplicity and speed.

Business schools obviously have another group of key customers apart from businesses – the MBA students themselves. The Aspen research has also approached this area of research from the perspective of the programme participants and finds that:

> 'Surveyed students believe that today's corporate leaders privilege the shareholder over other stakeholders in business decision making, but the students report that they personally would favour a more balanced stakeholder approach. Secondly, a high percentage of surveyed students believe that they "will have to make decisions during their business career that will conflict with their values". Interestingly, most believe that they would look for another job rather than trying to work within an organization whose values clash with their own'. (Aspen Institute, 2003)

Thus, the 'needs/demands' disconnect is confirmed – students acknowledge that business leaders must address the broader 'church' of stakeholders but do not believe that this is the prevailing practice or belief in the business world. They are pessimistic about value-driven change and predict clashes of personal integrity and commercial demands. It is important to remember that these findings are from MBA students; intelligent and able individuals with high job choice – the war for talent is relevant here. The 'new psychological contract' discussed earlier highlights that more and more employees expect their personal needs to be met in their working environment. A new generation of managers who look for congruity between their value system and that of their employing organization will factor CSR issues into their job choices and career development.

This leaves business schools in an exciting, but challenging position, providing them with an opportunity to be proactive rather than reactive in their offerings and develop programmes, short courses and master classes that businesses almost do not know yet that they need. This begs the question of whether business schools should simply respond to the businesses that are their customers by providing what the customers articulate as their 'needs', or should they take a more defining role? It may well be so as many business schools teach speculative new product development, entrepreneurial skills that create markets that customers did not know they wanted, such as organic foods or tabletop refrigerators. The schools should actually be taking the lead here, shaping management thinking rather than simply responding to it, creating the market demand in the current void.

Defining the CSR syllabus

But still – what to teach? As a starting point it is, of course, essential to define the term 'CSR' in sufficient detail to be able to identify what needs to be taught by business schools. A concept so intimately tied into the social world must inevitably evolve over time as does society. Some 50 years ago the key issues were thought to be military manufacturing, the 'well-being' of employees and support for the arts. By the 1970s product and personal safety, environmental pollution and preservation had surfaced as the main focus, along with unethical advertising and other issues, such as sexual and racial discrimination. The last 20 years have seen further changes to concerns over white collar crime, fraudulent trading, environmental disasters, world poverty, child labour and the demographics of the workforce. So, the focus of the ideas underpinning the concept of CSR have changed, broadened and increased over the years. And then of course, having defined and taught 'it', we must address the thorny issue of how do we measure or assess that teaching and learning?

Given the current knowledge and attitude framework around CSR issues, there is a clear dilemma for business schools. These are issues that are generally still framed as part of a discipline distinct from business. Therefore the option is to offer more discrete, stand-alone courses about ethics in business – an approach that could be described as:

'Saving the whales on the weekends'. (Samuelson, 2005)

The alternative is to frame the issues as integral to and inseparable from the fundamentals of contemporary business operations. This would require a comprehensive overhaul of most MBA programme content – an overhaul that would review each session in the light of its relevance to the intersection of business needs and wider societal concerns and the management of this complex interdependency. Such a radical rethink is probably a rather daunting thought for most MBA faculties and their supporting administrators! Yet, this change must be made. When we business schools stop asking the question 'can or should we teach ethics?' and start framing that question as 'how can we help managers deal with the complexity of the relationship between business needs and their rights to trade freely, with wider societal concerns and their responsibilities to trade beneficially?' then the picture of possibility begins to look different. Integrating CSR into mainstream business function teaching will see marketing classes addressing the impact of drug pricing decisions and finance classes that investigate the economics of investing in bottom of the pile (BOP) third world economies. Operations and strategy classes will consider the social impacts of outsourcing production, and so on – true integration will change the picture dramatically.

To deal with this complexity, the teaching of CSR in an MBA programme must be designed to deliver learning outcomes that cover both knowledge and skills – it is not sufficient simply to present theoretical, or even case based information about topics: students need to be able not only to understand the issues, but also to work with them and be able to manage and influence them. In broad terms, MBA programmes need to be designed to meet the following objectives.

- To increase students' awareness and knowledge of the changing social pressures and legislative requirements that are redefining the role of business in society.
- To encourage students to consider how these forces will impact on corporate governance and their individual leadership roles.
- To provide the tools and frameworks to integrate CSR into the mainstream business practices the students will be engaged in when they are in employment.
- To demonstrate how leading companies are responding to these challenges to build effective and successful business strategies and to consider the options available to businesses.

We are really talking here about several distinct but related aspects of syllabus coverage. First of all is the need to consider societal change. The social context in which business operates has shifted significantly from the Milton Friedman view that 'the business of business is business' (Friedman, 1970). Issues in this area include the difficulties of OECD countries to provide acceptable levels of social welfare provision, particularly in the light of recent environmental disasters such as the tsunami which devastated Southern Asia on 26 December 2004.

The role of individual responsibilities in this context is key. Examples would be personal donations to disaster funds, and the control of those funds, passive smoking and personal responsibility for the health of others. In general the concept that there is an interdependency between personal, individual decisions and the broader social context must be highlighted and acknowledged. Specifically, it is important for students to be aware of the fact that their personal decisions as managers will significantly affect the way other people live their own lives.

Secondly, MBA programmes should introduce students to the changing regulatory frameworks within which organizations must operate, now and in the future. The increasing pressure from shareholders and governments for companies to be more responsible has led to demands for increased transparency and has made direct links to changes in corporate governance around the world. Some of the issues here are around who owns a company that has separated ownership and control? What are the global trends in corporate legal frameworks and corporate governance codes? How do corporations deal with CSR in a way that enhances strategic direction and value creation rather than simply as risk management and control?

Within this framework MBA programmes must consider the options open to organizations. Programmes must inform students of what CSR means to organizations in practice and give information as to what they can actually engage in. The philosophical vs practical debate – is CSR critical for sustainable organizational growth or is it simply good PR? How can organizations tailor their CSR policies to their business? A good example of such tailoring is BP in China. Although under pressure from the state to support moves to deal with the AIDS threat in the country, BP have chosen to focus on road improvements within business sensitive areas. This has huge social benefits in providing improved transport and communication facilities for many local communities, but also facilitates BP's own operations in providing improved roads which minimize damage to vehicles and injury to transport staff. The ability to work out the business case for CSR should be a core skill that all MBA programmes develop in their students. Issues that need to be covered include the rise of single issue pressure groups and their impact on businesses. These include risks such as attacks by consumers, investors, the media or campaigning groups.

Power and politics should also be core topics in an ethically aware MBA programme. The dichotomies between corporate responsibility, the role of the individual and the power process of organizations are key determinants of CSR strategies and their implementation.

This last point is important. MBA programmes must deliver skills as well as knowledge to their students. This much is non contentious – most frameworks offered by institutions of education talk of learning outcomes in terms of skills and knowledge. However, the area of debate is around whether changes in attitudes and beliefs are also the responsibility of management development programmes. It is clear that management education should identify some of the main world views that inform responsible decision-making. What is less clear is how and why such education needs to identify a manager's personal view of these issues and whether a moralistic framework should be offered that can inform and guide an individual manager in their decision-making. If not a moralistic framework – then a measure of assessment as to how a manager is performing within a 'CSR aware' framework may be the answer.

A most useful development here has been the CSR competency framework developed by the CSR Academy, supported by the UK's Department of Trade and Industry (CSR Academy, 2004). The framework is a set of six competences that describe how managers need to act in order to integrate responsible business decision-making.

- The ability to understand society
  This involves a broad understanding of the role of each player in society, government, business, trade unions, non-governmental organizations and civil society.
- The ability to build capacity
  This means ensuring that organizations and individuals create the structures necessary to deliver CSR – using external partnerships and strategic networks and alliances as well as internal processes.
- The ability to question business as usual
  The necessity to be open to new ideas, challenging others to consider and adopt new ways of thinking.
- The abilty to develop effective stakeholder relations
  The ability to identify both internal and external stakeholders and develop relationships with them which involve consultation, and balancing demands.
- The ability to take a strategic view
  The ability to move from short-term thinking to longer and broader perspectives.
- The ability to harness diversity
  This is not simply a question of offering equal opportunities and complying with anti-discrimination legislation, but of respecting the

added value that diversity in people and practices can bring to the workplace.

Whilst determining what skills and competencies are to be required as part of CSR education is an important step forward, there is still the question of what standards and criteria must be applied, against which to assess these skills and competencies.

The CSR Academy framework outlined on the previous page can be mapped onto five different levels of attainment for each competence – awareness, understanding, application, integration and leadership – and is designed to operate across the full spectrum of business functions from operations to marketing.

Firstly, the context of the global socio-economic and political environment must be understood. The ways that organizations interact with stakeholders on a local, national and international level must be understood. This corresponds with the 'awareness' and 'understanding' levels of the CSR Academy framework.

Having set the context, possible organizational responses, options and alternatives need to explored, focusing on the business case for CSR, exploring the spectrum of possible avenues which can move CSR from being rhetoric to a reality in terms of strategy, policy and action. For example, Shell UK installed a new lighting system to increase both customer and staff sense of security on petrol forecourts. Automated sensors measure light conditions and enable an automatic switch off and on at optimum times. Nationwide this initiative led to environmental savings of an estimated 10,000 tonnes of CO_2 a year and a 12 per cent saving in related electricity costs. In addition, staff and customer morale received a significant boost. Examples such as this can be a vehicle for the understanding, application and integration levels of the CSR Academy framework.

Finally, the individual's role and response are considered, starting from the formation of attitudes and beliefs, through decision-making processes, to power and politics in organizations, culminating in the development of the individual as an ethical leader. This corresponds to the 'leadership' level of the framework.

The complexity implied by this framework is in line with research indicating that what the business world wants increasingly from business education, particularly MBA education, is not simply knowledge based, but also action oriented, and must also incorporate ways to develop and nurture integrity, judgement and intuition (Andrews and D'Andrea Tyson, 2004).

Future vision

Thus, MBAs must be redesigned to deliver essential business knowledge, but not in isolation. Programmes must provide the broad integrated range of business skills needed to negotiate the complexities of the business world with confidence. It is also understood that effective leadership is at the heart of business success, so the development of personal leadership skills underpins the learning. Students must be provided with tools and frameworks to integrate corporate responsibility into mainstream business practice and an understanding of how leading companies respond to these challenges to build sustainable business strategies.

If we are successful at integrating CSR teaching into our MBA programmes, our graduates will be able to articulate strategies to integrate corporate responsibility into mainstream business practice, taking account of the barriers and facilitators that affect the implementation of corporate social responsibility policies in practice. They will also be able to evaluate their own leadership capabilities in the context of socially responsible leadership and understand how these are underpinned by their personal ethical beliefs and value systems. And finally, they will be able to apply the theoretical concepts and ideas stemming from their learning to real world business situations.

At Ashridge Business School, we believe that future leaders want a broad framework for understanding the role that companies play in society and the expanded role that they, as managers, are being asked to play. MBA programmes must consider these challenges, develop frameworks and help future business leaders to develop a philosophy of management that will guide their day-to-day decision-making for years to come. The Ashridge MBA incorporates a 'Business in Society' module designed to provide a critical lens through which organizational performance on issues of social responsibility is viewed and evaluated.

In order to further develop the integration of the teaching of CSR and values-based leadership into the MBA programme, Ashridge is participating in a research programme called 'the Teaching Innovation Programme' (TIP). This is a two-year action learning project in collaboration with GE Crotonville, a consortium of corporations, and 11 leading international graduate schools of business. These are drawn from around the world, including USA, Europe, India, Mexico and Canada.

TIP is designed to create a 'tipping point' in business education to further the teaching of corporate citizenship and values based leadership, while providing a forum for cross-learning among consortium members.

A core driver of the programme is the exchange of ideas between and among leaders of corporate executive training and development, human resources and business school faculties. Ashridge is playing to its strengths in leadership development by looking closely at the concept of socially responsible leadership, its diagnosis and measurement, and the difference this can make to the performance of an organization.

There is no doubt that understanding the role of business in society today is both critical and complex. It is critical firstly because of the fundamental role of business in value creation, providing jobs, products and services and indeed in paying taxes for the maintenance of civilized society. It is also critical because of the power corporates are seen to have in today's world. In the UK, a national opinion poll found that most people believe that multinational companies have more power over their lives than the government. The legitimacy of this non-elected power is increasingly being questioned by individuals and pressure groups, making organizations more vulnerable to single issue politics.

Although there are no easy answers, business schools cannot afford to ignore the debates. Integrating CSR better into development activities such as the MBA should not be about reacting to past scandals – this is simply closing the stable door after the horse has bolted. Today's executives must juggle ambitious and sometimes ambiguous goals in the fast moving global world of business today. There are pressures to cut corners and to make short term decisions. But management education can go a long way towards providing the socially responsible awareness, knowledge and skills that are necessary to taking proactive steps before damage is done and to create socially responsible cultures which add value to society. Our business is the development of managers; it would be socially irresponsible of us to neglect this critical aspect of their education.

References

Andrews, N and D'Andrea Tyson, L (2004) The upwardly global MBA. *Strategy + Business* **36** 1–10

Aspen Institute (2003) *Where Will They Lead: MBA Student Attitudes about Business and Society.* Available at: http:// www.aspeninstitute.org

Banaji, M R, Bazerman, M H and Chugh, D (2003) How (un)ethical are you? *Harvard Business Review* Dec. 56–64

Brown, Gordon (2004) *Civil Renewal in Britain. National Council for Voluntary Organisations Annual Conference.* Keynote speech. 18 Feb. Available at: http://www.ncvo-vol.org.uk/Asp/search/ncvo/main.aspx?siteID=1&sID=18&subSID=206&documentID=1942

BusinessWeek Online (1999) Available at: http://www.businessweek.com/

Cowton, C (1998) Research in real worlds: the empirical contribution to business ethics. In: Cowton, C and Crisp, R (eds) *Business Ethics; Perspective on the Practice of Theory.* Oxford: Oxford University Press, pp 97–115

CSR Academy (2004) *CSR Competency Framework.* Available at: http://www. csracademy.org.uk/competency.htm

Cummins, J (1999) *The Teaching of Business Ethics.* London: Institute of Business Ethics

Friedman, M. (1970) The social responsibility of business is to incease its profits. *New York Times Magazine* 13 Sept.

Robertson, D (1993) Empiricism in business ethics; suggested research directions. *Journal of Business Ethics* **12** 585–599

Samuelson, Judith (2005) *TIP (Teaching Innovation Programme) Conference, Monterrey, Mexico, January.* Washington, DC: Aspen Institute

13

Towards a Responsible Capitalism

Geoffrey Chandler

The corporate world entered the 21st century at the zenith of its influence and near the nadir of its reputation. The rapidly increasing internationalization of the world economy had brought many benefits. But growing awareness of the collateral damage that companies could inflict in the course of their operations and the absence of any self-regulating mechanism which might temper profit with principle had led to deep public suspicion and distrust.

Yet by the turn of the century the landscape had begun to change and the responsibility of companies to society was on all agendas. There were in place a growing number of initiatives, many of which had already been adopted by a few leading companies and which, if embraced by the corporate world as a whole, could salvage reputation and lay a firm foundation for the future. It had been a long journey to this point in which external pressures and damage to reputation rather than company initiative had been the chief drivers of change. The journey remains unfinished: the demand for greater transparency and accountability has still to be met and the foundations of trust have still to be laid. The question now is whether companies will embrace change constructively, or, as in the past, resist attempts to bring their conduct into line with society's values without which they will have no assurance of a continuing licence to operate. A more fundamental question is whether the underlying philosophy of capitalism is inherently in conflict with socially acceptable behaviour.

The growth of corporate power

The ending of the Cold War, the demise of Communism and the discrediting of state control of national economies brought radical change to the world scene. Economic 'globalization' – the internationalization of the world economy – was not new in principle. What was new was the speed with which privatization and foreign investment were embraced by countries that had previously believed in state control of the economy, and technology which enabled financial transactions to be carried out around the clock regardless of national boundaries. Countries of the North and South now competed for the skills, technology, investment, management and access to markets that private companies could bring. Companies seized the opportunities offered. The supply chains of the supermarkets and the consumer goods industries spread ever wider and deeper into the developing countries of Asia, Africa and South America. Investment by the major transnational corporations (TNCs), in particular those in the oil and mining industries, moved into areas previously denied by political or ideological barriers.

The public limited company, operating increasingly across national boundaries, had become the primary instrument for economic growth. In a competitive market economy it had proved itself the most effective mechanism so far known for the generation of financial wealth and the provision of goods and services. But it was the richer nations which chiefly enjoyed the fruits of its dynamism and inventiveness as well as profiting from a trading framework biased in their favour. They, or at least the better off in their populations, were the chief beneficiaries of a dazzling array of technologies which transformed communication, transport and medicine, enjoying delicacies, once local and seasonal, which now filled the shelves of their supermarkets the year round as new sources of supply were found overseas.

To the developing world private companies also brought significant benefits. These included employment, at its best providing better conditions than local or state companies; at its worst seeking the lowest cost without regard for the conditions under which goods were produced. Companies brought financial wealth, though often at the cost of more traditional forms of wealth. They touched countless people at many points: if they were prepared to conduct their operations in a principled manner it lay in their power to help to raise standards.

The new risks

With the new opportunities also came risk. Few companies had adequate understanding of the dangers inherent in countries with governments that lacked any democratic legitimacy and where corruption, injustice, internal conflict and human rights violations prevailed. Supply chains could involve exploitative child labour, sweatshops and discrimination, even forced labour. The extractive industries faced similar problems, but in addition confronted new challenges of physical security for personnel and plant and of working under governments which blatantly violated human rights. Their presence inevitably gave both economic and moral support to the regime in power. In such a context companies could incur the accusation of complicity in the interest of profit if they lacked explicit policies in support of international human rights standards. Complicity had yet to find a legal definition, but had strong moral connotations. An increasingly alert and critical world, aided by the internet, acted as watchdog, leaving companies no hiding place for what they did.

Lacking an understanding of the challenges and without appropriate policies to confront them, companies could not avoid involvement in abuses. While their spread and influence grew, their reputation sank. Survey after survey showed companies to be as little trusted as politicians. If, in the 1930s, capitalism had been threatened by its apparent failure, it was now endangered by the manifest success which by its own narrow measures it enjoyed. Financial scandals and excessive rewards to top executives aggravated mistrust, but its fundamental cause lay in the prevailing belief that companies did not care about the labour conditions of their employees, did not care about conditions in their ever-expanding supply chains, did not care about their impact on the physical environment or on the communities in which they operated – so long as they were making money. It was a belief sustained by accumulating examples of bad behaviour, fuelling the suspicion that profit was invariably put before principle. It was a belief unfair to those few leading companies that had by now adopted principles which applied to the totality of their operations. But the behaviour of the bad inevitably tainted the reputation of all and the world did not readily forget that even those companies now in the vanguard had required reputational damage and external pressure to stimulate change.

The pattern of challenge and response had long been set. Companies believed in the virtues of continual growth when others were beginning to question it. Right-wing economists argued that the wealth created by investment would 'trickle down' to the population as a whole and that social and political advancement would be the inevitable concomitant of economic growth. Similarly, the watchword of the Thatcher era in the UK had been 'a rising tide floats all boats'. Unfortunately, neither was true: these were siren voices. In many countries government corruption proved itself fully competent to staunch any 'trickle down' and the rising tide of financial wealth often floated only armaments, prestige buildings or the Swiss bank accounts of governing elites, leaving any real development or poverty alleviation untouched.

Resistance to change

Change had come gradually. From the 1960s onwards there was increasing recognition of the fragility of the planet and of the impact of business activity on the environment. The rise of non-governmental organizations (NGOs)[1], reflecting public disillusion with the ability of conventional politics to meet social aspirations, brought new dimensions to the debate. Rachel Carson's *Silent Spring* (1962), the Club of Rome's *Limits to Growth* (Meadows *et al.*, 1972) and Barbara Ward and René Dubos's *Only One Earth: Care and Maintenance of a Small Planet* (1972) were potentially seminal landmarks, though companies did no more than challenge their analysis while failing to appreciate the validity of the underlying warnings. By the 1970s the environment movement, strengthened by the foundation of Friends of the Earth and Greenpeace in 1971, had become a significant influence on international opinion and on the performance of companies. Today there are few major companies that do not have environmental policies, even if practice lags behind. The world was becoming sensitive to the environmental impact of companies, but was slower to recognize and grapple with their impact on human rights.

Unlike the environmental movement, the human rights movement came late to seeking engagement with business, regarding governments as its traditional target. Human rights organizations had sporadically exposed and condemned direct corporate involvement in human rights violations, but had been slow to attempt to recruit the influence of the corporate world for the protection of such rights. Efforts in the UK in the early 1990s to engage major transnational companies in discussions on human rights met with rebuff. Some companies failed even to perceive the violations that went on around them. Human rights, seen narrowly as political and civil rights, were regarded as a matter for governments. Companies rejected any role in their defence, viewing involvement on their part as a slippery slope into politics on to which they could only venture at their peril.

It was the rejection of such involvement and the resulting disaster for corporate reputation that proved the catalyst for change. In late 1995 the failure of Shell, the largest foreign investor in Nigeria, to speak out against the arbitrary execution of Ken Saro-Wiwa and eight other Ogonis until the last moment led to international condemnation. This episode, following on the heels of the international outcry that had greeted Shell's plans to jettison the Brent Spar oil platform in the deep ocean, proved a watershed for the company, for the human rights movement and for the whole debate on corporate responsibility. It was not that companies lacked principles – Shell had issued its first statement of general business principles in 1976, recognizing indivisible responsibilities towards all its stakeholders (though that term had yet to come into common usage[2]): the reality was that the world and society's expectations had changed more rapidly than company perceptions.

A new framework – codes, guidelines and reporting

The United Nations Universal Declaration of Human Rights (UDHR), adopted by the UN General Assembly in 1948, was now explicitly accepted as applicable to companies, first by Shell, to be followed by BP, similarly suffering from reputational damage as a result of its operations in Colombia (United Nations, 1948). A barrier had been breached and change accelerated. Codes and initiatives now multiplied (Leipziger, 2003)[3]. The 'Global Sullivan Principles' were published by the Reverend Leon Sullivan in February 1999, analogous to those he had published for company behaviour under the South African apartheid regime (International Foundation for Education and Self-Help, 1999). Those objectives were 'to support economic, social and political justice by companies where they do business; to support human rights and to encourage equal opportunity at all levels of employment'. The OECD Guidelines for Multinational Enterprises, comprehensively addressing all aspects of corporate behaviour, had been first adopted by member governments in 1976, but were little known. They were revised in 2000 to make them more relevant and to give them greater impact in practice (OECD, 2000). The United Nations Global Compact, proposed by the Secretary General, Kofi Annan, in 1999 and launched in 2000, set out nine principles for corporate behaviour covering human rights, labour and the environment (United Nations, 2000) deriving from the UDHR, the International Labour Organization's Declaration on Fundamental Principles and Rights at Work (International Labour Organization, 1998) and the Rio Declaration on Environment and Development (United Nations, 1992). These instruments enjoyed universal consensus and could not be rejected on the grounds of cultural relativity. A tenth principle, concerning corruption, was added later.

Reporting frameworks and verifiable standards were developed to cover all aspects of company operations. AccountAbility 1000 (AA 1000; 1999) (Institute of Social and Ethical Accountability, 1999) defined best practice in social and ethical auditing, accounting and reporting, with stakeholder engagement as an integral part. Social Accountability 8000 (SA 8000; 1997) (Social Accountability International, 1997) provided a certification standard designed to make the workplace more human. The Global Reporting Initiative (GRI) launched the Sustainability Reporting Guidelines in June 2000, providing a framework for economic, social and environmental reporting with the mission 'to elevate the quality of reporting to a higher level of comparability, consistency and utility' (Global Reporting Initiative, 2002).

Language was changing. The 'triple bottom line'[4] – the simultaneous management and reporting of the economic, environmental and social impact of a company's operations in place of the exclusively financial 'bottom line' – gained increasing currency. 'Sustainability' entered the business vocabulary, prompted by the threat of climate change, though with no precise definition in the corporate context. 'Corporate social responsibility' (CSR) now headed all agendas, the 'business case' for the exercise of such responsibility being the lever used to access boardroom thinking. Both provided a way into the discussion. But both were deeply flawed. CSR rapidly spawned an academic industry and a rash of consultancies and conferences, but was mired in definitional confusion between philanthropy and the principled conduct of operations, most definitions opting for a voluntary add-on rather than the application of principle to a company's core business (Chandler, 2003)[5]. The 'business case', although a useful passport, was essentially amoral in arguing the necessity of an economic rationale for doing what was right. Moreover it fell far short of being applicable to the full range of company responsibilities and could have the perverse effect of making conformity with the law, for example in the avoidance of pollution, an economic calculation rather than a principle if a fine proved less costly than preventive investment.

Progress in patches

There was little lacking for companies that wished to construct appropriate principles and to report on their implementation. In fact there was too much. The plethora of codes and other initiatives, inevitable at the formative stage of developments, required consolidation. The lack of comparability of non-financial performance, which the GRI aimed to remedy, meant that market forces, potentially the most important influence of all, could make no judgement on company performance other than on the traditional criterion of money. Companies complained of 'code fatigue', but had only themselves to blame because of their own failure to play a part in stimulating initiatives, almost all of which came from outside business. On the positive side, a growing number of companies were developing their own comprehensive codes and acknowledging the relevance of the UDHR to their operations[6]. The early 1990s saw the beginning of ethical supply chain management, with Levi Strauss & Co. developing its Terms of Engagement in 1992. The UK Ethical Trading Initiative, formed in 1998, brought together supermarkets, NGOs and trade unions, with funding from the government, to identify and promote good practice in supply chains. Sectoral initiatives, among them rugs, clothing, electronics, coffee and timber, offered common standards, enhanced certification and labelling, but ran the risk of providing no more than a lowest common denominator.

The financial institutions, responsible for the bulk of investment in a world in which the individual shareholder as an active participant had virtually disappeared, remained an obstacle. Remote from the direct risks and challenges that companies faced, particularly in the developing world, and so far largely immune from any reputational implication for financing projects which damaged the environment or human rights, it was difficult to influence a concept of fiduciary duty based exclusively on short-term financial gain. Nonetheless the growth of the socially responsible investment (SRI) movement and new stock exchange categories for companies meeting certain social and environmental criteria made inroads into conventional financial thinking.

The responsibility of companies for the direct impact of their operations was clear-cut. In the context of conflict, corrupt governments or failed states they faced more complex challenges. The misuse by government of revenues paid legally by companies, the need for physical protection by ill-disciplined state forces, involvement in the chain from mine to market, most notoriously in the case of diamonds which were fuelling civil war in Africa, all demanded a joint response on the part of companies, NGOs and governments. Legal payments by companies to governments, for example for oil concessions in Angola and Equatorial Guinea, were frequently stolen by the ruling parties for their own purposes, leaving the bulk of the population untouched by the country's wealth. The UK Government's Extractive Industries Transparency Initiative (2002) and the NGO-led *Publish What You Pay* initiative (2002) both called for disclosure by companies of such payments to enable the people of a country to monitor the revenues paid to their government. The use by companies of state forces for protection had led to cases of brutal oppression of protesters.

In December 2000 the US and UK governments (later joined by the Dutch and Norwegian governments) announced the Voluntary Principles on Security and Human Rights for extractive industries, bringing pressure to bear on companies initially reluctant to join (Foreign & Commonwealth Office/US State Department, 2000). The Kimberley Process, a joint government, diamond industry and civil society initiative, sought to stem the flow of 'conflict diamonds' used to finance wars by rebel movements against legitimate governments (Kimberley Process, 2002).

NGOs were gaining in confidence and capability to engage constructively with companies; they were also learning, albeit slowly, the value of joining together in coalition to tackle this vital constituency. Both NGOs and companies began to recognize that they could not succeed in their objectives without cooperation. NGOs could not succeed in their aims for development, poverty alleviation and protection of human rights without the corporate sector playing a positive role; the corporate sector, lacking capability in these areas, would not succeed without the expertise of NGOs. Each had to surmount a legacy of mutual stereotyping, ignorance, hostility and suspicion which has yet to be fully overcome.

Distrust of companies

If so much was being done, why did trust in companies remain so low? There were two prime reasons. First, throughout the history of the company the interest of every stakeholder other than the shareholder, whether labour, the physical environment or the community, had been protected by external pressure and legislation, not by corporate initiative. Second, the absence of any criticism from within business of actions that brought the whole activity into disrepute implied an activity incapable of self-regulation.

The bleakest aspect of the scene was the absence of collective corporate leadership. There is indeed principled leadership within companies, but it stops at the company gate. There is little willingness to break out of the defensive box that has unthinkingly fought regulation, or to initiate change in the parameters within which the market operates. As has been (but is no longer) the tradition of journalism, dog does not eat dog: actions that bring business into disrepute are not condemned by business. Redress for the victims of Bhopal in India (perhaps the worst corporate crime of the post-war period) or of asbestosis in South Africa finds no champions in the business community. When inadequate safety measures in the Bhopal plant of the American company Union Carbide led to the death of thousands of people, whose families to this day remain inadequately compensated, not a breath of criticism was heard from the business world: nor a murmur of disapprobation from the United States Council for International Business (USCIB), a body presumably concerned with the reputation of the activity it represents.

When the British company Cape plc abandoned South Africa, it left its former employees suffering from asbestosis, refusing compensation on the grounds that the conduct of its wholly owned subsidiaries was not its responsibility. Not a word of criticism was heard from the International Chamber of Commerce (ICC) or the Confederation of British Industry (CBI) or any corporate leader. In any other walk of life – medicine, the law or sport – bringing the activity into disrepute would bring condemnation. Not so with companies. This is a self-inflicted wound, the responsibility lying squarely on the shoulders of the corporate world, and if it is to be remedied it is up to the corporate world to act.

What was needed was consensus about the principles which should underlie corporate behaviour throughout the world and a system of reporting which would enable comparison to be made between company performance on these principles. Without these there was no hope of market forces bringing influence to bear on anything other than financial results. Two developments offered a way forward – the GRI and the United Nations Human Rights Norms for business. The first was already being used or referenced by nearly 600 companies. The second was to become the focus of a debate which illuminated how far the corporate world still had to travel to meet the legitimate expectations of society.

The Human Rights Norms – a flawed attempt at consensus building

The Norms[7] were the outcome of a four-year initiative of the UN Sub-Commission on the Promotion and Protection of Human Rights. This tackled one of the foremost challenges of the 21st century – the need to ensure that companies, now the dominant influence in the post-Cold War world economy, reflect the values of contemporary society in their behaviour. These values, deriving from a very wide range of human rights instruments and treaties of which the chief are the UDHR, the Convention on the Rights of the Child (United Nations, 1989) and the core International Labour Organization conventions, already served as the basis for the OECD Guidelines and the UN Global Compact. Both of these, particularly the latter, had helped to raise the profile of the issues involved; both were voluntary; both contained a generalized requirement to observe human rights; but neither spelt out the human rights responsibilities of companies in any detail and neither had sufficient visibility to help the market to judge and influence company performance. A growing number of companies committed themselves to both, but remained a small minority of the total, with no guarantee that commitment would be reflected in policies and practice. The Norms offered a comprehensive elaboration of the human rights' obligations of companies and represented the behaviour a civilized society was entitled to expect from its corporate citizens. They were no more subject to legal enforcement than the Guidelines and the Compact, but could with formal UN endorsement provide a visible measure of comparable non financial performance for investors and the public at large and, most importantly, for the market.

The Norms made clear that states have the primary responsibility for the promotion and protection of human rights and that the Norms addressed 'the respective spheres of activity and influence' of companies. In other words, we are not entitled to expect companies to solve world problems of poverty, disease, the environment, conflict and human rights violations. But we *are* entitled to expect that they should not aggravate these problems through what they do. We *are* entitled to expect that the manner in which they operate should help to diminish problems rather than create or increase them.

Two issues were repeatedly debated: were the Norms to be for transnational companies (TNCs) only, or were they for all businesses? Were they merely voluntary, or did they have legal status? The debate was not helped by the obvious ignorance of the nature of business on the part of some of the experts and some of the non-governmental organizations that played a part in the consultations. Some simply disliked private business much and TNCs more, seeing the latter as the only legitimate target. At the other end of the political spectrum, the United States Council for International Business (USCIB), the International Chamber of Commerce (ICC) and the International Organisation of Employers (IOE) objected to the singling out of TNCs (although the Norms in fact applied to all businesses), emphasizing – justifiably – that many local businesses and state enterprises behaved much worse than the better transnationals. There was failure on the one side to recognize that human rights standards are in principle as applicable to small- and medium-sized businesses as they are to large. On the other side there was failure to acknowledge that TNCs in the post-Cold War world have become the dominant players, with unprecedented influence, carrying in their wake innumerable smaller suppliers which are dependent on them.

The debate was not helped by the intemperate tone of the corporate opposition. It was not helped by supporters who defended the draft as holy writ, failing to accept that both its wording and its content gave hostages to fortune.

Nor was the draft itself blameless. In essence the exercise promised a set of principles for business distilled from a complex set of UN and other conventions which should be of value to investors, to the market, and to companies themselves. It should have been seen as an opportunity, not a threat, particularly since a growing number of leading companies already matched most of the requirements set out in the Norms in their own business principles.

What was being attempted was of profound importance. In practice, as draft followed draft, the need to change the title, to accommodate views without which there would be no further progress, meant that the elaboration of principles became increasingly complex and included wording, such as the precautionary principle (though this also featured in the Global Compact), which even the most progressive of companies would find difficult to follow to the letter. More damagingly to the central purpose, late in the process clauses were added about monitoring, proposing a possible role for the United Nations which would inevitably meet opposition from the home governments of TNCs.

Were the Norms voluntary or mandatory? Did they add to the legal requirements already imposed on companies by international human rights law? The straight answer to the second question was: no. As to the first, the reality was that, apart from those areas such as slavery, torture and genocide where international law applies to all, the Norms are voluntary in the sense that they cannot be enforced. However, as would apply to all aspects of human behaviour, there is a difference between the purely voluntary – that which can be followed or ignored at will (as is the case with the OECD Guidelines and Global Compact) – and the normative – standards which all are expected to observe.

The unanimous approval of the Norms by the Sub-Commission in August 2003[8] acted as a trigger for an impassioned debate and prompted the initiation of a consultation process by the UN High Commissioner for Human Rights. This provided a remarkably informative touchstone for the views of all the constituencies involved. NGOs, individual companies, business institutions and governments made submissions[9]. A large group of NGOs from both developed and developing countries expressed support for the Norms. Business institutions – the ICC, IOE, USCIB and CBI – voiced vigorous opposition, though the corporate world was divided between those who supported this institutional line and a small but significant group of companies, first seven, then ten in number, which set up the Business Leaders Initiative on Human Rights, one of whose aims was to test the applicability of the Norms to their own operations.

Opponents appeared to deny that human rights standards might apply to companies, though it should be obvious that the responsibility of companies for the health and safety of their employees and for their impact on the physical environment and on the communities in which they operate involves direct human rights responsibilities, regardless of the nature of the regimes under which they work, whether democracies or dictatorships. At the core of objections lay the contention that international human rights law pertained only to states, not to 'non state actors' such as companies, and that companies should simply comply with the law which it was up to governments to enforce. While it is highly desirable that all national governments should translate international human rights law into their domestic legislation, thus also embracing companies, this is an unlikely scenario for many countries where the worst violations take place. And it would anyhow not solve the problem of a fast-moving and rapidly changing transnational activity that can shift its legal domicile and ownership at will.

All, however, now supported dialogue, the business institutions welcoming what they saw as the sidelining of the Norms and expressing willingness to engage, though whether with the intent to frustrate or support an eventual outcome is still unclear. The United States government joined the critics in a submission whose tone and content differed little from that of the business institutions. The UK government, which had been instrumental in ensuring that debate on the issues should not be halted at an earlier stage, put forward a well-reasoned submission (Business & Human Rights Resource Centre, 2003)[10] suggesting that 'the exercise could be an opportunity to work towards a universally accepted collation and clarification of the minimum standards of behaviour expected of companies with regard to human rights' by 'building on what has already been achieved on corporate social responsibility'. It advocated the avoidance of legally binding treaty language and the setting out of principles in clear accessible terms. Certainly a simplification of language would be helpful, as would recognition that the term 'human rights' was now being used to encompass the whole of corporate responsibility, not just, as in the past, civil and political rights.

Progress and its obstacles

A clarification of standards or principles is the necessary next step. At the time of writing the story is unfinished and the ability of all involved to build constructively on the foundation laid by the Norms will be a test of statesmanship, particularly for the business community. Clearly in the longer term an international regulatory framework will be required for an infinitely diverse international business activity whose mobility makes national jurisdictions, even if reflecting international human rights law, inadequate for the task. A set of international principles could provide the consensual basis necessary to make such a framework effective, assist in providing a level playing field for the better performing companies and deter the piecemeal legislation which, in the event of failure at this stage, will be a real possibility, threatening the dynamism which lies at the heart of the corporate contribution to the world economy.

Much has been achieved. We have reached a plateau where there is sufficient recognition in principle of corporate responsibility for human rights to make it immune from economic recession or a fight-back from outdated Friedmanism, but where inertia and outright opposition still dominate. This plateau is not a destination, but needs to be a point of take-off. Corporate responsibility is moving slowly in the right direction, though the unhappy phrase 'corporate social responsibility' continues to obscure its meaning. There is growing acknowledgement of stakeholders. But many company initiatives remain distant from core operations, forming no part of prior human rights or environmental assessments or long-term strategy. Even leading companies demonstrate the conflict between competitive pressure and commercial opportunity and the principles they have set out for themselves. These are genuine dilemmas, but constitute a test of adherence to company principles. BP, for example, a company committed to the support of human rights, found itself challenged on the host government agreement negotiated with Turkey to protect the Baku–Tbilisi–Ceyhan pipeline which appeared to conflict with that commitment. Company lobbying activities, rarely if ever divulged, can be at variance with professed aims in seeking from government lower social or environmental standards[11].

There is a danger that the avalanche of words – in company brochures, conferences, consultancies and academe – may obscure the inadequacy of applied practice. Forward movement is stultified by the debate between voluntarism and regulation, a debate made sterile by the unreality of the extremes at both ends of the argument – the proponents of voluntarism ignoring history and the evidence of current practice, the advocates of international regulation (however necessary) ignoring the political obstacles and the need for the establishment of principles and national legislation first. The overwhelming lesson of history, from the abolition of the slave trade onwards, is that legislation has been required to secure corporate adherence to the contemporary values of society. And it is legislation that has enabled the market economy to survive, not as a 'free' market, but as one which retains its dynamism within a moral framework.

The purpose of business – legal and moral responsibility

What we have witnessed and continue to witness today is a wholly unnecessary conflict: a conflict between a corporate world that supports voluntarism and the primacy of the shareholder and a growing consensus that believes that companies have a responsibility for all their stakeholders, of whom the shareholder is only one, and that regulation is needed for an otherwise inadequately accountable international business. There are sufficient companies today, if still a small minority, that show such conflict to be unnecessary, but whose principles, genuinely held, continue to be tested by what appears to be an inherent contradiction between the values to which they aspire and the current philosophy of business.

The contention that the purpose of the company is to 'maximize value to shareholders' – 'value' being represented by money – underpins that philosophy. It is a purpose, as senior executives are increasingly rewarded with stock options, that leads logically, and with unscrupulous people inevitably, to the corruption of Enron and WorldCom. It conflicts with the perception of responsible managers who daily recognize a duty of care to all their stakeholders, a competitive return to shareholders being part of that duty if the enterprise is to survive – a condition, but not a purpose. Given the existence of countervailing powers – with employees able to organize and with the environment and community protected by NGO vigilance or government intervention – a balance can be found empirically. But where the elements for such a balance do not exist, companies can ride roughshod over other interests in the pursuit of returns to shareholders. Moreover, the corporation's 'legally defined mandate', argues Professor Joel Bakan in his brilliant book, *The Corporation* (Bakan, 2004), 'is to pursue relentlessly and without exception, its own self-interest, regardless of the often harmful consequences it might cause to others. As a result, the corporation is a pathological institution, a dangerous possessor of the great power it wields over people and societies'.

It is difficult to believe that society's intention in according the privilege of limited liability to companies was simply to profit a relatively small, constantly changing and often anonymous group of people with no reciprocal obligation to the enterprise, but free to buy and sell at whim. Common sense would suggest that it was to provide conditions under which goods and services could be provided profitably on a continuing basis – a service to society.

If the law is truly an impediment to responsible behaviour, then the law needs to be changed to enforce a broader duty of care[12]. Bakan concludes that new ways are needed to control the corporation – by improving the regulatory system, strengthening political democracy, creating a robust public sphere. However, an external framework of regulation alone is unlikely to be successful in making so protean an activity as international business, mobile both in geographical location and legal jurisdiction, fully accountable. We can legislate for behaviour, but we cannot legislate for virtue. Business requires a moral imperative as its starting point, a recognition of a moral case for applying society's values to its operations – a case for doing right because it is right, not because the law enforces it or economic interest justifies it.

If the corporate world lacks a sense of moral responsibility or moral liability for its actions, if it responds only to the law or the stimulus of profit, it will neither win back public trust nor attract the intellect and idealism of a younger generation without which it will not flourish.

Capitalism to be sustainable needs a moral base. We need a new paradigm of business – a recognition of the company as the servant of society, providing goods and services profitably and responsibly, not simply as the generator of cash for shareholders. We need business institutions that are the guardians of a business version of medicine's Hippocratic Oath instead of representing the lowest common denominator of corporate attitudes. We need to recognize that an injunction to do no harm is as relevant to business as to the medical profession and that the standards of business cannot differ from those applicable to the rest of society.

We cannot afford to regard such aspirations as utopian: they would accord with the beliefs and values of the great majority of ordinary people who work in business. But it will require business leadership, which at present shows no signs of appearing, if radical transformation is to be brought about. In the meantime progress will slowly continue to be made as investors and markets take into account social and environmental performance, but we will also see continuing guerrilla warfare – satisfactory to neither side – between NGOs and companies and an increasing resort to whatever law may be available (*The Changing Landscape of Liability*, 2004)[13]. Recourse to the 18th century United States Alien Tort Claims Act (US House of Representatives, Office of the Law Revision Counsel, 1992) is increasing. It is a crude and inadequate weapon, but in the absence of appropriate legislation that could deter malpractice as well as punish it by making parent companies responsible for any misdeeds of their subsidiaries, it remains a useful weapon to stimulate company action.

The anti-capitalists who were successful in disrupting World Trade Organization meetings have helped to raise the profile of the economic and political injustices in the world, but offer nothing to put in the place of the present system, opposing those who try to reform it. But they provide an important warning of the vulnerability of the present scheme of things if changes are not made. Kofi Annan, the UN Secretary General, had stated the case more temperately when he proposed the Global Compact at the World Economic Forum in January 1999. He said that traditionally national markets have been held together by shared values. In the face of economic transition and insecurity, people have known that, if the worst comes to the worst, they could rely on the expectation that certain minimum standards will prevail. But in the global market people do not yet have that confidence. 'Until they do have it, the global economy will be fragile and vulnerable – vulnerable to backlash from all the "isms" of our post-cold-war world:

protectionism, populism, nationalism, ethnic chauvinism, fanaticism and terrorism. What all those "isms" have in common is that they exploit the insecurity and misery of people who feel threatened or victimized by the global market. The more wretched and insecure people there are, the more those "isms" will continue to gain ground. What we have to do is to find a way of embedding the global market in a network of shared values' (cited in Eide, 2000).

Kofi Annan was prescient. Political injustice and economic inequity may have a long fuse, but they are ultimately explosive ingredients. And in a world of international terrorism, whatever its motivation, it is as well to realize that the dispossessed provide a friendly sea in which the terrorists can swim. The solution lies primarily in the hands of governments, but the behaviour of companies is also relevant and needs to be a contributory factor to that solution. The immediacy of daily contact with millions of people throughout the world gives companies a greater potential for good or harm than any other constituency. A living wage throughout their supply chains, care for the environment and communities where they operate, and a voice for human rights would all help to raise standards and diminish inequities.

All the elements are now available except the necessary political will. The acceptability of companies will depend both on the law and voluntary action. It will depend on companies playing a responsible role in a broader concept of governance – not simply lobbying governments for their own advantage, but playing a constructive role in the devising of a framework which protects the interests of a full range of stakeholders. Governments too will need to subordinate their aims and actions to principle. They have so far failed, nationally and collectively, to grasp the nettle of a mandatory framework which sets clear lines of behaviour and minimum standards. They cannot use companies as a substitute for their own failure to take action over human rights violations.

At the end of the day it will only be when business performance harmonizes with the values of contemporary society and with the dictates of the individual human conscience, when it performs as the servant, not the exploiter, of society, that the future of capitalism will deserve to be assured.

Notes

1   The collective term of 'NGO' has come to denote bodies ranging from organizations with international spread and repute, such as Oxfam, Save the Children Fund, Amnesty International and Greenpeace, to local interest groups

with a social or political aim, or pressure groups monitoring the activities of a single company. Their defining features are clarity of purpose or 'mission', frequently devoted to a single issue, the voluntary and unpaid nature of their governance, activities which are not for profit, and significant (sometimes exclusive) dependence on financial contributions from the public or their membership. They have a role as gadflies, catalysts and experts and constitute an essential component of civil society and democracy. Their legitimacy derives from public support for the issues they represent which are inadequately catered for by government or private enterprise. Their capacity, competence and probity can be as varied as those of any other walk of life and their survival ultimately depends on the judgement society makes on their work. In many cases their own transparency and accountability do not match up to the standards they demand from the corporate world. They do not uniquely hold the moral high ground, but hold a significant place on it.

2   Stakeholders are those who contribute directly to the success of a company or are affected by its operations. They comprise shareholders, employees, customers and the community and physical environment in which operations take place. Broader definitions, which may include NGOs, the media and government, make practical application of the concept meaningless. 'When everyone is somebody, Then no one's anybody'.

3   This invaluable source book provides details of the main codes and standards for companies. The promulgation of such codes has proved useful in stimulating a climate of public awareness about corporate responsibilities and putting pressure on companies to respond. They are, however, unlikely to have real impact without a commitment from companies to amplify and extend their own internal codes and consequent practice in order to match the evolving values of society.

4   A phrase coined by John Elkington of SustainAbility.

5   This describes the confusions surrounding the CSR debate more fully.

6   The Business & Human Rights Resource Centre website provides a running list of these companies.

7   The full cumbrous title, the product of compromise necessary to secure the unanimous agreement of the 26 country experts of widely diverse nationality, was UN Norms on the Responsibilities of Transnational Corporations and Other Business Enterprises with Regard to Human Rights (2003).

8   This approval was given by the initiating body. The UN Commission on Human Rights was quick to point out that this did not constitute formal approval by the UN Commission or the UN General Assembly – a distancing seized upon by governments and companies hostile to the Norms.

9   The Business & Human Rights Resource Centre website provides full coverage of the submissions.

10   Submission to the Office of the High Commissioner for Human Rights. See the Business & Human Rights Resource Centre website for the full text.

11   For example, American companies' membership of the USA*Engage coalition, formed to oppose United States governmental sanctions on oppressive regimes, could be interpreted, in the absence of any corporate policies of their own on human rights, as preparedness to connive at human rights violations in pursuit of commercial gain.

12 In 2004 a Bill before the UK House of Commons included such a provision, but found no support from government.
13 This provides an admirable analysis of the changing moral and legal liabilities which the Boards of large companies face today.

References

Bakan, J (2004) *The Corporation: The Pathological Pursuit of Profit and Power.* New York: Free Press
Business & Human Rights Resource Centre (2003) Available at: http://www.business-humanrights.org
Carson, Rachel (1962) *Silent Spring.* Boston: Houghton Mifflin
Chandler, G (2003) The curse of 'corporate social responsibility'. *New Academy Review* 2:1 Spring
The Changing Landscape of Liability: A Director's Guide to Trends in Corporate Environmental, Social and Economic Liability (2004) London: SustainAbility.
Eide, Asbjorn (2000) *Human Rights and the Oil Industry.* Antwerp: Intersentia
Extractive Industries Transparency Initiative (2002). Available at: http://www2.dfid.gov.uk/news/files/extractiveindustries.asp
Foreign & Commonwealth Office/US State Department (2000) *The Voluntary Principles on Security and Human Rights.* Available at: http://www.voluntaryprinciples.org/
Global Reporting Initiative (2002) *Sustainability Reporting Guidelines.* Available at: http://www.globalreporting.org
Institute of Social and Ethical Accountability (1999) *AA1000 Assurance Standard.* Available at: http://www.accountability.org.uk
International Foundation for Education and Self-Help (1999) *The Global Sullivan Principles of Social Responsibility.* Available at: http://www.thesullivanfoundation.org/gsp/principles/gsp/default.asp
International Labour Organization (1998) *Declaration on Fundamental Principles and Rights at Work.* Available at: http://www.ilo.org
Kimberley Process (2002) Available at: http://www.kimberleyprocess.com
Leipziger, D (2003) *The Corporate Responsibility Code Book.* Sheffield: Greenleaf Publishing
Meadows, Donella A *et al.* (1972) *Limits to Growth.* New York: Potomac Associates
Organisation for Economic Cooperation and Development (2000) *OECD Guidelines for Multinational Enterprises.* Available at: http://www.oecd.org/daf/investment/guidelines
Publish What You Pay (2002) Available at: http://www.publishwhatyoupay.org/english/
Social Accountability International (1997) *Social Accountability 8000.* Available at: http://www.cepaa.org/
United Nations (1948) *Universal Declaration of Human Rights.* Available at: http://www.ohchr.org/english/law/index.htm
United Nations (1989) *Convention on the Rights of the Child.* Available at: http://www.ohchr.org/english/law/crc.htm

United Nations (1992) *The Rio Declaration*. Available at: http://www.un.org/documents/ga/conf151/aconf15126–1annex1.htm

United Nations (2000) *The Global Compact*. Available at: http://www.unglobalcompact.org

United Nations Draft Norms on the Responsibilities of Transnational Corporations and other Business Enterprises with Regard to Human Rights (2003). Available at: http://www1.umn.edu/humanrts/links/NormsApril2003.html

US House of Representatives, Office of the Law Revision Counsel. United States Alien Tort Claims Act 28 U.S.C.§1350. (1992) Available at: http://uscode.house.gov/

Ward, Barbara and Dubos, René (1972) *Only One Earth: Care and Maintenance of a Small Planet*. London: Deutsch

Index